An Introduction to English Phonetics

TITLES IN THE SERIES INCLUDE

Visit the Edinburgh Textbooks on the English Language website at
www.edinburghuniversitypress.com/series/ETOTEL

An Introduction to English Phonetics

Second Edition

Richard Ogden

EDINBURGH
University Press

Edinburgh University Press is one of the leading university presses in the UK. We publish academic books and journals in our selected subject areas across the humanities and social sciences, combining cutting-edge scholarship with high editorial and production values to produce academic works of lasting importance. For more information visit our website: edinburghuniversitypress.com

Edinburgh University Press Ltd
The Tun – Holyrood Road,
12(2f) Jackson's Entry,
Edinburgh EH8 8PJ

Typeset in Janson by
Servis Filmsetting Ltd, Stockport, Cheshire,
and printed and bound in Great Britain by
CPI Group (UK) Ltd, Croydon CR0 4YY

A CIP record for this book is available from the British Library

ISBN 978 1 4744 1175 2 (hardback)
ISBN 978 1 4744 1176 9 (paperback)
ISBN 978 1 4744 1177 6 (webready PDF)
ISBN 978 1 4744 1178 3 (epub)

Contents

Figures and tables

Figures

Tables

To readers

Immediately I had agreed to write a book with the title *An Introduction to English Phonetics*, I realised that describing the phonetics of 'English' is problematic because English is so phonetically heterogeneous. So the result is a book that is more about phonetics, with illustrations from around the English-speaking world. It is not a complete description of any one variety; rather, my intention has been to try to provide enough of a descriptive phonetic framework so that readers can describe their own variety in reasonable detail.

I have tried in this book to concentrate on how to go about doing phonetics, and to show how phonetics can inform our understanding of categories like 'voicing', and explain sound changes like the vocalisation of laterals, and how phonetic details relate to meaning and linguistic structure on many levels. I have tried to take a broad view of what 'meaning' is, so the book is not limited to phonemes and allophones. Following J. R. Firth, I use the word 'sound' as a neutral term. Consequently, this book contains many things that many introductory textbooks don't. Glottal stops are included among the plosives; clicks and ejectives find a place; and where possible the data comes from naturally occurring talk, without giving too much weight to citation forms. This is, I admit, a controversial decision; but my own experience has been that students want to be able to engage with the stuff of language that surrounds them, and with appropriate help, they can do that.

In common with many introductory books on phonetics, this one leaves out much explicit discussion of rhythm, intonation and other 'prosodic' features. This isn't because I think they are unimportant; but teaching them often involves working with hunches and intuitions, and any framework for description moves quickly into phonological representations that can be complex. So only the bare bones are covered in this book.

Likewise, assimilation, a common topic of introductory textbooks, is not covered much in this book. When considered as a phonetic phenomenon, recent work shows that it's much more complex than traditional descriptions imply. The chapters here, I hope, will give students enough grounding in observing and understanding the phonetic organisation of talk so that understanding phenomena such as assimilation will be easier.

Acknowledgements

I owe a great debt of thanks to many people who have helped me with data for this book. These include the secretary of the IPA, Katerina Nicolaidis; Dom Watt; Esther Grabe; Bill Haddican; and many of my own students, who over the years have collected a lot of material full of wonderful detail.

Thanks also to Alex, Hazel, Jennifer, Julianne, Lis, Malcolm, Nan and Roger, my panel of non-phonetician readers who took the time to read parts of this and helped to make it understandable; to my friend Joyce Trotman (plenty love, Joyce!), who read and annotated the first edition so carefully and helped me to see where the second edition needed revisions; to Selina for help with Chapter 11; to my colleagues who let me have the time to bring this to completion; and to fellow phoneticians who have kept me enthused about working with speech. The acoustic representations in the book were made using PRAAT (www.praat.org), developed by Paul Boersma and David Weenink. Ester Grabe kindly gave permission to use files from the IViE Project (www.phon.ox.ac.uk). Where recordings from this have been used, they are referred to with the preface IViE, followed by the identifier.

The IPA chart is reprinted with permission of the International Phonetic Association. Copyright 2005 International Phonetic Association. I am grateful to the IPA for permission to use material from the *Journal of the IPA*, the *Handbook of the International Phonetic Association* and the accompanying recordings, which are available to members via the IPA website. Where images are based on IPA recordings from the website above, they are marked (IPA) in the accompanying captions. Information about IPA membership can be obtained from the IPA website: https://www.internationalphoneticassociation.org

THE INTERNATIONAL PHONETIC ALPHABET (revised to 2005)

CONSONANTS (PULMONIC)   © 2005 IPA

	Bilabial	Labiodental	Dental	Alveolar	Postalveolar	Retroflex	Palatal	Velar	Uvular	Pharyngeal	Glottal
Plosive	p b			t d		ʈ ɖ	c ɟ	k ɡ	q ɢ		ʔ
Nasal	m	ɱ		n		ɳ	ɲ	ŋ	N		
Trill	B			r					R		
Tap or Flap		ⱱ		ɾ		ɽ					
Fricative	ɸ β	f v	θ ð	s z	ʃ ʒ	ʂ ʐ	ç ʝ	x ɣ	χ ʁ	ħ ʕ	h ɦ
Lateral fricative				ɬ ɮ							
Approximant		ʋ		ɹ		ɻ	j	ɰ			
Lateral approximant				l		ɭ	ʎ	L			

Where symbols appear in pairs, the one to the right represents a voiced consonant. Shaded areas denote articulations judged impossible.

CONSONANTS (NON-PULMONIC)

Clicks		Voiced implosives		Ejectives	
ʘ	Bilabial	ɓ	Bilabial	'	Examples:
ǀ	Dental	ɗ	Dental/alveolar	p'	Bilabial
ǃ	(Post)alveolar	ʄ	Palatal	t'	Dental/alveolar
ǂ	Palatoalveolar	ɠ	Velar	k'	Velar
ǁ	Alveolar lateral	ʛ	Uvular	s'	Alveolar fricative

OTHER SYMBOLS

ʍ Voiceless labial-velar fricative

w Voiced labial-velar approximant

ɥ Voiced labial-palatal approximant

ʜ Voiceless epiglottal fricative

ʢ Voiced epiglottal fricative

ʡ Epiglottal plosive

ɕ ʑ Alveolo-palatal fricatives

ɺ Voiced alveolar lateral flap

ɧ Simultaneous ʃ and x

Affricates and double articulations can be represented by two symbols joined by a tie bar if necessary.

k͡p t͡s

VOWELS

Where symbols appear in pairs, the one to the right represents a rounded vowel.

SUPRASEGMENTALS

ˈ Primary stress

ˌ Secondary stress

ˌfoʊnəˈtɪʃən

ː Long   eː

ˑ Half-long   eˑ

˘ Extra-short   ĕ

| Minor (foot) group

‖ Major (intonation) group

. Syllable break   ɹi.ækt

‿ Linking (absence of a break)

DIACRITICS   Diacritics may be placed above a symbol with a descender, e.g. ŋ̊

	Voiceless	n̥ d̥		Breathy voiced	b̤ a̤		Dental	t̪ d̪
	Voiced	s̬ t̬		Creaky voiced	b̰ a̰		Apical	t̺ d̺
ʰ	Aspirated	tʰ dʰ		Linguolabial	t̼ d̼		Laminal	t̻ d̻
	More rounded	ɔ̹	ʷ	Labialized	tʷ dʷ	˜	Nasalized	ẽ
	Less rounded	ɔ̜	ʲ	Palatalized	tʲ dʲ	ⁿ	Nasal release	dⁿ
	Advanced	u̟	ˠ	Velarized	tˠ dˠ	ˡ	Lateral release	dˡ
	Retracted	e̠	ˤ	Pharyngealized	tˤ dˤ	̚	No audible release	d̚
	Centralized	ë	˜	Velarized or pharyngealized	ɫ			
	Mid-centralized	e̽		Raised	e̝	(ɹ̝	= voiced alveolar fricative)	
	Syllabic	n̩		Lowered	e̞	(β̞	= voiced bilabial approximant)	
	Non-syllabic	e̯		Advanced Tongue Root	e̘			
	Rhoticity	ɚ a˞		Retracted Tongue Root	e̙			

TONES AND WORD ACCENTS

LEVEL			CONTOUR		
e̋ or	˥	Extra high	ě or	ˇ	Rising
é	˦	High	ê	ˆ	Falling
ē	˧	Mid	e᷄	᷄	High rising
è	˨	Low	e᷅	᷅	Low rising
ȅ	˩	Extra low	e᷈	᷈	Rising-falling
ꜜ		Downstep	↗		Global rise
ꜛ		Upstep	↘		Global fall

1 Introduction to phonetics

1.1 What is phonetics?

Language is one of the distinctive characteristics of human beings. Without formal instruction, we learn from infanthood the skills that we need to be successful users of a language. For most of us, this will be spoken language, though for some it will be a signed language. In acquiring language, we learn words, and how to put them together; we learn to link words and sentences to meaning; we learn how to use these structures to get what we want, to say how we feel, and to form social bonds with others; and we also learn how to sound like members of the community around us – or perhaps choose to sound different from them.

Linguistics is the formal study of language. Its main sub-disciplines are: syntax, the study of sentence structure; semantics, the study of meaning; pragmatics, the study of meaning in context; morphology, the study of word structure; sociolinguistics, the study of language in its social context; phonology, the study of sound systems; and phonetics, the study of the sounds of speech. In this book, we will be mindful that linguistically significant aspects of the sounds of a language have to do with meaning on some level, whether it is to distinguish words from each other, to join together words of particular kinds, to mark (or do) something social, such as where the speaker comes from, or to handle the flow of talk in a conversation.

Language and speech are often distinguished in linguistics. For many, linguistics constitutes a set of claims about human beings' universal cognitive or biological capacities. Most of the constructs of linguistics are attempts at explaining commonalities between members of communities which use language, and they are abstract.

Phonetics on the other hand is the systematic study of the sounds of speech, which is physical and directly observable. Phonetics is sometimes seen as not properly linguistic, because it is the outward, physical manifestation of the main object of linguistic research, which is language (not speech): and language is abstract.

On the other hand, setting aside Deaf signing communities, speech is the commonest and primary form of language. Most of our interactions, with family members, colleagues, people we buy things from or whom we ask for help, are done through the medium of speech. There is a primacy about the spoken form of language which means that for us to understand questions like "what is the possible form of a word?", "how do you ask questions in this language?", "why does this speaker use that particular pronunciation, and not some other?", we need to have an understanding of phonetics.

Speech is produced by the controlled movement of air through the throat, mouth and nose (more technically known as the vocal tract). It can be studied in a number of different ways:

- **articulatory phonetics** (how speech sounds are made in the body)
- **acoustic phonetics** (the physical properties of the sounds that are made)
- **perception** (what happens to the speech signal once the sound wave reaches the listener's ear)

The linguistic phonetic study of a language involves working out how the sounds of language (the 'phonetic' part) are used to make meaning (which is what makes it 'linguistic', and not just the study of the sounds we can make with our bodies): how words are shaped, how they are put together, how similar (but different) strings of sounds can be distinguished (such as 'I scream' and 'ice cream'), how particular shades of meaning are conveyed, and how the details of speech relate systematically to its inherently social context.

One of the central paradoxes of phonetics is that we make observations of individuals in order to understand something about the way groups of people behave. This is good in the sense that we can use ourselves and the people around us as representatives of groups; it is bad in that we cannot always be sure how representative someone is, and there is always the possibility that what we observe is just an idiosyncratic habit. In this book, we will mostly skirt round this issue: there are (surprisingly) still many things that are not known about English phonetics, so in this book, we will make observations of English-speaking communities and individuals in order to show how the phonetic potential of the vocal tract is used by speakers of English, in various settings.

1.2 What this book covers

Because the English-speaking world contains so many diverse communities, scattered over a wide geographical area with different historical and cultural backgrounds, our basic stance is that it is not really possible to describe the phonetics of 'English' as such. Even in the British Isles, there is huge variability in the way that English sounds. Traditionally, British textbooks on English phonetics concentrate on **Received Pronunciation** (**RP**), a variety of English which traditionally has had high social status, but is spoken nowadays by few people. So in this book we explore the phonetic potential of the vocal tract, and illustrate it from English; but also you, the reader, are encouraged to reflect on what is true for you and your community. Despite its being one of the most written-about languages, there are still many discoveries to make about English, and perhaps you will make one of them.

In making our observations, we will look at the way that sounds are articulated, and think about how the articulations are co-ordinated with one another in time. We will look at how the sounds of English can be represented using the Phonetic Alphabet of the International Phonetic Association. We will look a little at acoustic representations so that we can see speech in a different way; and we will look at speech in a number of different settings, including carefully produced tokens of words and conversational speech.

1.3 Ways to talk about sounds

Talking about sounds is something that most native English-speaking children do from a very young age. One reason for this is our writing system, which is based, however loosely, on a system where a set of twenty-six symbols is used to represent the forty-five or so sounds of English. So we learn, for example, that the letter <m> stands for the sound [m], and the letter <c> can usually stand for either a [k] or a [s] sound. Learning this way gives priority to letters over sounds. For example, if we want to describe how to say a word like 'knight', we have to say something like 'the "k" is silent'. The problems do not end there: <igh> stands for what is often called 'a long "I"-sound', which in phonetic transcription is often represented as [aɪ]. These ways of talking also cause us problems. What does it mean to say that the word 'knight' 'has a "k"', when we never pronounce it? It is temptingly easy to talk about words in terms of the letters we write them with rather than their linguistic structure.

We will discuss ways of representing sounds in Chapter 3. For now, we just observe that for English, there is no one-to-one mapping of letter to sound, or of sound to letter (which is what is meant when people say English is not 'spelt phonetically').

In this book, we will use the word 'sounds' as a semi-technical term. Phonetics and phonology have a well-developed vocabulary for talking about sounds in technical ways, and many of the terms used are very specific to particular theories.

1.3.1 The phoneme

Many theories of phonology use the concept of the **phoneme**. The phoneme is the smallest unit of sound which can differentiate one word from another: in other words, phonemes make lexical distinctions. So if we take a word like 'cat', [kat], and swap the [k] sound for a [p] sound, we get 'pat' instead of 'cat'. This is enough to establish that [k] and [p] are linguistically meaningful units of sound, i.e. phonemes. Phonemes are written between slashes, so the phonemes corresponding to the sounds [p] and [k] are represented as /p/ and /k/ respectively. Phonemes are phonological (not phonetic) units, because they relate to linguistic structure and organisation; so they are abstract units. On the other hand, [p] and [k] are sounds of speech, which have a physical dimension and can be described in acoustic, auditory or articulatory terms; what is more, there are many different ways to pronounce /p/ and /k/, and transcribing them as [p] and [k] captures only some of the phonetic details we can observe about these sounds.

Phoneme theory originated in the early twentieth century, and was influential in many theories of phonology; however, in recent decades, many phonologists and phoneticians have seen phonemes as little more than a convenient fiction. One reason for this is that phonemic representations imply that speech consists of units strung together like beads on a string. This is a very unsatisfactory model of speech, because at any one point in time, we can usually hear cues for two or more speech sounds. For example, if you say the words 'cat', 'kit', 'coot' and isolate the [k] sounds, you will notice that they are different from one another. The tongue makes contact with the roof of the mouth at slightly different places (further forward for 'kit', further back for 'coot' and somewhere in between for 'cat'), and the lips also have different shapes. These things make the [k] sounds sound different from one another. Now, we have the feeling, as native speakers of English, that these sounds are at some level 'the same'; and this is what phoneme theory attempts to explain. These different sounds are **allophones** of the phoneme /k/: they have some things in common, and the differences between them arise from the context they are in. The differences are not seen as linguistically important, because they are predictable.

Another way to look at this is to think of the consonant as telling us something about the vowel that is coming: if you hear the kind of [k] which goes in the word 'kit', then before you even hear the vowel sound for real, you can tell what kind of vowel sound is coming. So in a way, the consonant and the vowel are being produced at the same time. The question for us as phoneticians is what we make of this, and how we explain it. In this book, we will use the word 'sound' as an essentially neutral word which does not take one stance or another towards what we hear. It is a term chosen so as to allow us to be as descriptively rich as we would like, without committing us one way or another to whether the best account is a phonemic one or something else.

Sounds will be written enclosed in square brackets, such as [k], [a], [t] or [kat]. Phonemes, where we refer to them, will be enclosed in slash brackets such as /k/, /a/, /t/. And letters will from now on be enclosed between angled brackets like this: <c> <a> <t>; but when referring to words, the convention will be: 'cat'. We will use English spelling quite a lot, and this might seem counterintuitive in a book on English phonetics. But remember that speakers of English do not all pronounce the same words with the same phonemes, let alone the same sounds; and the only neutral way to write English is in fact its orthography: this is one reason why English spelling has been so resistant to change over the years.

1.4 An overview of the book

The book begins by taking an overview of the mouth, nose and throat, where we cover the main details of the production of speech. We introduce a lot of essential terminology there, and get a broad picture of the sounds of English. Next, we take a look at ways of representing sound on paper: a difficult problem, since the material for our study is grounded in time, ephemeral and short-lived, whereas the printed word is static and long-lasting. We cover aspects of phonetic transcription and take a simplified look at acoustic representations. After this, we look at the larynx and matters of breathing, pitch and voice quality.

Next comes a series of chapters on the main kinds of sound in English, beginning with vowels. We start with vowels because they are a fundamental building block of speech, and in English many consonants take on properties of their adjacent vowels. After vowels, we move through the main consonant types in English: approximants, plosives, fricatives and nasals. Finally, we look at some less common sounds where the air is moved into or out of the vocal tract by some other mechanism than the lungs.

Each chapter ends with some exercises and suggestions for further reading. Discussion of the exercises can be found at the end of the book, though for many of the exercises there are no clear-cut answers. When terms appear in **bold**, this is a first mention, and a glossary containing these terms is provided at the end of the book.

By the end of this book, you should have some understanding of ways to represent spoken English. You should understand something about the way sounds are made in the vocal tract, and something of the complexity and detail of spoken English. Most importantly of all, by the end of the book you should have some skills for making some phonetic observations of your own.

Further reading

Many books on linguistics provide an overview of the place of phonetics and phonology within linguistics, and the relations between them, e.g. Fromkin et al. (2007), which also discusses the phoneme.

English phonetics is discussed from a phonemic point of view in e.g. Jones (1975) and Cruttenden (2001).

2 Overview of the human speech mechanism

2.1 The complexity of speech sounds

Human speech is complex, and lay people are not used to describing it in technical ways. On the other hand, many people have some inkling of how to describe music. We could describe the rhythm (where are the beats? what is the tempo?), the melodic structure (what key is it in? what scale does it use? are there recurrent themes?), instrumentation and so forth. All of these are different aspects of music, and all of them contribute to the totality of what we hear.

Describing speech is a similarly complex task. Speech involves the careful co-ordination of the lips, tongue, vocal folds, breathing and so on. The signal that we perceive as successive sounds arises from skills that we learn over years of our lives, even as our bodies grow and age. In producing even the simplest of speech sounds, we are co-ordinating a large number things. Phonetics involves something like unpicking the sounds of speech and working out how all the components work together, what they do, and when. It is a bit like hearing a piece of music and working out how the score is constructed.

One problem we face is exactly the interconnectivity of the parts: in a way, we need to know something about everything all of the time. The purpose of this chapter is to give you an overview of the speech mechanism. The terms and concepts that are introduced here will be developed in more detail in later chapters, but understanding even the simplest things about speech is easiest if we have an overview of the whole system: so this chapter introduces a lot of basic terminology of phonetics.

2.2 Breathing

Speech sounds are made by manipulating the way air moves out of (or sometimes into) the vocal tract. There are a number of ways of doing this, as we will see in Chapter 10, but universally across languages sounds of speech are produced on an out-breath. This kind of airflow is called **pulmonic** (because the movement of air is initiated by the lungs; the Latin word for lung is 'pulmo') and **egressive** (because the air comes out of the vocal tract; 'e-', 'out', '-gress-', 'move forwards'): all spoken languages have pulmonic egressive sounds.

Try an experiment. Take a lungful of air and then hum or say 'aaah' until you have to stop. Time yourself; it should take you quite a long time before you run out of air. Now repeat this, but breathe out first. This time, you will see that you cannot sustain the same sound for anything like as long. This is enough to show you that a simple sound like 'aaah' ([ɑː]) or 'mmm' ([mː] – [ː] is the diacritic for long) requires an out-breath with a reasonable amount of air in the lungs.

Now try breathing in while you say 'aah' or 'mmm'. You probably will find that this is quite hard, and you will probably get a more 'croaky' voice quality. If you try saying your name while breathing in, you will notice that it feels both unpleasant and difficult; and it doesn't sound very good either. This is because the vocal tract works best for speech when breathing out, i.e. on an egressive airflow.

The lungs are large spongy organs in the thoracic cavity (chest). They are connected to the outside world via the trachea, or windpipe. The lungs are surrounded at the front by ribs, and at the bottom by the diaphragm. The ribs are attached to one another by intercostal muscles. In breathing in, the diaphragm lowers and the intercostal muscles make the rib cage move upwards and outwards. This increases the size of the thoracic cavity, and so it lowers the air pressure. As a result, air flows into the lungs, and they expand and fill up with air. Once inhalation stops, the diaphragm and the intercostal muscles relax, and exert a gentle pressure on the lungs. Air is forced out of the lungs, generating a pulmonic egressive airflow.

2.2.1 In-breaths to project talk

In beginning to speak, people often make audible in-breaths. In-breaths are one way to communicate: "I am about to say something."

Extract (1) shows a question–answer pair, where the answer is given in overlap with the question. (Where two speakers speak at once, this is marked with '[' and ']', with the respective talk lined up. The codes before data extracts are an index to the original sources.)

(1) (Voc9/02.01.04;0342 acid)

1	P	Marguerite you need a little bit of acid
2		in there to get a s[et as

3	M	→		[hːː↓
4	P		[well is that right]	
5	M		[you wouldn't] with redcurrants	

P and M are talking about making jam. In line 1, P asks M whether some acid is needed to make it set. In line 3, M marks that she is about to speak, by producing an audible in-breath (transcribed [hːː] with [↓] to indicate that the air is coming into the body, not out) and then gives her answer while P1 in line 2 produces the end of his question. Audible in-breaths like this are one way for a speaker to display "I have something (more) to say." Here, the "something to say" is an answer, and M produces her in-breath at a point relative to P's talk where it is clear what kind of answer is relevant in the context. Producing audible in-breaths is a common device that allows speakers to co-ordinate turn-taking in conversation.

2.3 The larynx and voicing

The **larynx** (Figure 2.1) is a structure built of cartilage. Its main purpose is as a kind of valve to stop things going down into the lungs. We will look at the larynx in more detail in Chapter 4.

You should be able to locate your larynx quite easily. You probably know it as your 'Adam's apple' or voice box. It is often visible as a notch at the front of the neck.

The larynx contains the **vocal folds** (also known as the **vocal cords**, but this suggests that they are like strings on a stringed instrument, which they are not). When we breathe, they are kept wide apart, which allows air to pass freely across the **glottis**, the space between the folds; but during speaking, the vocal folds play an important role because they can be made to vibrate. This vibration is called **voicing**. Sounds which are accompanied by voicing are called **voiced** sounds, while those which are not are called **voiceless** sounds.

You can sense voicing by a simple experiment. Say the sound [m] but put your hands over your ears. You will hear quite a loud buzzing which is conducted through your bones to your ears. Now repeat this saying a [s] sound, and you will notice that the buzzing stops. Instead, you will hear a (much quieter) hissing sound, which is due to the turbulent airflow near the back of the teeth. If you now say a [z] sound, you will notice that everything is the same as for [s], except that there is the buzzing sound because [z] is voiced. Voicing is caused by the very rapid vibration of the vocal folds. Voicing is one of the most important features of speech sounds, and we will look at it in more detail in Chapter 4.

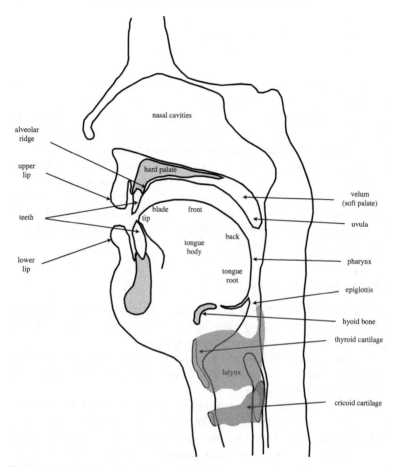

Figure 2.1 Cross-section of the vocal tract.

2.4 Airflow

Air passes out of the vocal tract through the mouth or the nose. The way that it comes out affects the sound generated, so we need a framework to describe this aspect of speech.

2.4.1 Central and lateral airflow

Central airflow is when the air flows down the middle of the vocal tract. If you say the sound [s], hold the articulation and then suck air in, you should feel that it goes cold and dry down the middle of your tongue and the middle of the roof of your mouth. The cold and dry patches will be more or less symmetrical on each side of your mouth. All languages have sounds with central airflow.

Lateral airflow is when the air flows down one or both sides of the vocal tract. If you say the sound [l], hold the articulation and then suck air in, you should feel this time that it goes cold and dry down one or both sides of the mouth, but not down the middle. The sides of the tongue are lowered, and the air passes out between the back teeth.

In theory, lateral airflow can be produced at the lips too: to do this, keep the sides of the lips together and try saying something like 'Pepé bought a pencil'. It will both sound and look strange. It is probably not a surprise that no language has lateral airflow caused by constricting the lips at one side, and this combination is blocked out in the chart of the International Phonetic Association.

2.4.2 Oral and nasal airflow

Air can exit the vocal tract through the nose or the mouth. This is controlled by the position of the **velum**. The velum is a sort of valve that controls airflow through the nose. If the velum is raised, then the nasal cavities are blocked off. Consequently, air cannot pass through them, and it must exit the vocal tract through the mouth. Sounds with airflow exiting through the mouth only are said to have **oral airflow**. If the velum is lowered, air flows through the nasal cavities, and out through the nostrils. If the air flows through the nose, the airflow is **nasal**.

If you say a [s] sound and pinch your nose, you will notice that you can easily continue the [s] sound. This is because [s] is oral: the velum is raised and makes a tight seal, preventing escape of air through the nose. On the other hand, if you say a [m] sound and pinch your nose, you will notice that you can only continue the [m] sound for a very short time. This is because the lips are closed, making oral escape impossible, but the velum is lowered, so that the airflow is nasal. By pinching your nose, you effectively seal off the only remaining means of escape for the air.

A third possibility exists, where air escapes through the nose and the mouth. For these sounds, the velum is lowered, but there is no **complete closure** in the oral tract, as we had for [m] (where the complete closure is at the lips). A good example would be a **nasalised** vowel, as in the French word 'pain', [pã], 'bread'. You might try making a nasalised [s] sound, [s̃], but you will notice that it is much quieter and less hissy than it should be, with as much noise caused by air coming through the nostrils as through the mouth.

2.5 Place of articulation

The vocal tract contains some discrete physical landmarks which are used primarily in producing and describing consonants. In describing the place of articulation, we are describing where in the vocal tract a sound is made.

Articulators are the parts of the oral tract that are used in producing speech sounds. They are often grouped into two kinds, active and passive. **Active articulators** are ones that move: the tongue tip is an active articulator in sounds like [s t n], since it moves up to behind the teeth. **Passive articulators** are articulators that cannot move, but are the target for active articulators. In the case of sounds like [s t n], the passive articulator is the bony ridge behind the upper teeth, known as the alveolar ridge.

Most places of articulation are described by reference to the passive articulator. We start our description of them with the lips, working our way down the vocal tract.

2.5.1 Bilabial

Bilabial sounds are sounds made at the lips. 'Bi-' means 'two', and 'labial' is an adjective based on the Latin word for 'lips'. In English, the sounds [p b m] are bilabial. If you say [apa aba ama] and look in the mirror, you will see that they look identical. If you say the sounds silently to yourself and concentrate on your lips, you will feel that the two lips touch one another for a short period, and the action is basically the same for all three sounds.

2.5.2 Labiodental

Labiodental sounds are made with the upper teeth ('dental') against the lower lip ('labio'). In English the labiodental sounds [f v] occur. Logically speaking, labiodental sounds could involve the lower teeth and the upper lip, but this is difficult for most people to do: it involves protruding the jaw, and most people have upper teeth that sit in front of the lower teeth. Labiodental sounds can be made with the teeth against either the inside surface of the lip (endolabial) or the outside edge of the lip (exolabial).

2.5.3 Dental

Dental sounds involve an articulation made against the back of the upper teeth. [θ ð] in English (as in the initial sounds of 'think' and 'then') are often dental; they can also be interdental, that is, produced with the tongue between ('inter' in Latin) the teeth, especially in North America. Dental forms of [l] and [n] are used in words like 'health' and 'tenth', where they are followed by a dental; and dental forms of [t] and [d] are regularly used in many varieties of English (e.g. some forms of Irish or New York English, and in Nigeria) as forms of [θ ð].

2.5.4 Alveolar

Alveolar sounds are made at the alveolar ridge. This is a bony ridge behind the upper teeth. If you rest your tongue on the upper teeth then gradually move it backwards, you will feel a change in texture from the smooth enamel to the bumpier gum. Just behind the teeth you should be able to feel the alveolar ridge. This sticks out a bit just behind the teeth. People's alveolar ridges are very variable: some are very prominent, others hardly noticeable. Alternatively, try isolating the consonant sounds in the word 'dent', and you should feel that the tongue tip is making contact with the alveolar ridge. Sounds with an alveolar place of articulation in most varieties of English are [t d n l r s z].

2.5.5 Postalveolar

Postalveolar sounds are made just behind ('post') the alveolar ridge. There are four of these in English, [ʃ] and [ʒ], the sounds spelt <sh> in 'ship', [ʃɪp], and <si> in 'invasion', [ɪɱveɪʒən], and the sounds [tʃ dʒ] as in 'church' and 'judge'. It can be hard to feel the difference in place of articulation between alveolar and postalveolar sounds, but if you produce a [s] sound, then a [ʃ] sound, and suck air in immediately after each sound, you should feel that part of the roof of the mouth which goes cold and dry is further back for [ʃ] than for [s].

Special symbols for dentals and postalveolars only exist for the fricatives. If dental or postalveolar articulations need to be distinguished, this can be done using **diacritics** – characters which modify the basic value of letters, and are placed over or under simple letters. We can modify the basic alveolar symbol [t] with diacritics: [t̪] marks dental, so [t̪] stands for a voiceless dental plosive, and [ˍ] marks '**retracted**' (i.e. further back), so [t̠] stands for a voiceless postalveolar plosive.

Postalveolars are reported occasionally in dialects which are on their way to losing distinct [r] sounds. Hedevind (1967) reports a contrast between dentals/alveolars and postalveolars (transcribed [n̪, z̪, t̪] in pairs such as those below in a dialect from Dent (Cumbria, Northern England).

(2) own   [aːn̩]   brain ('harn')   [aːn̩]
     mows   [maːz]   mars   [maːz]
     shot   [ʃɔt̩]   short   [ʃɔt̩]

If you slowly move your tongue away from the alveolar ridge and slide it back along the roof of your mouth, you will feel a change in texture (it will get smooth and hard) as well as a distinct change in shape (it will feel domed). This domed part is known as the hard palate. (You may be able to curl your tongue even further back, when you will feel a change in texture again – it will feel soft – and it might feel a bit uncomfortable; this is the velum, or soft palate.)

2.5.6 Retroflex

Retroflex sounds are made with the tongue curled ('flex') back ('retro') to the hard palate. (This is one case where the 'place of articulation' refers to the active articulator.) The symbols for retroflex sounds are easy to remember: they all have a rightward-facing hook on the bottom: [ʈ ɖ ɳ ʂ ɭ ɻ ɽ].

Retroflex [ʈ ɖ ɳ] are frequently used in Indian varieties of English instead of alveolars for the sounds [t d n]. (Many Indian languages have dental and retroflex or postalveolar sounds, but not alveolar.) The retroflex fricative sound [ʂ] also occurs in some varieties of English, notably some Scottish and North American varieties, as a combination of [r] + [s], as in 'of course', [əv kɔːʂ]. And many varieties of American English use [ɻ] for the r-sound; this is also known as 'curled-r'.

2.5.7 'Coronal'

On the IPA chart, sounds are described according to where in the mouth they are made; but it is equally important to think about which part of the tongue is used to make them. Dental, alveolar, postalveolar and retroflex sounds are all made with the front part of the tongue, the tip (the very frontmost part of the tongue) or the blade (the part just behind the tip). There is a lot of variability among English speakers as to which part of the tongue they use to articulate dental, alveolar and postalveolar sounds, so usually this factor is ignored, since it seems to play no linguistic role for English. In the phonology literature, sounds made with the front part of the tongue are often called **coronal**, a term which does not appear on the IPA chart. (The Latin word 'corona' means 'crown'; this is the term used to refer to the front part of the tongue.)

2.5.8 Palatal

Palatal sounds are made with the tongue body, the massive part of the middle of the tongue, raised up to the hard palate, or the roof of the mouth. Palatal sounds aren't common in English, except for the sound [j], which is usually spelt <y>, as in 'yes', 'yacht', 'yawn'; or as part of the sequence [ju] represented by the letter <u> in words like 'usual', 'computer'.

2.5.9 Velar

Velar sounds are made with the tongue back (or **dorsum**) raised towards the soft palate. The soft palate is at the back of the roof of the mouth, and is also known as the velum. The sounds [k g] are velars, as is the sound [ŋ], represented by <ng> in words like 'king', 'wrong', 'hang'; but as we will see in Chapter 7, there are in fact many variations in the precise place of articulation in English.

The velum also acts as a kind of valve, because it can be raised and lowered. When it is lowered, air can pass into the nasal cavities and escape through the nose. When it is raised, the nasal cavities are sealed off, and air can only escape through the mouth.

2.5.10 Uvular

Uvular sounds are made with the uvula (which is Latin for 'little egg', the shape of the uvula). The uvula is the little fleshy appendage that hangs down in the middle of your mouth at the back. If you gargle, the uvula vibrates. French, German, Dutch and Danish all use uvular articulations for orthographic <r>; and in fact, one variety of English (around the north east of England) has, in its more archaic forms, a uvular sound too in this position.

2.5.11 Pharyngeal

The pharynx is the cavity behind the tongue root and just above the larynx. Pharyngeal sounds are made by constricting the muscles of the neck and contracting the pharynx; this kind of articulation occurs rarely in English.

2.5.12 Glottal

Glottal sounds are made at the glottis, the space between the vocal folds, which are located at the larynx. English uses a number of such sounds:

[h] as in 'head' and its voiced equivalent between two vowels, [ɦ], as in 'ahead'; and the glottal stop [ʔ], which is often used alongside or in place of [t] (as in many Anglo-English – that is, the English of England – pronunciations of words like 'water', [wɔːtə, wɔːʔə]), and in words that begin with vowels (as in many American and Australian pronunciations of phrases like 'the [ʔ] apple').

2.6 Manner of articulation

As well as knowing where a sound is made, we need to know how it is made. Consonants involve at least two articulators. When the articulators are brought closer together, the flow of air between them changes: for instance, it can be stopped or made turbulent. The channels between any two articulators govern the pressure and flow of air through the vocal tract, and in turn this affects the kinds of sound that come out. The way a sound is made (rather than where it is made) is called manner of articulation. Most manners of articulation are combinable with most places of articulation.

2.6.1 Stop articulations

Stop articulations are those sounds where a complete closure is made in the oral tract between two articulators; this stops the air moving out of the oral tract. Stop articulations include a whole range of sound types, which vary according to the kind of airflow (oral vs. nasal) and whether the closure can be maintained for a long time or not.

Plosives are made with a complete closure in the oral tract, and with the velum raised, which prevents air escaping through the nose. English plosives include the sounds [p t k b d g]. Plosives are 'maintainable' stops because they can be held for a long time, and the closure portion arises from a deliberate articulation. The term 'plosive' relates to the way the stop is released – with what is sometimes called an 'explosion'. We look at the release of plosives in more detail in Chapter 7. It is worth pointing out that many phoneticians use the word 'stop' to mean 'plosive'. We are using the word 'stop' in Catford's (2001) sense.

Nasals are made with a complete closure in the oral tract, but with the velum lowered so that air escapes through the nose. For English there are three main nasal sounds, [m n ŋ], bilabial, alveolar and velar respectively. Nasals are usually voiced in English.

The other kinds of stopped articulation are trills and taps. In these sounds, a closure is made only for a very short time, and the closure arises because of aerodynamics or the movement of articulators from one position to another.

Trills are rare in English, but they are one form of 'rolled r': they involve the tongue tip striking the alveolar ridge repeatedly (usually three to four times). They have a very restricted occurrence in English, primarily among a very particular kind of theatrical performer, though they are often thought of as typically Scottish.

Taps on the other hand are quite common in English. These consist of just one short percussive movement of the tongue tip against the alveolar ridge. They occur in many varieties of English, but are especially well known as kinds of /t/ or /d/ sound in many North American varieties in words like 'bu[ɾ]er', 'wri[ɾ]er', 'a[ɾ]om'.

2.6.2 Fricative articulations

Fricative articulations are the result of two articulators being in **close approximation** with each other. This is a degree of stricture whereby the articulators are held close enough together for air to pass between them, but because the gap between them is small, the airflow becomes turbulent and creates friction noise. (In lay terms, we might talk about a 'hissing' sound.) Fricatives in English include [f v θ ð s z ʃ ʒ], the sounds represented orthographically by the underlined portion: fish, vow, think, then, loose, lose, wish, vision. Notice that there are not very consistent representations particularly for the sounds [ʃ ʒ] in English spelling.

Fricative articulations can be held for as long as there is sufficient air to expel. The amount of friction generated depends on the amount of air being forced through the stricture and on the degree of stricture. If you produce a [s] sound and then push more air out, you will notice an increase in the loudness (intensity) of the friction. If you do this and at the same time make the tongue tenser, the intensity of the friction will increase and the friction will sound 'sharper'. On the other hand, if you relax the articulators in producing a [s] sound, you will notice that the friction gets quieter and that it changes quality, becoming 'flatter'.

Affricates are plosives which are released into fricatives. English has two of these: [tʃ dʒ], both postalveolar, as in 'church' and 'judge'.

The sounds [h ɦ] as in 'heart' and 'ahead' are voiceless and voiced glottal fricatives respectively. These sounds are produced with friction at the glottis.

Tongue shape plays a determining role in the overall sound of fricatives. We will return to this in Chapter 8.

2.6.3 Resonant articulations

If articulators are held so as not to generate friction, but to allow air to pass between them smoothly, then we get articulations known as **resonant**. The degree of stricture is known as **open approximation**, and consonant sounds generated this way are called **approximants**. Vowels are another kind of resonant articulation.

Approximants in English include the sounds [j w l r]. (Note: [j] stands for the sound usually written <y> in English, as in 'yes'. The phonetic symbol [y] stands for a vowel.) [j w] are often called glides, because they are closely related in phonetic terms to the vowels [i] and [u], and can be thought of as non-syllabic versions of these vowels. [l r] are often called liquids, and they have certain similarities in the places where they occur in consonant clusters. We will use the symbol [r] for now to represent any kind of [r]-sound, though for the majority of English varieties, a more accurate symbol would be [ɹ].

The English approximants [w j r] are central and [l] is lateral. Approximants are among the phonetically most complex of sounds in English because they typically involve more than one articulation; so we shall leave further discussion of English approximants to a later chapter.

Summary

There are three main aspects of the production of speech sounds in English: voicing, place of articulation and manner of articulation. We have introduced much terminology for describing speech sounds. In later chapters, we will look at place, manner and voicing in much more detail. We will focus on those aspects of the sound of English which relate to meaning in its broadest sense: word meaning, utterance meaning and social meaning. To do this, we will make extensive use of the categories of the International Phonetic Alphabet.

Exercises

1. What is the place and manner of articulation of the consonants in the following words? Remember to refer to the sounds you make in pronunciation, which do not always straightforwardly correspond with the letters in the spelling!

a. club   f. Dutch   k. psychology
b. heavy   g. contact   l. hearing
c. deaf   h. community   m. perform
d. kiss   i. industry   n. translate
e. raised   j. night

2. Divide each of the following groups of symbols into two sets of three, each of which has something in common phonetically. The first one is done for you.

	Symbols	Set 1	Set 2
a.	p m t n k ŋ	p t k (oral plosives)	m n ŋ (nasals)
b.	s l p m v ʃ		
c.	f j w l z θ		
d.	s v h ð ʒ θ		
e.	r k n l w g		
f.	t w s m b g		
g.	ʃ ʒ t̞ θ ð t̞		
h.	h z ɦ l ʔ s		
i.	n a p k j w		
j.	j w b d ɖ ɹ		

Further reading

Overviews of the production of speech and discussion on the classification of speech sounds can be found in Abercrombie (1967), Catford (2001) and Ladefoged (2005, 2006). Ball (1993) is aimed at clinicians, but is very approachable. More advanced readings include Laver (1994) and Pike (1943). For discussion relating to English more specifically, Jones (1975) and Gimson's work (Cruttenden 2001) are classics.

3 Representing the sounds of speech

3.1 Introduction

One of the problems that phonetics needs to solve is how to represent speech, an ephemeral and time-bound phenomenon, so that it is available in a more permanent form.

In this book we will look at two ways to represent speech. The first is phonetic **transcription**: the use of alphabetic symbols to represent the sounds of speech. This is the kind of representation found in dictionary entries, for instance, to represent the pronunciation of words with inconsistent spellings, like 'plough', 'tough', 'trough', 'cough', 'although'.

English, like all languages, has a set of conventions to relate letters to sounds; but it has fewer one-to-one mappings between letter and sound than many other languages that use the Roman alphabet. Phonetic transcriptions are built on the apparently simple **alphabetic principle** of one symbol for each sound.

The second kind of representation we will look at gives us quite different information. These are representations that have a basis in acoustic analysis, such as waveforms and spectrograms. They provide a different perspective on the organisation of speech. Acoustic representations help us to see that despite our impressions, reinforced by an alphabetic writing system, the sounds of speech are constantly changing, are interwoven with one another, and are not discrete in the way that letters are. Acoustic representations are commonly used in phonetics, and they make it possible to see individual aspects of sounds separately.

3.2 Phonetic transcription

The practice of using written letters to represent the sounds of speech is called phonetic transcription. Transcriptions represent an analysis of the sounds we can hear, so transcriptions often have a linguistic status. ('Often' and not 'always' because some transcriptions are more impressionistic and try to capture what we hear rather than make claims about the significance of what we hear for making meaning.) It is useful for phoneticians to write down what we can hear, and we need to do this in a way that is systematic, easy to use, easily understood by others, and portable – a notepad and a pencil predate modern recording equipment by many years, and remain the cheapest tools of the phonetician's trade.

How we transcribe is not a simple matter. Using just the letters of the Roman alphabet is problematic for a number of reasons.

First, the phonetic values of letters are variable. For instance, the letter <g> is regularly used in most European languages with the value of a voiced velar plosive, [g]. In Dutch <g> is pronounced like the <ch> in Scottish 'loch'; in French and Portuguese before an <e> or <i> it has the same value as <si> in 'invasion', [ʒ]; in Swedish in the same context <g> is pronounced like English <y> in 'yes'; in English (sporadically) and Italian (regularly) [dʒ], as in 'gem'.

Within English, letters can have very different values, as in <g> in 'get' and 'gem', or <a> in 'sofa', 'hat' and 'hate'. These differences are due to different spelling conventions being used at different times in the history of the language, or spelling conventions reflecting the etymology of words, and through the conservative approach to spelling reform adopted in the English-speaking world.

Secondly, the Roman alphabet has no symbol for some sounds of English, so that we use digraphs (combinations of two letters) like <th> for the different sounds of 'thick' ([θ]) and 'this' ([ð]) or <sh> for the [ʃ] sound in 'ship'; but 'facial', 'admission', 'station' and 'louche' also contain this sound, where it is represented differently. So the alphabetic principle in English writing is weak.

A number of writing systems built on phonetic principles have been invented over the centuries, but the one that is most widely used is the alphabet of the International Phonetic Association.

3.2.1 The main tool of transcription: the IPA alphabet

The commonest tool for phonetic transcription is the alphabet of the International Phonetic Association. A little confusingly, both the Association and the Alphabet are commonly known as 'the **IPA**', a practice maintained here. The Alphabet is approved by the Association; amendments are made to it regularly on the basis of practical experience and scientific advice. For this reason, phonetics textbooks from different years contain slightly different versions of the Alphabet. (In particular, over the years there have been substantial changes to the number of vowels the IPA represents.)

'Alphabet' is perhaps also not the best way to refer to the IPA. The letters of the alphabet, {A, B, C . . .}, occur in a random order, with vowels scattered among consonants, and the consonants not grouped according to any linguistic principle. The IPA, however, is a set of tables containing symbols organised into rows and columns which are labelled with terms that have agreed meanings.

The rows of the Consonant chart group sounds according to manner of articulation. The first row contains plosives: [p b t d ʈ ɖ c ɟ k g q ɢ ?]. The rows below have sounds with progressively more open stricture. The columns organise symbols by place of articulation, with the left-most column containing symbols that stand for bilabial sounds, and subsequent columns containing symbols for sounds made progressively further down the vocal tract, so that the rightmost column contains symbols for glottal sounds.

The symbols of the IPA are presented in a number of tables, the main ones being pulmonic egressive consonants and vowels. The other tables contain non-pulmonic consonants, diacritics (small marks that combine with letter symbols to represent sounds not on the chart, as we have already seen) and suprasegmentals, aspects of sound which relate to things like length, phrasing, intonation and so on. There is also a collection of 'other symbols', which stand for sounds that do not easily fit in the main scheme.

3.2.2 The principles of the IPA

The IPA, like any system that is used for analysis, makes some assumptions about the nature of speech. Not all of these assumptions are shared by all phoneticians, but it is important none the less to understand them. They are set out in the IPA *Handbook* (IPA 1999: 3–4).

According to the IPA, 'Some aspects of speech are linguistically relevant whilst others . . . are not.' Phonetic transcriptions should only contain information that is linguistically meaningful.

If two speakers from the same speech community say the same thing in the same accent (for instance, 'Come in!'), then they will none the less sound different, although we recognise them as saying the same thing. Physical differences, caused by things such as gender, age or physical state (like being out of breath), mean that people sound different; but these are physical, not linguistic, differences, so a phonetic transcription does not capture them. Except in clinical situations, phonetic transcriptions generally ignore speakers' individual quirks, preferring to work on the language of a community, and not just of an individual.

On the other hand, think about ways of saying 'Shut up!': in particular, how are the two words joined? In the north west of England, you might hear a [ɹ] sound (as if it were written 'shurrup'); in many parts of the English-speaking world, you will hear a glottal stop, [ʔ], or a tap, [ɾ] (as in 'shuddup', defined in the online *Urban Dictionary* as 'what Donald Duck says to Goofy Dog'). In most places, you could hear an alveolar plosive with a puff of air (aspiration), [tʰ]. Most speakers will have a choice about how to join these words, with [tʰ] probably being the sound that has the highest social status. These differences are certainly socio-linguistically meaningful, and for that reason, phoneticians want to be able to represent them.

Secondly, 'Speech can be represented partly as a sequence of discrete sounds or **segments**.' 'Segment' means a piece of something that has been chopped up: in the case of speech, 'segments' means a piece of the speech signal, which is actually continuous. This is the principle that makes the use of the IPA alphabetic: the claim is not that speech is made of segments, but that we can represent it as segments. It is a useful working assumption in many ways, and it is familiar to people who use an alphabetic writing system.

Thirdly, the IPA establishes two major types of segment, **consonant** and **vowel**. Consonants are those sounds which are produced with some kind of constriction in the vocal tract. We can feel, see and hear where these constrictions are made, and what kind of constriction they are.

Vowels, by contrast, are produced without a constriction in the vocal tract, and it is harder to sense how they are articulated. The IPA's terminological framework for describing consonants and vowels is different.

Suprasegmentals are aspects of speech which persist over several segments, such as duration, loudness, tempo (speed), pitch characteristics and voice quality; they are often thought of as the 'musical' aspects of speech, but may include other properties like lip-rounding. They are called suprasegmentals because they function over ('supra' in Latin) consonants and vowels.

The effect of suprasegmentals is easy to illustrate. In talking to a cat, a dog or a baby, you may adopt a particular set of suprasegmentals. Often, when doing this, people adopt a different voice quality, with high pitch register, and protrude their lips and adopt a tongue posture where the tongue body is high and front in the mouth, making the speech sound 'softer'.

Suprasegmentals are important for marking all kinds of meanings, in particular speakers' attitudes or stances to what they are saying (or the person they are saying it to), and in marking out how one utterance relates to another (e.g. a continuation or a disjunction). Both the forms and functions of suprasegmentals are less tangible than those of consonants and vowels, and they often do not form discrete categories.

3.2.3 Types and levels of transcription

Perhaps surprisingly, for any utterance there is more than one appropriate phonetic transcription. Different situations make different demands of a transcription, so we need to understand how transcriptions can vary.

For example, if we encounter a new language or a new variety for the first time, there is no way of knowing initially what might turn out to be important, and what might not. In this case it is common to transcribe as many details as possible so that we have rich working notes to refer to. These transcriptions might be personal memoranda to remind ourselves of what we heard. (Most phoneticians have a good auditory memory: reading detailed transcriptions is one way to recall what was heard.)

We might be working on data for a specific linguistic reason, for instance to work out something about the details of place of articulation for [t] sounds within a given variety. In doing this it is best to concentrate on things that are relevant to the problem in hand, so some parts of the transcription might be detailed, while others will be sketchier.

One important dimension is the amount of detail that a transcription contains. At one end of the spectrum, transcriptions can contain representations of as many details as we can observe. This kind of transcription is often called **narrow**. At the other end of the spectrum are transcriptions that use a restricted set of symbols, and which therefore gloss over many phonetic details on the grounds that they are predictable from the context, and not important in distinguishing word meanings. Such transcriptions are often called **broad**. Transcriptions in dictionaries are typically broad.

A **simple** transcription is one which uses familiar Roman letter shapes in preference to non-Roman letter shapes. E.g. the /r/ sound in English is often pronounced as [ɹ]; but it can be represented with [r] in a simple transcription unambiguously because although [r] stands for a voiced alveolar trill on the IPA chart, alveolar trills do not usually occur in English.

Transcriptions are sometimes used to compare sounds. For instance, we might want to compare the pronunciation of /r/ in Scottish English and Irish English, so we could use symbols such as [ɾ] (tap), [r] (trill), [ɹ] (approximant), etc., so as to make comparison easier. Transcribing different varieties of a single sound when we hear them produces a **comparative** (also narrower) transcription.

Systematic transcriptions limit the number of symbols used to a given set. In some circumstances, there are choices about how to represent sounds. Phonemic transcriptions are by definition systematic. For example, the word 'hue' starts with palatal approximation, voicelessness and friction. In a systematic transcription, the set of available symbols is restricted. Since [h] and [j] are needed independently (for e.g. 'who' and 'you'), the combination [hj] represents the sound at the start of 'hue' unambiguously, without introducing a new symbol, although the symbol [ç] represents a voiceless palatal fricative and is equally accurate in this case. We return to this problem in Section 6.2.3.

Phonemic transcriptions embrace the concept that one linguistically meaningful sound should map onto one symbol. ('Linguistically meaningful' in this context usually means 'capable of distinguishing words'.) So the velar plosives in the words 'kick', 'cat', 'cool', 'skim', 'school', 'look' and 'sick' (which are all slightly different) are all transcribed as [k]. Phonemic transcriptions are necessarily broad. Allophonic transcriptions capture such details, even though they are predictable. Allophonic transcriptions are narrower than phonemic ones. Phonemic and allophonic transcriptions constitute the basis for a phonemic analysis of speech.

A transcription which uses the full potential of the IPA to record much observable detail is called **impressionistic**. Impressionistic transcriptions (or 'impressionistic records') are necessarily narrow.

3.2.4 Systematic transcription of English consonants

Table 3.1 contains the set of symbols used in this book for representing the consonants of English at a systematic level. The transcription is broad and general, and does not attempt to represent differences between varieties. Illustrations of the sounds that the symbols stand for are underlined. For many consonants, the phonetic symbol is generally the same letter we are familiar with from English spelling: [p, t, b, d] for the letters <p, t, b, d> respectively, for example. The examples include words with 'silent letters' such as in 'gnat' or 'lamb'. For some sounds, such as [dʒ], there are several ways to write them: <j>, <dg(e)> and <g> can all represent this sound.

The sound [ʍ] is put in brackets because some speakers do not use this sound, but use [w] in its place. Where letters of English spelling appear between parentheses, this shows that not all speakers will have appropriate examples of the relevant sound; for example, not everyone pronounces the final <r> of 'error'.

Table 3.1 Systematic transcription of English consonants.

p	pip, happy, spot, lamp
t	take, hot, matting, stop, rant
k	cake, sticky, scan, rank, queen
b	baby, hobby, rub, bulb
d	dad, rudder, hand
g	gig, ghost, ragged, rag
tʃ	church, inch, itchy
dʒ	judge, edgy, gem
m	mat, hammer, ram, lamp, lamb
n	not, gnat, knife, honour, phone
ŋ	sing, finger, rank
f	fall, offer, if, philosophy, laughter, rough
v	velvet, delve, love, over
θ	think, ether, truth, tenth
ð	though, rather, breathe
s	sigh, scene, hiss, ice, grassy, fancy
z	zoo, fuzzy, rise, haze, lazy
ʃ	ship, fish, Russia, station, facial
ʒ	invasion, pleasure, beige
h	hall, hollow, ahead
l	look, hilly, all, play, help
r	red, erro(r), sorry, write
w	wall, away, (wh)ite, witch
(ʍ)	white, while, which
j	young, computer, beauty

Table 3.2 shows some of the commonest correspondences from English spelling to phonetic values for the consonants, using most of the same words as in Table 3.1. Some of the mappings from spelling to phonetic symbol are rather complicated. This is partly because the Roman alphabet was designed for Latin, a language which had fewer consonants than English, so English spelling uses combinations of letters like <sh> or <th> to represent the single sounds [ʃ θ] respectively. Another reason is that in its history, English has taken in words from languages with different spelling traditions, and generally has not changed the spelling. So we have some spellings that go back to Anglo-Saxon times (when writing was pioneered by Irish monks), words from French, then later words from Latin and Greek, each with slightly different conventions about the phonetic value of letters. For example, almost all words with the combination <ph> for the sound [f], as in 'phonetics' or 'photo', are Latin transliterations of Greek; when [ʃ] is spelt <sh> it is usually

Table 3.2 Common phonetic values of consonants in English spelling.

Letter (spelling)	Common phonetic value	Examples
b	b	baby, hobby, rub, bulb
c	k	cake, sticky, scan
c + i, e, y	s	cent, ice, fancy
c + i + vowel	ʃ	facial, conscious
ch, tch	tʃ	church, inch, itchy
d	d	dad, rudder, hand
f	f	fall, offer, if
g	g	gig, ragged, rag
g + i, e, y	g	get
	dʒ	gem, gin, gyrate
gh	various, including f	rough
		laughter
h	h	hall, hollow, ahead
j	dʒ	jump
k	k	keep, kick, rank, cake
l	l	look, hilly, all, play, help
m	m	mat, hammer, ram, lamp, lamb
n	n	not, honour, phone
n + k, n + g	ŋ	tank, fang
p	p	pip, happy, spot, lamp
ph	f	philosophy, photo
q + u	kw	queen
r	r	red, error, sorry
vowel + r	vowel + r or long vowel/diphthong	star, hair, pure
s	s	sigh, gas, hiss
s + h	ʃ	ship, fish, washer
s between vowels	z	ease
s + i + vowel	ʃ, ʒ	Russia, Asia, fusion
t	t	take, hot, matting, stop, rant
th (content words: noun, verb, adjective)	θ	think, ether, truth, tenth
th (between vowels); initial in function words	ð	rather, breathe, though, they, this
t + i + vowel	ʃ	station, partial
v	v	velvet, delve, love, over
w	w	wall, away, witch
wh	w, ʍ	white, while, which
wr	r	write, wrong
x	ks, gz, z	axe, exit, xylophone
y	j	yacht, yes, you
	i/ɪ	happy, silly, funny
z	z	zoo, fuzzy, haze

a word from Old English, but when it is spelt <ti> (as in 'station' or 'spatial') it usually has its origin in Latin, via French.

The phonetic transcription system then has complex mappings: many sounds can be written orthographically in several ways, and many letters or combinations of letters have more than one phonetic value. So when learning to transcribe English phonetically, it is important to pay attention to the way a word sounds, and not to fall back too much on how it is spelt.

For vowels, it is even more difficult to provide a systematic transcription system. One reason for this is that vowels are extremely variable across varieties of English, and the mappings between spelling and sound are very complicated. We look at vowels of English in more detail in Chapter 5, including some of the issues of transcribing and representing vowels.

3.2.5 Examples of transcription

Now we will look at how one piece of speech can be transcribed in a variety of ways, and comment on the transcription.

We will look at a series of transcriptions of the utterance 'I think I need some shoes for that.' (The context is two young women chatting about a night out at a graduation ball that they are planning to go to. One of them is discussing the clothes she wants to buy.)

The **citation form** is the form of the word when spoken slowly and in isolation; this is the form found in dictionaries. Using a standard English dictionary, we could transcribe this sentence as in (1):

(1) Citation form transcription:
     [aɪ θɪŋk aɪ niːd sʌm njuː ʃuːz fɔː ðat].

This transcription, which uses the symbols taken from Tables 3.1 and 3.2, simply concatenates the citation forms for each word in the sentence. Notice how [n d s m n f] in 'need', 'some', 'new' and 'for' are the same in the phonetic transcription as they are in the spelling; but others are initially unfamiliar, such as [θ] for the sound at the start of 'think', [ŋ] for the velar (not alveolar) nasal in 'think', [ʃ] for the fricative at the start of 'shoes' and [ð] at the start of 'that'.

When we look up words in citation form, what dictionaries provide is usually a broad phonetic transcription – that is, some indication of how to pronounce it – and information about stress patterns. Stressed syllables are transcribed using the symbol ['] for the main stress. The words in the utterance above are all monosyllabic (they have only one syllable); but words with more than one syllable have the stress marked: for example, 'mountain', ['maʊntɪn]; 'arrival', [ə'raɪvəl]; 'repeat', [rɪ'piːt].

In this sentence, some words do not carry stress while others do. Furthermore, many function words (such as prepositions, auxiliary verbs, conjunctions, pronouns, etc.) in English have other forms called 'weak' forms, which occur when the word is unstressed. The word 'for' is one such word. Here it is transcribed as [fɔː], as if it were stressed, so that it is **homophonous** with 'four'. But in this context, a more natural pronunciation would be [fə], like a fast version of the word 'fur'. (This is true whether you pronounce the <r> in 'fur' and 'for' or not!) Likewise, the word 'I' is often pronounced in British English as something like [a] when it is not stressed, and 'some' as [səm]. So a more realistic transcription of the sentence as it might be pronounced naturally is:

(2) Citation form + weak forms:
    [a 'θɪŋk a 'niːd səm 'njuː 'ʃuːz fə 'ðat].

This is a broad transcription; it is also phonemic because all the symbols used represent sounds that are used to distinguish word meanings. It is systematic because it uses a small and limited set of transcription symbols.

We could add some allophonic details to the transcription and make it 'narrower'. Vowels before nasals in the same syllable – as in 'think' – are often nasalised. This means that the velum is lowered at the same time as a vowel is produced, allowing air to escape through both the nose and mouth. Nasalisation is marked by placing the diacritic [˜] over the relevant symbol.

Voiced final plosives and fricatives (as in 'need', 'shoes') are often produced without vocal fold vibration all through the consonant articulation when they occur finally and before voiceless consonants; this is marked by placing the diacritic [̥] below the relevant symbol.

(3) Citation form + weak forms + some allophones:
    [a 'θĩŋk a 'niːd̥ sə̃m 'njuː 'ʃuːz̥ fə 'ðat].

If we know the sounds and the contexts, these phonetic details are predictable for this variety of English. Not including them in the transcription saves some effort, but the details are still recoverable so long as we know how to predict some of the systematic phonetic variation of this variety of English. This transcription is not only narrower, it is also allophonic: the details we have added are predictable from what we know of English phonetics and phonology.

This sentence was spoken by a real person and without prompting, and there is a recording of her doing so. This means that the details are available for further inspection, and therefore can be transcribed.

Now we will look at some of the details and illustrate what it means to produce an impressionistic transcription.

The transcriptions so far imply that sounds follow one to another in discrete steps. In reality, things are more subtle. To get from [z] (a voiced alveolar fricative) at the end of 'shoes' to [f] (a voiceless labio-dental fricative) at the start of 'for' requires voicing to be stopped and the location of the friction to switch from the alveolar ridge (for the end of 'shoe[z]') to the lips and teeth (for '[f]or'). These two events do not necessarily happen simultaneously. First we get [alveolarity +friction +voicing], [z], but then the voicing stops, so we have [alveolarity +friction −voicing], which we can transcribe as [z̥]. Since labiodental articulations do not involve the same articulators as alveolar ones, the two articulations can be produced at the same time, so we get a short portion of [alveolarity +labiodentality +friction −voicing]: a period of voiceless friction at two places of articulation. We can represent this as [z͡f]: the symbol [͡] means that two articulations occur simultaneously. The alveolar constriction is then removed, leaving just labiodental friction, [f]. So in all, the fricative portion between these two words can be narrowly transcribed as [z z̥ z͡f̥ f]. This could imply four different 'sounds', and at some level, there are: there are four portions that are phonetically different from each other, but really there are only two parameters here: voicing goes from 'on' to 'off', and the place of articulation changes from 'alveolar' to 'labiodental'.

The end of this utterance is produced with creaky voice. This is where the vocal folds vibrate slowly and randomly (Chapter 4). As well as this, the final plosive is not in fact alveolar; like many speak-ers, this one uses a glottal stop instead. So the last two syllables can be partially transcribed as [fəðaʔ]. The dental sound in 'that' is produced without friction: it is a 'more open' articulation (i.e. the tongue is not as close to the teeth as it might be, and not close enough to produce friction): this is transcribed with the diacritic [ˎ] ('more open'); and there is at least a percept of nasality throughout the final syllable. This might be because the velum is lowered (the usual cause of nasal-ity), but sometimes glottal constrictions produce the same percept. We can't be sure which is the correct account, but the percept is clear enough, and in an impressionistic transcription, it is best not to dismiss any detail out of hand. (For all we know, the percept of nasal-ity might be a feature regularly used by this speaker to mark utterance finality.)

(4) Impressionistic transcription:
   [a ˈθĩŋk a ˈniːd̥ sə̃m ˈnjuː ˈʃuːzz̥z̥f͡fə̰ ˈð̰ã̰ʔ].

This probably looks a bit frightening, but it is worth remembering that (a) this is a transcription of one utterance on one occasion by one speaker, and (b) the transcription is based on a set of rather simple observations of what we can hear: it's more important to understand that relationship than to worry about the details of the transcription. It is important not to fetishise transcriptions, but to see the linguistic patterns that lie beyond them.

These impressionistic transcriptions, as can be seen, use the full range of IPA symbols and diacritics in an attempt to capture details of pronunciation whose linguistic status is not clear. There is no point including details of voice quality in an English dictionary because voice quality does not systematically distinguish words one from another. On the other hand, if it turns out that the speaker whose speech we have transcribed regularly uses creak to mark utterance finality (one possible explanation for what we have found), then transcribing it will have served a useful purpose. Impressionistic transcriptions are therefore often preliminary to further analysis, because they raise a lot of questions.

3.2.6 'Correct' transcriptions

Students learning phonetics frequently worry whether they have the 'correct' transcription. Whether a transcription is correct or not depends partly on what kind of transcription it is. The appropriateness of a transcription depends on what it is to be used for and the style of transcription that is adopted. As we have seen, the same thing can be transcribed in a number of different ways; and each transcription is useful for noting different kinds of thing. For example, the word 'thing' is never likely to be pronounced [tɪg], so that transcription is most likely 'wrong' under any circumstances. But this is a relatively trivial case. For a dictionary entry, something like [θɪŋ] is most appropriate, because it is broad – it uses a small set of symbols in a systematic way – and representative of the pronunciation of many English speakers. Many speakers will say [fɪŋ] for this word, because they systematically produce /θ/ as [f], or (to put it in a slightly different way), the distinction between /θ/ and /f/ is lost for them; so [θɪŋ] is not an accurate transcription of their production. If on the other hand we had a speaker in front of us and we wanted to make an impressionistic transcription, [θɪŋ] might only be a starting point. We might want to mark that the [θ] sound was made with the tongue between the teeth, rather than at the teeth; that the vowel was slightly nasalised; or that we could hear a [g]-like ending to [ŋ] as the tongue was released. If the purpose of our listening is to observe whatever we can, then [θɪŋ] may not be the most informative transcription we could produce.

None the less, certain kinds of mistake are easy to make. Common ones include: transcribing the same sounds differently (or different sounds the same); importing letters from spelling (like [c] for [k], or 'silent' letters like <k> in <kn->); using strong vowels where weak ones are more usual (e.g. [fɔː, fɔr] for [fə, fər] in 'for'). The main problem that arises with transcriptions as a working tool is when they are inconsistent; which means that the transcription style needs to be decided at the outset. It is also good practice to state briefly what conventions have been used for transcription: e.g. '[r] stands for [ɹ]'; 'the transcription is phonemic'; 'the transcription is impressionistic and focuses on nasalisation'.

3.3 Acoustic representations

The sounds of speech are made by changes to air pressure that are caused by airflow through the vocal tract. As the air moves, it causes perturbations, which the ear picks up. The ear converts physical movements in the air into electrical signals that are sent to the brain, which is where processing of other kinds (such as detecting meaningful units like sounds, words, sentences and so on) occurs.

Technology makes it possible to convert these changes of air pressure into pictures; and being static and unchanging, these pictures allow us to examine more of the detail of talk as it happened. This kind of phonetics is known as acoustic phonetics, and in this book we use some acoustic representations to show some of the details of talk. The aim of this section is to enable you to understand that there is a connection between articulation and acoustics. There are two main kinds of acoustic representations we will use in this book: waveforms and spectrograms. We will approach these representations as pictures which can show us particular aspects of speech and as a useful complementary tool to transcriptions.

3.3.1 Waveforms

Waveforms are a kind of graph. Graphs have an x-axis, which runs horizontally, and a y-axis, which runs vertically. In waveforms of speech, the x-axis represents time and is usually scaled in seconds or milliseconds, while the y-axis shows (to simplify a great deal) amplitude, a representation of loudness.

Figure 3.1 shows a waveform of a vowel. On the x-axis, time is marked at 0.1 second (or 100 ms) intervals. On the y-axis, there is a

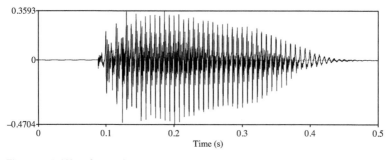

Figure 3.1 Waveform of a vowel.

line marked 0 (the zero crossing) which goes through the waveform. The bigger the displacement from this line, the louder the sound is. The beginning and end of this waveform have no displacement from the zero crossing line, so the recording begins and ends with a period of silence. The sound starts just before 0.1 s into the recording, and is loudest around 0.2 s. From a little after 0.2 s to around 0.45 s, the sound gets quieter: or, a little more technically, the amplitude decreases. By about 0.45 s, the signal has died away.

With a little experience and practice, various other kinds of sound are also evident in waveforms. We will look at these after we have considered spectrograms.

3.3.2 Spectrograms

Spectrograms are pictures of speech: in spy movies they are often called 'voiceprints', which although inaccurate conveys the idea that they show a picture of someone speaking.

Spectrograms provide more complex information than waveforms. Time, as in waveforms, is marked on the x-axis. The y-axis shows frequency. Amplitude is reflected in darkness: the louder a given component in the speech signal is, the darker it appears on the spectrogram.

3.3.3 Three types of sound and their appearance

There are three main kinds of sound that are easily distinguishable on a spectrogram, corresponding to three acoustic categories. Sounds can be **periodic** (that is, regularly repeating) or **aperiodic** (that is, random). Aperiodic sounds in speech can be either continuous (like fricatives such as [s f θ]) or **transient** (that is, short and momentary), like [p t k]. Each has a different appearance on a spectrogram and in waveforms.

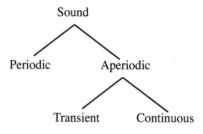

Figure 3.2 Three types of sound.

3.3.4 Periodic sounds

Waveforms which repeat themselves are called periodic. (In reality they are not perfectly periodic, but for simplicity we will think of them as such.) In speech, periodicity is associated with the vibration of the vocal folds, so periodic waveforms are associated with voicing. Each one of the major peaks in a periodic waveform corresponds to one opening of the vocal folds. Figure 3.4 shows the waveform of the section between 0.3 and 0.4 s of Figure 3.3, in the middle of the vocalic portion.

One complete repetition is called a cycle or period. There are about 10.5 cycles in Figure 3.4. This reflects the number of times the vocal folds open in the time represented. The number of complete cycles the vocal folds make in one second is called the **fundamental frequency (f0)**; it is measured in **Hertz (Hz)**. A **frequency** of 1 Hz means that there is one complete cycle per second. A frequency of 100 Hz means that there are one hundred complete cycles per second, or alternatively one complete cycle every 0.01 s (every one hundredth of a second). In the waveform in Figure 3.4, there are approximately 10.5 cycles in 0.1 s, which means the fundamental frequency in this stretch of speech is about 105 Hz.

In spectrograms, periodic signals have two important visual properties. First, there are vertical **striations** which correspond to the opening of the vocal folds: each time the vocal folds open and air escapes, there is a sudden increase in amplitude. This shows up in the striations in the spectrogram which line up with the peaks in the waveform. Voicing is seen in regular spikes in a waveform, and corresponding regular striations in a spectrogram.

Secondly, there are darker horizontal bands running across the spectrogram known as **formants**. There are three clearly visible formants in the periodic part of Figure 3.3, one centred at around 700 Hz (labelled 'F1'), another around 1800 Hz (labelled 'F2'), and a third one around 2800 Hz (labelled 'F3'). There are in fact more formants, but usually only the first three are of interest.

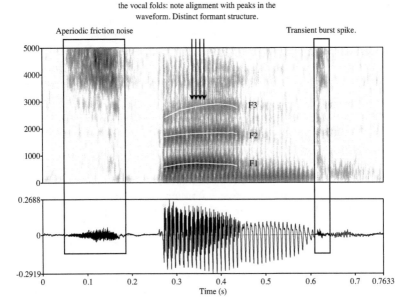

Figure 3.3 Spectrogram of the word 'spend', with periodic, aperiodic and transient sounds marked.

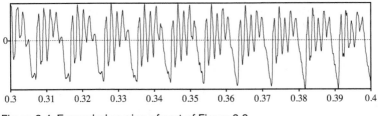

Figure 3.4 Expanded version of part of Figure 3.3.

Formants are named counting upwards. The first one is called the first formant, or Fl. The next one up is called the second formant, or F2; and so on.

Formants are natural **resonances**. Each configuration of the vocal tract has its own natural resonance. Most of us are familiar with the idea of resonances. Imagine a home-made xylophone made of glass bottles. If the bottles are different sizes and shapes, or if there are varying amounts of water in the bottles, then when they are tapped, they will produce different notes. The big bottles will have a deeper 'ring' to them than the little ones, or the ones with more water in them. The vocal tract exhibits similar (though more complex) properties: when the sound wave from the vocal folds passes through the vocal tract, some parts of the acoustic signal are made louder, and some quieter. The frequencies which get amplified (made louder) are the natural resonances of the vocal tract, and are determined by its size and shape. In turn, the size and shape of the vocal tract depends on the position of the tongue, velum, lips and all the other articulators, so that different sounds of speech have different natural resonances; and in turn, they look different on a spectrogram.

To illustrate this, produce any vowel sound (say, [iː] as in 'bee'), and then round and unround your lips. As you do this, you change the length of the vocal tract and the shape of its frontmost cavity. Acoustically, the effect of this is to change the sound that comes out, by changing the location of the formants relative to one another. When the lips are rounded, the vocal tract is a little longer; so the formants will all be a little lower.

Say the vowel [iː]; now make a glottal stop by holding your breath. If you flick your larynx gently, you will excite the first formant. You will hear a low-pitched knocking sound each time you flick. If you now try this with a vowel like [a], you will hear an altogether different, higher note. This is because the shape of the vocal tract has been changed by moving the tongue and opening the jaw. If you make a vowel like [u] you will hear a lower note again.

In summary: periodic sounds in the vocal tract are caused by voicing. Periodicity is seen in a regular waveform, striations in the spectrogram, and visible formants in the spectrogram. Vowels and the sounds [w j l ɹ m n ŋ] all illustrate these properties well.

3.3.5 Aperiodic, continuous sounds

For aperiodic sounds there is no repetition, but rather random noise. This kind of sound is called aperiodic. Figure 3.5 shows 0.1 s of the voiceless fricative [s] sound. If you compare this with Figure 3.4, you will see that it looks very different: [s] has no repeating waveform, and the amplitude varies apparently randomly.

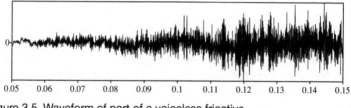

| 0.05 | 0.06 | 0.07 | 0.08 | 0.09 | 0.1 | 0.11 | 0.12 | 0.13 | 0.14 | 0.15 |

Figure 3.5 Waveform of part of a voiceless fricative.

Friction noise is generated when the airflow between two articulators is turbulent. The correlate of this in a waveform is a very much more irregular, random pattern than we find for periodic sounds; it lacks the regular ups and downs of a periodic waveform.

In Figure 3.3, the aperiodic portion lacks the clear formant structure and the vertical striations we saw for periodic portions. However, the pattern of the frequencies does change. As the lips close to form the [p] sound, the [s] sound changes, and sounds as though it gets lower in pitch: this can be seen in the end of the segment marked 'aperiodic'.

A combination of voicing (periodic) and friction (aperiodic) is also possible; we will see this in Chapter 8.

3.3.6 Transient sounds

Transient sounds are aperiodic sounds which come and go quickly. Examples from everyday life are a knock on a door, the sound of one piece of cutlery rattling against another, or a firework exploding. In speech, the main source of transient sounds is the explosive release of a closure, such as releasing a closure for [p] or [k]. Other common transient sounds in speech are the tongue or lips coming apart as someone starts to speak, bubbles of saliva bursting in the mouth, the velum being raised, or the sides of the tongue making contact with the teeth or cheeks.

In a waveform, transients show up as a spike. On spectrograms, they appear as dark vertical lines which last only a short time.

In Figure 3.3, there are two transients. One, at about 0.25 s, corresponds to the lips opening for the sound [p], the other, marked with the box just after 0.6 s, corresponds to the tongue coming away from the alveolar ridge, for [d].

Figure 3.6 shows the waveform of a transient (the start of [d] in 'spend') in more detail. The transient portion T lasts less than 30 ms. It has an abrupt start and then fades away.

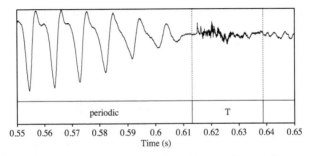

Figure 3.6 Transient portion (T) for the initial plosive of 'spend'.

3.4 Acoustic representations and segments

Acoustic representations are rarely static in the way that transcriptions are. In the waveform and spectrogram of 'spend' (Figure 3.3), many things change simultaneously: the amplitude of the signal and the formants in particular are not static. In speech, many articulations do not start and stop quite synchronously. Looking at the spectrogram we can identify six or seven more or less stable portions. On the other hand, this utterance is transcribed broadly as [spɛnd], which implies five discrete units.

Transcriptions and acoustic representations capture different kinds of truth about speech, [spɛnd] captures the fact that English speakers conceive of this word as having five distinct sounds. English speakers' intuitions about how many segments there are do not match up with what our eyes might tell us. The acoustic representation captures the fact that in speaking, the articulators are rarely static. When articulators move, these movements have acoustic consequences, and this very fluidity helps to make everyday speech easier to perceive. Both the acoustic and written representations convey important but different information about speech.

Transcriptions may have a generality to them which acoustic representations do not. A broad transcription represents many of the important details of the speech of a whole community of speakers, which is why such transcriptions are used in dictionaries. On the other hand, acoustic representations capture details and facts about one utterance on one occasion by one speaker (as may an impressionistic transcription); if the speaker changed, or if the same speaker produced the same word e.g. more slowly, then many of the details of the acoustic representation would also change. So acoustic representations may be less useful from the point of view of representing facts about language.

3.5 Representation and units in phonetics

From both written transcriptions and acoustic representations, it should be clear that all forms of representation of speech are partial, and none gives a complete picture of speech. In the same way, an architect or an estate agent will describe a house in different ways, reflecting different purposes and different levels of detail.

Both transcriptions and (perhaps more surprisingly) acoustic representations have an element of subjectivity in them. As phoneticians, we train ourselves to listen more objectively. Ways to make transcription more of a 'science' and less of an 'art' include regular practice, collaborating with others whose judgements are trustworthy, or combining the activity of transcription with acoustic observation, which allows for a slower, more piecemeal approach to work and can make it possible to check impressions against acoustics. If our records open the way to other work, then they have served a useful purpose.

Acoustic representations seem more objective: after all, any two people can put the same acoustic signal in and get the same representation out. However, such representations are less objective than they appear. For instance, it is possible to manipulate the way the acoustic signal is processed and the way that spectrograms are drawn so that they appear sharper; or to emphasise the temporal organisation of the signal over the frequency aspect (or vice versa); or to draw spectrograms in colour rather than black and white; and the Hertz scale does not by any means represent the way the ear and brain analyse the signal. So there are also many unknowns with this kind of representation.

For all these reasons, it is wise to be wary of ascribing to any one form of representation some kind of primacy. Made and used carefully, they are all informative in some way.

Summary

In this chapter we have looked at two forms of representation of speech: transcription and acoustic representations. We have seen that each has a place, and each type of representation has both advantages and drawbacks.

In later chapters, we will use verbal descriptions, transcriptions and acoustic representations to try to give some impression of the way the sounds of English are produced, and to try to show some of the details of those sounds where using words is not straightforward. Phonetics is special in linguistics for the way it combines the production and perception of sounds, the auditory, visual and kinaesthetic aspects of the subject: this means that learning phonetics can be a multi-sensory experience. It is worth persisting, if frustration sets in, to try to put the various forms of phonetic description and representation together, because it results in a richer understanding of the embodied nature of human speech.

Exercises

1. Consider the functions of phonetic transcriptions in the following circumstances: a speech therapist with a client; a fieldworker working out a writing system for an unwritten language; a dictionary aimed at learners of English as a foreign language. What demands and needs might each situation make?

2. Below is a text and various phonetic transcriptions of it (representative of a variety of Anglo-English where <r> is pronounced only before vowels). For each transcription, comment on its properties: how broad is it, how simple, how systematic?

'He was really tired, because he didn't get any sleep the night before either.'

a.   [hi wɒz rɪəli taɪəd bɪkɒz hi dɪdənt gɛt ɛni sliːp ðə naɪt bɪfɔːr aɪðə]
b.   [i wəz ɹɪːli tʰaɪəd bɪkəz i dɪdən? gɛ? ɛni sliːp ðə naɪt bɪfɔːr aɪðə]
c.   [i wəz rɪːli tʰaɪəd bɪkəz i dɪdən? gɛ? ɛni sliːp ðə naɪt bɪfɔːr aɪðə]
d.   [ʔi wəzʷ ɹʏwɪːli taːɪə̰b̚ pə̥xeẓ i dɪŋ? gɛ? ɛ̥ni sliːp̚ d̪ðə nɑɹp̚
     bɪ̥fʷɔːɹʏʷ aɪðə̰]

3. The spectrogram and waveform in Figure 3.7 represent a production of 'took off his cloak', [tʊk ɒf ɪz kləʊk], spoken by a speaker of RP. Identify the following things:

a.   four periods of voicing
b.   four transients
c.   the first three formants
d.   two portions with low F2, one with high F2
e.   portions where there is aperiodic (friction) noise

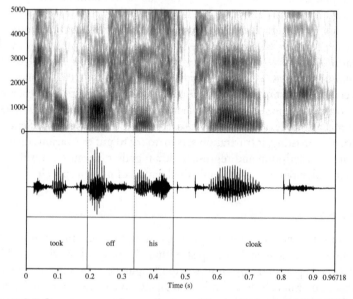

Figure 3.7 Spectrogram of a production of 'took off his cloak' (RP) (IPA).

Further reading

Bell (2004) discusses English spelling in an approachable but critical way. The *Handbook of the International Phonetic Association* (IPA 1999) provides a short overview of the principles of the IPA and transcription styles. Abercrombie (1967), Kelly and Local (1989), Laver (1994) and Jones (1975) contain more thorough discussion of transcription styles, and Pullum and Ladusaw (1996) is a useful guide to IPA and other phonetic symbols. For more practice at transcription, Lecumberri and Maidment (2000) has lots of exercises and discussion. Heselwood (2013) is an exhaustive overview of the history, theory and practice of phonetic transcription.

For a more technical introduction to acoustic phonetics, Ladefoged (1995) is very approachable; Denes and Pinson (1993) and Johnson (2002) are also recommended.

4 The larynx, voicing and voice quality

4.1 Introduction

In this chapter, we look at the production of voicing, the construction of the larynx, and the mechanism which gets the vocal folds vibrating. We will then move on to look at ways this vibration can be controlled to produce different pitches and voice qualities.

Good examples of pairs of sounds distinguished by voicing in English are [s f] (voiceless) and [z v] (voiced). Produce a [s] or [f] sound; close your eyes and concentrate on how it feels to produce this sound; and then make a [z] or [v] sound instead. Now produce chains of sounds like [s z s z s . . .] or [f v f v . . .] without inserting a pause between them. If you put your fingers in your ears, you will notice a humming or buzzing for [z v] which is not there for [s f]. With the fingers resting very lightly on your larynx, you will notice that [z v] involve a vibration that you do not feel for [s f].

Voicing is produced when the vocal folds vibrate. The vocal folds are located in the larynx (Figure 4.1), which sits just below where your jaw meets your neck. For males, there is a rather prominent notch at the front of the larynx, and it is a couple of centimetres below the jawbone; for females, the larynx is less prominent and may be a bit higher up the neck. If you watch yourself in a mirror, you will probably be able to see your larynx bob down and then up again as you swallow.

The larynx is constructed from three main cartilages: the **thyroid**, **cricoid** and **arytenoid** cartilages. Of these three, the thyroid is the most obvious. It is the largest and is at the front of the larynx, and forms the 'box' of the larynx. It consists of two plates which are joined at an angle at the front. Female thyroids are at a wider angle than male thyroids, so the notch where the plates meet is more obvious in males than in females. The thyroid cartilage is attached by muscles to the hyoid bone higher up in the neck.

The cricoid cartilage is a sort of ring shape underneath the thyroid. It forms the bottom part of the 'box'. It has two spurs at the back, one on

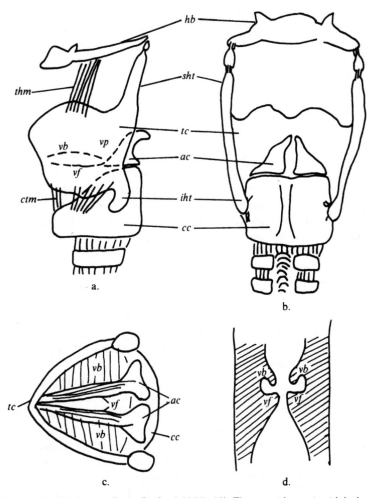

Figure 4.1 The larynx (from Catford 1977: 49). The most important labels for our purpose are: *vf*: vocal folds; *hy*: hyoid bone; *tc*: thyroid cartilage; *cc*: cricoid cartilage; *ac*: arytenoid cartilages.

each side, which reach up to behind the bottom part of the thyroid. The two arytenoid cartilages sit on top of the back of the cricoid cartilage. They can move together and apart, rock backwards and forwards as well as rotate.

The vocal folds are two ligaments (fibrous tissues) which are covered in mucous membrane. They are attached to the arytenoids at the back and the thyroid at the front. At the side, they are attached to muscle in the larynx. In the middle they are free, so that there is a gap or a space between them, known as the glottis. The arytenoids can move, but the thyroid is static; by manipulating the arytenoids, the tension across the vocal folds can be changed, as can their thickness and the way they vibrate.

4.2 How the vocal folds vibrate

The vocal folds form a kind of valve. Their primary function is to prevent anything entering the lungs, such as food or water, by forming a stoppage in the windpipe. For example, if when you swallow something 'goes down the wrong way' (a description which is actually rather accurate), the reflex reaction is to close the vocal folds tightly together, and then cough. Coughing involves an increase of air pressure below the closure at the glottis, and then releasing the closure forcefully in an attempt to expel anything that has fallen down too far. You can make a cough and then release it more gently: this release of the cough is a glottal stop, transcribed [ʔ]. We return to glottal stops in Chapter 7.

For breathing, the vocal folds are open and held wide apart so that air can pass in and out of the lungs unimpeded. If you breathe with your mouth open, you will hear only a gentle noise as the air moves in and out of your body. However, you can make a little more tension across the vocal folds, and you will get a [h] sound.

Sounds that are made with the vocal folds open, allowing the free passage of air across the glottis, are voiceless. In English, voiceless sounds include [p t k f θ s ʃ]. Voiceless sounds often have a more open glottis than the state of the vocal folds for breathing.

Voiced sounds are made with a more or less regular vibration of vocal folds. They include: [b d ɡ v ð z ʒ m n ŋ l r w j] and all the vowels. As we will see in later chapters, the way the phonological contrast between voiced and voiceless sounds is accomplished phonetically involves more than the presence or absence of vocal fold vibration.

We will now take a look at the mechanism by which voicing is produced. The vibration of the folds is not caused directly by commands from the brain telling the folds to open and close: it is caused by having the right amount of tension across the folds. When the folds are shut, the air below them cannot escape, yet the pressure from the intercostal muscles has the effect of forcing the air out. So the pressure builds up below the glottis. Once this pressure is great enough, it forces the folds to open from below, until eventually they come open. Once they are open, and air can pass through the glottis, the air pressure above the glottis and below the glottis equalises. Now the tension across the vocal folds forces them back together again, making a closure again. The process now repeats itself: the folds are closed, air cannot escape through the glottis, so the pressure builds up, the folds are forced open, the pressure equalises, the folds close again.

This cycle of opening and closing is an aerodynamic effect called the **Bernoulli effect**. When the vocal folds vibrate making complete closure along their full length (that is, with no gaps in contact between the vocal folds), with regular vibration, and with no particular tension in the folds to make them especially thick (and short) or thin (and long), this is called **modal voicing**. Few speakers really achieve modal voicing, but since most people have a 'normal' setting (that is, one that has no particular distinguishing features for them), we often speak of modal voicing to mean a person's default voice quality.

4.3 Fundamental frequency, pitch and intonation

The rate of vocal fold vibration affects the perceived pitch of speech. The faster the rate of vibration of the vocal folds, the higher in pitch the speech signal will sound. Correspondingly, the lower the rate of vibration of the vocal folds, the lower in pitch the speech signal will sound.

4.3.1 Changing the rate of vibration of the vocal folds

The rate of vibration of the vocal folds is affected by several things. First, more tension across the folds creates a faster rate of vibration. If the folds are tightened (adducted) by the arytenoid cartilages, then they will start to vibrate more quickly, and the pitch will rise. If on the other hand they are relaxed, and the tension is lowered, then they will vibrate more slowly. You can get a sense of this by singing a very high note. If you hold that note silently, you will feel quite a lot of tension in your larynx. You may also be raising your larynx: this facilitates the tension across the folds. Now drop from a high note to a low note quickly, and you will feel a change in tension and possibly also in larynx height.

Secondly, the more air pressure there is below the folds, the more quickly they will vibrate, other things being equal. Under certain conditions (stress being one of them), we typically breathe more quickly. As a result, the average air pressure below the folds increases, and with it both the loudness of our speech and its average pitch. On the other hand, if there is rather little air in the lungs, the air pressure below the folds will be low. Speech produced like this is more likely to sound 'tired' because it requires less energy to produce. But this can also be used as a more linguistic device: when coming to the end of a topic, one iconic device we can use to mark this in our speech is to talk quietly and with a low pitch.

4.3.2 Pitch and fundamental frequency

The **pitch** of speech is related to the rate of vibration of the vocal folds: grossly speaking, the higher the rate of vocal fold vibration, the higher the pitch. This is not a straightforward relationship because of the way our hearing mechanism works, and as we have seen, the relationship between air pressure, airflow and vocal fold vibration is not quite simple. We use the term 'pitch' to refer to a percept rather than a physical event. The rate of vibration of the vocal folds is often called the fundamental frequency, because it is the lowest component frequency of speech. Fundamental frequency is often abbreviated as f0.

The relation between pitch and fundamental frequency is not a linear one, but is more logarithmic in nature. Linear relationships are where an absolute difference of a certain number of units always has the same effect: for example, if the f0 : pitch relation were linear, then the difference between 100 Hz and 200 Hz would sound like the same difference as that between 200 Hz and 300 Hz: a difference of +100 Hz in each case.

For logarithmic relations, the important factor is the proportionality. For example, the difference between 100 Hz and 200 Hz sounds the same as the difference between 200 Hz and 400 Hz, because in each case the second figure is twice the first one: a proportion of 1 : 2. The difference between 200 Hz and 300 Hz is not in the proportion 1 : 2, but 1 : 1.5.

Figures 4.2 and 4.3 show a pitch trace for a production of 'oh thank you for calling' by a female speaker. The figures are scaled according to this speaker's range: her lowest pitch is 80 Hz, and her highest pitch is 585 Hz. Her average pitch is 220 Hz, marked on the right. Figure 4.2 shows a linear pitch trace: the steps 200–300–100–500 Hz are equal on the y-axis. The speaker's average pitch seems rather low in her range on this graph, and certainly lower than half way through her range.

Figure 4.3 shows the same thing on a logarithmic scale. Here, the distance between 100 Hz and 200 Hz is the same as that between 200 Hz and 400 Hz, because the proportion 100 : 200 is the same as 200 : 400, that is 1 : 2 – the second number is twice the value of the first. On this representation, the higher frequencies appear squashed together; and the speaker's average pitch is more in the centre of the graph. This is closer to what we perceive.

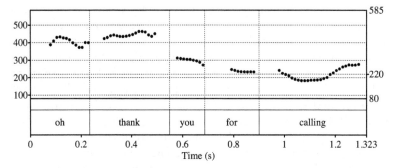

Figure 4.2 f0 on a linear scale.

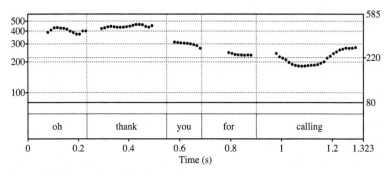

Figure 4.3 f0 on a logarithmic scale.

4.3.3 Parameters for describing f0

Speakers cannot produce f0 above or below a certain level, for physical reasons; or to put it another way, f0 is produced within a certain range. The bottom of the range refers to a speaker's lowest f0 value, while the top of the range refers to their highest f0 value. This range varies from individual to individual, but it also varies according to extralinguistic factors such as state of health, the loudness of the speech and the time of day.

Average values for male speakers are around 120 Hz, while female speakers' averages are around 220 Hz. A typical f0 range in conversation is something like 120–300 Hz for females and 70–250 Hz for males.

The reason for so much individual variation in f0 is that it is a product of individuals' vocal tract shapes, their larynx and their habitual way of speaking. However, we can draw some generalisations about relations between f0 and speaker age and gender. Female speakers have a higher average f0 than male speakers. This represents anatomical differences in the construction of the larynx. The thyroid cartilages are at a wider angle in female larynxes than in male ones, which means that the average tension across the folds is higher for female speakers than for males. There are cultural effects too: in English-speaking cultures, it is common for males to enhance their intrinsically lower f0 by lowering their larynx, and for females to enhance their intrinsically higher f0. The other difference is to do with age. Children of both sexes have roughly the same f0 and are anatomically alike until the onset of puberty, when boys' voices start to become lower in pitch. As people age, the cartilages harden and the mucous membranes which coat the vocal folds become drier, making it harder for speakers to produce such a wide range of f0 as in their younger years. The data in Table 4.1 is taken from Baken and Orlikoff (2000); it shows how gender and age impact on mean f0.

Table 4.1 Average f0 values (Baken and Orlikoff 2000).

Gender	Mean age	Age range	No. subjects	Mean f0 (Hz)
Male	20.3	17.9–25.8	25	120
Male	85	80–92	12	141
Female	24.6	20–29	21	224
Female	85	80–94	10	200

4.4 Phrasing and intonation

All languages use changes in pitch to handle some aspect of meaning. In English, changes in pitch are associated with sentence- or utterance-level meanings and not e.g. word meanings. **Intonation** is the linguistic use of particular f0 contours in the production of speech. These contours can be described using labels that refer to their shapes such as 'fall' ([\]), 'rise' ([/]), 'fall-rise' ([\/]), 'rise-fall' ([/\]), 'level' [\], sometimes accompanied by a reference to where in the speaker's overall range the contour is: 'a high fall', 'a fall to low', 'a low rise'.

In English utterances, intonation contours start on stressed syllables. When stressed syllables bear an intonation contour, they are said to be **accented**. This means that pitch movement starts on the stressed item and carries on over any subsequent syllables up to the next accent, or the end of the phrase. Let's start with words with one syllable:

(1)   Ann
       Will

If you are trying to get Ann's or Will's attention, one option is to use a rising contour which ends high in the speaker's range. We will mark the rise with /. The underlining indicates the accented syllable:

(2) /A̲nn
     /Wi̲ll

To see that the rising contour belongs with the stressed syllable, we can replace the names with slightly longer ones:

(3) /A̲nna
     /Wi̲lliam

Notice that although these names are longer, the rise starts in the same place in the word, and ends at the end of the word. On the other hand, the rise cannot start on the unstressed syllables:

(4) * A̲/nna
     * Wi̲/lliam

If you substitute the rising contour for a different one, such as a fall, you can probably imagine other appropriate occasions for their use: \A̲nna, \Wi̲lliam, \/A̲nna, \/Wi̲lliam and so on.

In any given English utterance, there is at least one accented syllable. Take a simple sentence: 'It's a small firm.' This can be produced with an accent on 'small': 'it's a \sma̲ll firm'. Or it can have an accent on 'firm': 'it's a small \fi̲rm'; or on both: 'it's a \sma̲ll \fi̲rm'. The placement and choice of contours in English is linguistically complex, and depends on the context. We will touch on some of the factors governing these choices in this chapter.

Figure 4.4 shows f0 traces for three utterances: 'hello', [hɛ\ləʊ]; 'hello', [hɛ/ləʊ]; and 'hello there', [hɛ/ləʊ ðɛː]. The difference between the falling and rising contours should be visible enough. (It is safe to ignore the smaller movements of f0 on the unstressed syllables: they are not auditorily prominent in the way that movements on stressed syllables are.) In 'hello (3)', the f0 contour is the same as in 'hello (2)', but it is distributed over more material.

Here are two speakers assessing a third person:

(5) nrb/reluctant lover
1   K   she's really ni̲ce | i̲sn't she
2   J   →   she i̲s nice

Our focus of interest is line 2, 'she is nice'. In the first line, K assesses another person as 'really nice', and invites J to agree with her ('isn't she'). J responds by repeating K's words: 'she is nice'. In English, when words

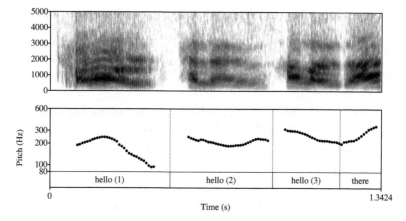

Figure 4.4 (1) 'hello', [hɛ\ləʊ]; (2) 'hello', [hɛ/ləʊ]; (3) 'hello there', [hɛ/ləʊ ðɛː].

are repeated, it is normal for the stress to shift to a different word from the first time round: the 'nice' in line 2 is 'deaccented'. The main stresses in the utterances are marked with underlining.

Now let us imagine different intonation contours here. With a falling intonation contour ('she \is nice'), the pitch would be high on 'is', and fall to low at the end of 'nice'. Most English speakers would say that line 2 produced this way expresses straightforward agreement. If the contour is different, then the meaning is different. If line 2 had a fall followed by a rise ('she \/ is nice'), where the pitch is high on 'is', but then falls and is low at the start of 'nice', rising up again at the end of 'nice', then most English speakers would say that the next word is likely to be 'but'. A fall–rise intonation contour in this context usually says: there is an upcoming disagreement.

In fact, this is how the conversation actually went:

(6) nrb/reluctant lover (ctd).

1	K	she's \really \ nice	\isn't she
2	J	she \/ is nice
3		I do find though that she says stuff
4		for the sake of saying stuff

In lines 3–4, J qualifies her agreement that the other person is 'nice'. This illustrates that in English intonation handles utterance-level meanings: the fall vs. fall–rise contours here mark different types of agreement.

Here are two examples of the word 'yes', both located after an assessment. They differ in intonation, loudness, pitch range, and in their location relative to the previous turn at talk; and they also differ in the meanings they convey.

(7) njc.nice feet.l0;15

1	W		Vic had slip-ons on
2	M		yes I saw Vicky
3	W		[I quite liked those]
4	M		[I thought she had quite nice] feet
5	W	→	↑ \ YES
6	M		I thought she had really nice feet
7	W		yeah I did

(8) gw/00.washing machine

1	H		but it's better than \tokens /though
2			(0.4)
3	E	→	yes it\ is better than /token [s
4	H		[cos like you always
5			went to the porter and he said "oh we've got none"
6			like went back two days later and he still had none
7	E		.mt we-uhm (1.0) my card always says bad card all the time

In (7), Marion and Wendy are discussing a character from a soap opera. Marion says she thought she had 'quite nice feet', and Wendy agrees with her. She does her agreement in line 5 almost immediately after Marion has assessed Vicky's feet. She does her agreement loud (represented with capital letters here) and with quite high pitch (represented by [↑]).

The second case, 'washing machine', also has a 'yes', in line 3. In this extract, Elizabeth and Helen are discussing the system used to pay for the launderette at college, which has changed from tokens to a smart card. Helen says the new system is 'better than tokens though'. Elizabeth agrees with this, but her agreement comes late (almost half a second later). Agreeing late weakens the sense of agreement; notice that Helen comes in and explains her assessment of the new system as 'better', and the next thing Elizabeth does is to find a reason why the new system is not very good (lines 7–8). So the 'yes' here is not whole-hearted, especially in comparison with the 'yes' of the first example. Perhaps unsurprisingly, the strength of agreement is audible too: the 'yes' in line 3 of the 'washing machine' extract is quiet, low pitched, and slow – a direct contrast with the 'yes' in line 5 of the 'nice feet' extract.

Here, then, we have two instances where 'yes' is produced, but the intonation, along with other things, affects the 'meaning' of the 'yes', making it stronger and more affirmative, or weaker and prefacing a disagreement.

Phrasing and intonation give speakers clues about the syntax that organises words into structures. This is one of the main interfaces between phonetics and syntax and semantics. Talk is chunked up into phrases, whose boundaries reflect major syntactic boundaries. The symbols [| ||] mark minor and major intonational phrase boundaries. Phrases have some or all of the following characteristics (roughly):

- at the start: speeding up, re-setting of pitch
- at the end: slowing down, quieter, near the bottom or top of the speaker's pitch range
- a pause before or after
- congruence with syntactic or pragmatic boundaries

Take the following sentence:

(9)   We didn't go to the museum because it was raining.

Did we go or not? If the sentence is spoken on a monotone, it is not possible to tell. But if an intonation contour is placed on the sentence, then two different meanings are possible:

(9a)   ‖ We \ didn't go to the mu \ seum be \ cause it was \ / <u>rai</u>ning ‖
(9b)   ‖ We \ <u>did</u>n't go to the museum | because it was \ <u>rai</u>ning ‖

In the first one, there is one phrase and the last word has a falling + rising intonation contour on it. It means: we did go to the museum, but for some other reason than the fact that it was raining. In the second one, there are two phrases, with a slowing down at the end of 'museum', and two falling contours, one on 'didn't', the other on 'raining'. This means: we did not go to the museum and the reason is that it was raining.

4.5 Voice quality

Speakers can control not just the rate of vibration of the vocal folds, but also the way in which they vibrate. This is known as **voice quality**. Aside from modal voice quality, we will look at four voice qualities which are regularly used in certain situations, to convey e.g. a particular stance towards the thing being talked about. There is also some evidence that varieties of English have habitual settings for voice quality: that is, speakers belonging to certain sociolinguistic groups share a common voice quality. None the less, there remains much work to be done on the function and use of voice quality in English.

4.5.1 Breathy voice

Breathy voice is produced by incomplete closure along the length of the vocal folds as they vibrate. There is an opening which allows air to flow out during voicing, generating both voicing and some friction noise. Breathy voice impressionistically is 'soft', and tends to be quieter than modal ('normal') voicing. In English-speaking cultures it is often associated with female speakers, and is often exploited in e.g. adverts for chocolate or cosmetics. Many people (of either gender) regularly use a slightly breathy setting in their ordinary speech.

Breathy voice is transcribed with the diacritic [..], which sits below the symbol, e.g. [mm̤m], 'mhm'.

English [h] is often produced as a stretch of breathy voicing: for example, in the phrase 'a happy holiday', the words 'happy' and 'holiday' have voicing at their start, accompanied with breathiness. We could transcribe this as [ə ɦapi ɦɒlideɪ], or alternatively – and equivalently – as [ə a̤api p̤ɒlideɪ].

4.5.2 Creak

Creaky voice can be produced in a number of ways. It involves closure along the vocal folds leaving an opening at the front end; the folds are loosely pressed together and are thicker than in other settings. The subglottal pressure is often low. Creak often leads to a more irregular pattern of vibration, and always to a slower one than is normal for the speaker. This means that the f0 of creaky voice is low, and in fact it is sometimes possible to hear individual pulses as the folds open. When speakers reach the low part of a falling f0 contour, they may switch into creaky voice: there is a close relationship between low f0 and creak. The symbol for transcribing creak is the diacritic [ˍ], which sits under another symbol. A creaky production of the word 'yeah' could be transcribed [jḛa̰]. (Remember that the diacritic for nasal sounds looks the same as this one, but it goes over the symbol: so [ã] means a nasalised [a], and [a̰] means [a] produced with creaky voice; [ã̰] means nasalised and creaky!)

Figure 4.5 shows a spectrogram of a stretch of speech where creak is used. The speaker is describing a fizzy drink as 'disgusting yeuagh' (a 'nonce' word, invented for the occasion), [dɪsɡʊstɪŋ jø̰a̰ːː]. The latter part of this is produced with very marked creaky voice, which can be seen in the way that vertical striations change from being rather regularly spaced to being irregularly spaced, and further apart from one another.

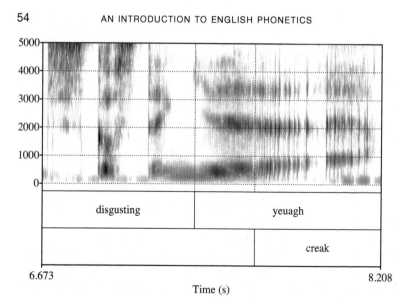

Figure 4.5 Creaky voice.

4.5.3 Whisper

Whisper is produced by narrowing the vocal folds so that the glottis is not closed, and the folds do not vibrate; none the less the glottis is narrow enough so that when air passes through it, the airflow becomes turbulent. Whisper is used by speakers as a way to speak 'quietly', or 'secretively': this seems to be a very widespread practice among linguistic communities. It is sometimes also used to mark stance, as in (10) below. The IPA has no symbol for marking whisper.

(10) tlj-sum04-damsongin

1	if you like / damson / <u>jam</u>
2	if you like stewed / <u>dam</u>sons
3	if you like \ {_{wh}da_{wh}} mson \ {_{wh}gi_{wh}} n,
4	which is gorgeous . . .

4.5.4 Falsetto

Falsetto involves the raising of a speaker's average f0 to way beyond their normal range. To produce falsetto, the vocal folds are stretched and lengthened and the glottis is not completely closed. Falsetto can be used in singing, but also occurs in conversational speech. The IPA has no symbol for marking falsetto.

Here are two cases of falsetto from everyday talk. The first one is part of a complaint from Lesley to her friend Joyce about an acquaintance of theirs, who has offended Lesley. At line 8, she goes into falsetto, probably marking some kind of stance such as 'outrage' at the way she has been treated. (We will return to this story in Chapter 10.)

(11) Field C85.4

1	L	and he came up to me and he said
2		"oh hello Lesley, still trying to buy something for
3		nothing?"
4	J	[ǀ ɑ ₒ ↓ ː] ((a click followed by a sharp in-breath))
5		[ooh
6	L	[ooh
7	J	isn't [he
8	L	[{Falsetto what do you say Falsetto}
9	J	oh isn't he dreadful

The second example is a woman describing to a friend her feelings towards a man. She compares her earlier stance towards him with her current view of him: she is now much more favourably disposed towards him than she was. She uses the same words to express her stance towards him, but the second time round, she speaks in falsetto, as well as speaking much more slowly and loudly.

(12) smc/sweet guy

1	B	much more attractive in every way
2	A	hahahaha
3	B	not even just physically just like in every way than
4		he was before
5		it's like before when he did something that was
6		really sweet it was just like
7		"oh that's really sweet=that's Tim"
		{fast ─────────────}
8		.hh and now it's like "o:h that's ↑really sweet"
		{falsetto ─────────}
		{loud, slow ─────────}

In both of these examples, by moving into falsetto, the speaker is able to use a higher pitch range than her normal one, which means that the difference between the highest and lowest values of the f0 range is expanded. The high pitches the speakers can reach (as high as 673 Hz in the first example and 572 Hz in the second one) may be used to mark out their current talk as conveying something 'noteworthy', or something that the other person is expected to comment on. In both these cases, the speakers are involved in presenting a strong stance towards the person they are talking about: in the first case as part of a complaint, and in the second case as part of a positive, upgraded stance compared with an earlier one. Perhaps falsetto is used to mark an attitude towards the subject matter which is at one extreme or the other – but not neutral.

4.5.5 Voice quality as a sociolinguistic marker: Glasgow

Glasgow is one of the major cities of Scotland, with a strong Scottish and distinctively Glaswegian identity. Glasgow English is one of the few varieties of English whose voice quality has been systematically studied (Stuart-Smith, in Foulkes and Docherty 1999). This study showed that voice quality in Glasgow varies with age, gender and class. Male speakers overall are more creaky than female speakers.

There are also differences in 'articulatory settings' – that is, in the habitual postures that speakers use throughout their speech. Here we list some of the main ones. Male speakers have overall a more nasalised setting than female speakers: they keep the velum slightly lowered, allowing nasal escape of air. Working-class speakers tend to speak with a more open jaw, with a more raised and backed tongue body, perhaps also with their tongue roots more retracted: this gives the auditory effect of a constriction in the throat and makes speech sound lower in pitch and harsher in tone. Middle-class speakers have no particular traits, just an absence of working-class ones.

'Voice quality', then, can be used as a sociolinguistic marker, but it is worth noting that the description of voice quality for Glasgow does not just involve laryngeal settings: it involves a cluster of features involving the whole vocal tract.

Summary

In this chapter, we have seen how speakers control the vibration of the vocal folds to bring about changes in pitch and changes in voice quality. Voicing is also implicated in distinguishing certain pairs of sounds in English. Both pitch and voice quality are used linguistically in English, but with a complex range of meanings, none of them lexical.

There is comparatively little work on voice quality in English, either in terms of its functions in small stretches of conversation or in terms of its more generic function in marking speakers as belonging to a particular community: this is another area of English phonetics which is ripe for research.

Exercises

1. Using the IPA chart, identify which of the sounds of English we looked at in Chapter 3 are voiced, and which voiceless. For each sound, find a pair of words or phrases which highlights the contrast. The pairs should be as alike as possible. For example: [f – v]: 'proof', 'prove'. For some sounds, you will not be able to find pairs; try to produce the sound with/without voicing.

2. The texts below (based on spoken material) have no punctuation. Punctuate them with <. , ( ) ? !> etc., and read them out loud. What differences to pronunciation does the punctuation indicate? Are there places where some kind of punctuation is impossible? Or obligatory? Are there any cases where the meaning is ambiguous depending on how you phrase the words?

a. now politics is competitive so obviously when people are trying to score points off each other you will find imaginative use of language
b. you're a caterer with a big firm small firm your own firm
c. I was so off my face on a wonderful collection of drugs it was a great experience
d. you know looking back at the photos now she was like a sort of you know like one of those film stars for the time she was just a normal you know regular person in the nineteen forties in the war time
e. as I understand it Marguerite is that right it's a pound of sugar to a pint of juice
f. now you grow your own fruit which is fantastic but not too happy about your jam mate are you

Further reading

Baken and Orlikoff (2000), primarily aimed at clinicians, is an extensive survey of the voice and its measurement. Laver (1994: ch. 7) provides a classificatory overview of voicing and voice quality. For more detailed descriptions of English intonation, see Couper-Kuhlen (1986), Cruttenden (1997) or Wells (2006) (who all take a traditional 'British' approach); Ladd (1996) presents a more contemporary theoretical overview.

5 Vowels

5.1 Introduction

In the remaining chapters we turn our attention to the vowels and consonants of English, beginning with vowels. Vowels play a central role in the phonetics of English. While words can consist of vowels alone (e.g. 'eye', 'awe'), they cannot consist of consonants alone. Typically, consonants adapt to an adjacent vowel, but not vice versa. When an English speaker starts talking, we can often tell within a few syllables where they are from because of the vowels they use.

Vowels are syllabic sounds made with free passage of air down the mid-line of the vocal tract, usually with a convex tongue shape, and without friction. They are normally voiced; and they are normally oral. As we will see, there are exceptions to this generalisation.

There is considerable discussion about the definition of vowels which is beyond the scope of this chapter; suggestions for further reading are given at its end.

The vowels of English vary enormously by variety. In this chapter we introduce the concept of keywords, a way of referring to whole sets of vowels by using the spelling of English. Keywords are written here in small capitals. When we say 'The vowel of GOOSE', we mean the vowel of 'goose' and words like it, such as 'loose', 'boot', and 'rude'. More details are set out in Section 5.5.

5.2 Reference points for vowels: cardinal vowels

When describing consonants, it is relatively easy to sense where the articulators are, and what kind of posture they are making. With practice, we can sense the articulatory postures for [p v t l ŋ] and so on. But with vowels, it is much more difficult to do this because they are open articulations, and our sense of how the tongue should be positioned in order to produce a particular vowel quality is very weak. As well as this, the lay terms we have to describe vowels are far from useful phonetic labels: terms like 'flat', 'full' and 'crisp' are entirely impressionistic.

The IPA describes vowels using a set of reference vowels called **cardinal vowels (CVs)**. Cardinal vowels are a set of reference vowels that have predetermined phonetic values which must be learnt. The vowels of languages are described with reference to the cardinal vowels. A trained phonetician can say: this vowel sounds like cardinal vowel 2, but is a little more open; or, this vowel is half way between cardinals 6 and 7. One phonetician can replicate the sound described by another following the instructions given alongside the transcription.

The idea for the cardinal vowels is found in 1844 in the work of A. J. Ellis; but it was around the time of the First World War that Daniel Jones, a phonetician at University College, London, first worked out the system of cardinal vowels which is still in use today. Jones trained many phoneticians in Britain, for many years, and the oral tradition of learning and perfecting one's cardinal vowels is still strong among phoneticians in Britain, the USA, Germany, Australia and elsewhere who are trained in the 'British' tradition.

Cardinal vowels are best learnt from a trained phonetician. It takes much practice to get them right, and to learn them well, good feedback is needed.

The cardinal vowels represent possibilities of the human vocal tract rather than actual vowels of a language because they are established on theoretical grounds. They are independent of any particular language. None the less, the 'primary' cardinal vowels are so called because vowels like them are found in the majority of the world's languages.

There are eight 'primary' cardinal vowels, numbered 1 to 8. These are identified as primary cardinal vowels partly because they form a useful set: most languages of the world (including English) have vowels with qualities close to these. They are (in order 1–8): [i e ɛ a ɑ ɔ o u]. Figure 5.1 shows their arrangement in the chart on the IPA.

In what follows, we take a practical look at three of them, [i u ɑ]; move on to look at the full system; and then see how it has been applied to a few varieties of English.

5.2.1 Cardinal vowel 1, [i]

Produce a word beginning with a [j] sound: that is, something that begins with the letter <y> in the spelling, such as 'yes'. Hold the [j] sound. The sides of the tongue are pressed against the sides of the upper teeth, and the upper surface of the tongue is quite close to the hard palate. If you vigorously suck air in or out of the vocal tract, you should feel a cold, dry patch near the front part of the tongue and on the front part of the hard palate. Your lips should be spread, a little as though you are smiling. This articulatory posture is close to the posture of cardinal vowel 1, [i]. Now make your tongue a little tenser, and raise it a bit: you should generate friction by doing this, which sounds a bit like a [ʒ]-sound. The cardinal vowel is as extreme as a vocalic articulation can be while not producing friction, which is a consonant. So release some of the tension, and return to the frictionless sound.

This vowel is cardinal vowel 1 (CV1), [i]. It has a close (or high) and front tongue position; and it is made with spread lips. It is close to (but more extreme than) the sound spelt <ee> in many varieties of English: for example, the word 'bee' in RP is close to this.

5.2.2 Cardinal vowel 8, [u]

Now start to say a word that begins with a [w] sound, such as 'wet'. Hold the [w] sound silently, and reflect on your tongue. The back of the tongue is raised up towards the velum (or soft palate). Suck air in vigorously, and you should feel that the back of the tongue and the rear part of the roof of the mouth go cold and dry. The lips are pursed: you may need to purse them a bit more, as if you were about to blow out a candle, or as if holding a pen in your mouth. This is close to cardinal vowel 8 (CV8), [u].

Another way to approach this vowel is to whistle the lowest note possible, hold that posture, and then try to produce a vowel.

This vowel is cardinal vowel 8 (CV8), [u]. It has a close (or high) and back tongue position; and it is made with rounded lips. English does not really use this vowel sound, although very conservative varieties of both RP and General American come close to it. If you use it in words like 'soon', 'cool' or 'rude', you will probably sound very 'posh', 'conservative' or 'old fashioned'. In any case, do not be tempted to think of the sound of words like these as 'CV8': the English versions of this vowel are much too front for CV8.

Now move silently back and forth between [i] and [u]. The backward and forward movement of the tongue should give you a sense of the back–front dimension.

5.2.3 Cardinal vowel 5, [ɑ]

Cardinal vowel 5 (CV5) is a back, open vowel. Imagine a doctor asking you to 'say aahhh'; you open the jaw wide, and keep the tongue low in the mouth. This is close to CV5. If you take the tongue any further back, you will feel some friction, and a slight tickle caused by the back of the tongue making contact with the walls of the pharynx. CV5 is written [ɑ]: this is not the regular printed letter <a>, but more like the hand-written <a>. CV5 is an open, or low, back vowel. It is produced with open lips, which are neither rounded nor spread.

English has vowels like this, but not as far back. The vowel in the word 'father' in many varieties (including English in the south of England and much of the north) is like this; the vowel in 'hot' is like this in most American varieties.

Now move silently between [i] and [ɑ], and [u] and [ɑ]. The vertical movement of the tongue should give you a sense of the height dimension, with [i] and [u] as close vowels, and [ɑ] as an open vowel.

5.2.4 Dimensions of vowel description

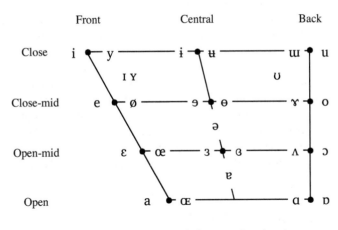

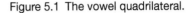

Where symbols appear in pairs, the one
on the right represents a rounded vowel.

Figure 5.1 The vowel quadrilateral.

The three vowels we have just described form three corners of the IPA's **vowel quadrilateral**. This represents, schematically, the **vowel space**: sounds articulated at the edge of or inside the box are vowels. The vowel space uses three dimensions for describing vowels: vowel height, frontness and backness, and lip posture (or rounding). If the tongue is raised any higher than the sounds along the [i]–[u] axis, then friction is generated, and so a fricative (i.e. a consonant sound) is produced. If the tongue is lowered or backed beyond the vowel [ɑ], then friction is also produced. The cardinal vowels take predetermined positions in the quadrilateral; other vowels are fitted in the spaces in between.

Vowel height is represented on the vertical dimension: from close through close-mid, and open-mid to open, along a continuum. The horizontal dimension of the chart (front – central – back) represents the second aspect of vowel description: **vowel frontness/backness**. The points between the extremes are chosen because they are useful reference points. In theory there is an infinite number of points between the extremes on each dimension.

The third aspect of vowel description is **lip posture**. The lips can be held in a large number of postures. Here are a few: spread and close (as if smiling), spread and protruded (as if to make a rectangular box between the lips and teeth), compressed and protruded (as if to make a polite kiss on someone's cheek), and open and rounded (as if to make a big O-shape). The IPA represents lip posture implicitly in symbols, with diacritics for deviations from what is implied.

There are two sets of cardinal vowels: the eight primary cardinal vowels [i e ɛ a ɑ ɔ o u] and the secondary cardinal vowels [y ɵ œ æ ɒ ʌ ɤ ɯ]. The primary cardinal vowels are, as the name suggests, the more important ones, because they represent the commonest types of vowel across the world's languages. The secondary cardinal vowels are less common. They are the same as the primary cardinal vowels with respect to tongue posture, but they have the lip posture of the vowel with the same height on the opposite side of the chart: for example, [y] has the same tongue position as [i], but the same lip posture as [u]; [ɯ] has the same tongue position as [u], but the same lip posture as [i].

5.2.5 Cardinal vowels 2–4 and 6–7

[i ɑ u] are the easiest vowels to define in articulatory terms. The other CVs fit in between the cardinal vowels in auditorily equidistant steps. Articulatory descriptions of the cardinal vowels are impressionistic rather than factually correct: their definition is primarily an auditory and impressionistic one.

Between [i] and [a], there are CVs 2–4, [e – ɛ – a]. They are all made with the tongue front in the mouth, and CV4, [a], is made with the tongue low in the mouth (and/or with an open jaw). They are 'auditorily equidistant' from each other, which means that the step from [i] to [e] sounds like the same sort of step as from [e] to [ɛ], and from [ɛ] to [a], etc. These vowels have lip postures that change from 'close, spread' for [i] to 'neutral' for [a].

Between [ɑ] and [u], there are two more cardinal vowels, [ɔ] and [o]. These vowels have accompanying lip rounding, [ɔ] has the most open rounding, and the amount of rounding and protrusion changes through [ɔ – o – u] to become more puckered and closer. As with the front series, the vowels [ɑ – ɔ – o – u] are auditorily equidistant from one another.

If there is more lip-rounding than to be expected according to the IPA system, we can use the diacritic [̹]; if there is less, then we can use the diacritic [̜]. For example [o] with the rounding of [u] can be transcribed [o̹]. The diacritic [ʷ] is used for consonants that are accompanied by lip-rounding (as in e.g. RP [sʷɔː], 'saw'), but is also occasionally used to mark rounding at the end of a vowel, as a [w]-like off-glide into another sound, as in RP 'go away', [gəʊʷ ə'weɪ].

5.2.6 Secondary cardinal vowels

Secondary cardinal vowels have the same tongue postures as primary cardinal vowels, and have the lip posture of the vowel with the same height on the opposite side of the chart. So secondary CV1, [y], has the tongue height and frontness of CV1, [i], but it has the rounding of its opposite number, CV8, [u]. So to make [y], start with [i] then round your lips so they look like [u], but keep your tongue as for [i]. This is close to the vowel in the French word 'tu', [ty], 'you'; or the sound written <ü> in German. Vowels like [y] occur in English, especially in [ju] sequences in words like 'use', 'computer', 'you', which we could more narrowly transcribe with [jy].

Secondary CV2, [ø], has the tongue height and frontness of CV2, [e], but the rounding of CV7, [o], which is the same height, but is back not front and rounded. It is close to the French vowel in the word 'feu', [fø], 'fire'; or the German sound written <ö>. Vowels like [ø] occur in some varieties of English: for example, in broad Australian English and in some northern Anglo-English varieties, the vowel in words like 'bird' is often close to [ø]. In New Zealand, the vowel in this set of words is transcribed as [ø] and described as a front or central close-mid rounded vowel.

Conversely, secondary CV8, [ɯ], has the tongue height and backness of [u], but the spread lips of [i], and secondary CV7, [ɤ], has the tongue height and backness of [o], but the spread lip posture of [e]. (Be careful not to confuse [ɤ] with the symbol [ɣ]: the vowel [ɤ], like e.g. [e ɛ a] does not descend below the line, while [ɣ] – the symbol for voiced velar fricatives – does.)

There are two other vowels between CV1 and CV8, [ɨ] and [ʉ]. These represent close central unrounded and rounded vowels respectively. Vowels like these are not ones we expect to find in stressed syllables in English, but they are rather common in conversational productions of the word 'because'. It is often pronounced 'bec[ɒ]se', 'bec[ɨ] se', 'bec[ə]se' or 'bec[ʁ]se'.

Many varieties have a rather front vowel in words like GOOSE: even in varieties where this vowel is by convention transcribed [u], the sound is often closer to [y] than to [u]. The symbol [ʉ] represents a rounded vowel half way between the two: a close central rounded vowel. This symbol is commonly used in representing the GOOSE vowel of Australian and New Zealand English. Many varieties of English (including Scottish and North American) use a similar, but unrounded, vowel for the close unstressed vowel in words like 'fitt[ɨ]d', 'clos[ɨ]s': other varieties, such as RP, use a fronter vowel, [ɪ], in this position.

Many varieties of English (including RP, some Canadian varieties, Australia and New Zealand) have a back open rounded vowel, [ɒ], for the vowel of 'hot'; and the vowel of 'strut' is frequently transcribed as [ʌ], the unrounded sister of CV6, [ɔ].

5.2.7 'Float' symbols

The vowels represented by the symbols [ɪʏʊəæɐ] are not cardinal, but vowels that are none the less useful in the description of languages. Their values are stated relative to CVs, hence the name 'float' symbols. Transcriptions of English commonly use some of these symbols, so we will consider them in this section.

The symbol [ɪ] is commonly used for a short close spread vowel: the sound of RP or General American 'bid'.

The symbol [ʊ], in the opposite corner of the chart, stands in the same relation to [u] as [ɪ] stands in to [i]: somewhat more central and open. It is often used to represent the vowel of the word 'good'.

Both [ɪ] and [ʊ] are used to represent short vowels in opposition to the long vowels [i(ː)] and [u(ː)], as in pairs like 'beat' ([biːt] or [bit]) – 'bit' ([bɪd]), 'booed' ([buːd] or [bud]) – 'book' ([bʊk]) in e.g. RP and General American. Because the short vowels are also different in quality, the opposition is sometimes known as 'tense' [i] and [u] vs. 'lax' [ɪ] and [ʊ].

The symbol [æ] stands for a sound somewhere between CV3 and CV4. This is traditionally used to represent the short open vowel of the word 'bad' in many varieties. (The symbol was used traditionally to remind learners of English – especially French or German speakers – that the RP vowel is closer to [ɛ] than the [a]-like vowel found in many other languages.)

In between close-mid and open-mid is the vowel [ə], sometimes called 'schwa'. This stands for a mid central vowel, sometimes called a 'neutral' vowel, and it is used to transcribe unstressed vowels in words such as 'sof<u>a</u>', 'b<u>a</u>nan<u>a</u>', '<u>a</u>ssume', 't<u>o</u>day'. In varieties such as RP and Australian English, where <r> is only pronounced before vowels, unstressed syllables in words like 'butt<u>er</u>', 'lett<u>er</u>', '<u>per</u>haps' also have this vowel or the more open [ɐ]. Its precise quality is highly variable, partly because it is very short and strongly coloured by neighbouring consonants; this is one reason why a 'float' symbol, with no precise definition, can be a useful tool for transcription: it can cover a wide range of qualities in one symbol.

5.3 The acoustics of vowels

There is a relatively simple correspondence between height, frontness and backness, and the relative positions of F1 and F2.

Figure 5.2 shows spectrograms of the eight primary cardinal vowels. The formants are shown with white lines.

The first formant relates to vowel height. Close vowels have a low F1, and open vowels have a high F1. This means that CV1 [i] and CV8 [u] both have a low F1 of approximately the same value, while CV4 [a] and CV5 [ɑ] have an F1 which is comparatively high, because these vowels are both open. The scale used on spectrograms is normally linear, which means that e.g. an interval of 100 Hz is represented as an equal interval at all points in the graph. Our hearing, however, is not like this: the human ear is more sensitive to changes in frequency in the lower ranges than in the upper ranges; so the difference between e.g. 400 Hz and 600 Hz sounds much bigger than the difference between e.g. 2100 Hz and 2300 Hz. So although the differences between the F1 values for CV1 and CV4 do not look great, they are quite significant from the point of view of hearing.

The second formant relates to frontness and backness. Front vowels have a high F2, but back vowels have a low F2. Rounding the lips also

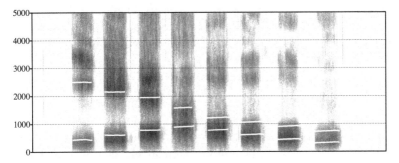

Figure 5.2 Spectrogram of cardinal vowels 1–8.

lowers F2, so as we move through cardinals 1–8, F2 gets progressively lower.

Knowing the F1 and F2 for vowels can be a useful way of working out where a particular vowel fits in the vowel space, especially if the vowel is short in duration or its quality is hard to hear.

5.4 Other vocalic features

Before we can tackle the vowels of English, the cardinal vowel scheme needs a little more expansion.

5.4.1 Retroflexion

Retroflexion means curling the tongue back. It is not represented directly on the IPA chart, but it is an important feature of [vowel] +<r> sequences in **rhotic** varieties, such as General American, Irish and Scottish English, where <r> is always pronounced after vowels. Any vowel sound can in principle be produced with retroflexion. The diacritic is [˞], added to the right of the vowel symbol. It is added mostly to the mid central vowels [ə] and [ɜ]: [ɚ ɝ]. These stand for the vowels found in American English words like the second syllable of LETTER, [lɛɹɚ], and in the word NURSE, [nɝs].

5.4.2 Diphthongs

The vowels so far are monophthongs: they are 'pure' and do not change. **Diphthongs** are monosyllabic vowels which have two discernibly different points, one at the start and one at the end. Most varieties of English have several diphthongs. The most obvious diphthongs are the vowels of CHOICE, MOUTH and PRICE in most standard varieties of English. These diphthongs start with open vowels and then raise to close vowels, generally in the area of [i] or [u]. These are called closing diphthongs for this reason. Diphthongs are transcribed by the start and end points. E.g. the vowel of CHOICE is transcribed in RP as [ɔɪ]: it starts with [ɔ] and ends with [ɪ].

5.4.3 Triphthongs

Diphthongs are vowels that have a start point different from their end point. **Triphthongs** get from the start point to the end point via some other, third, vowel in the middle. Or, alternatively, they are diphthongs with a vowel that forms an extension.

Triphthongs have been described for RP in words such as 'fire' and 'power', i.e. diphthongs which are followed by an <r> in the spelling. These words are pronounced monosyllabically with triphthongs such as [aɪə] and [aʊə]; but they are also susceptible to 'smoothing', giving pronunciations such as [faː] and [pɑː] respectively.

Triphthongs also occur in Southern US varieties. For example, in Alabama, the vowel of MOUTH is produced as [æɛɑ], that of CHOICE as [ɒɨ] and that of SQUARE as [aiæ].

Triphthongs are a more controversial unit than diphthongs, because they are not considered to have a phonological status. In RP, triphthongs can be analysed as diphthongs + phonemic /r/. The Alabaman triphthongs can be thought of as complex realisations of simpler underlying phonological units. Triphthongs can, at least in some varieties, distinguish words. For example, in RP, 'hire' (one **morpheme**) has a single syllable, [aɪɛ], and never two; but the word 'higher' (two morphemes, 'high+er') can be disyllabic, [aɪ.ə], which 'hire' cannot be.

5.5 Vowels in English 'keywords'

Vowels are perhaps the most important variable between varieties of English. If you think of a word in your own variety, and compare it with the pronunciation of that word in some other variety, you will easily be able to appreciate this.

First, there are systemic differences: i.e. differences in the structure of the vowel system. For example, most northern varieties of Anglo-English, and southern Irish, have five short vowels, [ɪɛaɒʊ], which in stressed syllables must be followed by a consonant (in words like 'hid', 'head', 'had'), but most other varieties have six: the five 'northern' ones plus [ʌ]. So in words like 'love', 'run', 'up', some varieties have [ʊ], while most have [ʌ]: [lʌv, rʌn, ʌp] vs. [lʊv, rʊn, ʊp].

Vowel length is a lexically contrastive (phonemic) feature of many English varieties. For example, Anglo-English usually has pairs of vowels like long /iː/ vs. short /ɪ/ ('beat' – 'bit', [biːt, bɪt]); long /ɑː/ vs. short /a/ ('heart' – 'hat', [hɑːt, hat]); long /ɔː/ vs. short /ɒ/ ('caught' – 'cot', [kɔːt, kɒt]). Speakers have to learn which words have long vowels, and which have short; it is a lexical property.

In Scottish varieties, vowels are traditionally short except before /r/, voiced fricatives, or a morpheme boundary. In these varieties, 'brood', [brʉd], is a morphologically simple word with a short vowel, but 'brewed' is 'brew'+'ed', [brʉːd], which conditions a long vowel. This is commonly called the Scottish Vowel Length Rule; the English of Northern Ireland has a similar pattern. Traditionally, this rule applied to all the vowels, but recent research shows that the system seems to be in flux.

While vowel length refers to phonological contrast, duration refers to how much time a sound is held. Here, the length contrast gets a little complicated. Vowel duration depends on a following syllable-final consonant. Before voiced consonants, vowels are regularly longer in duration; before voiceless consonants, they are regularly shorter in duration. So in the words 'heed', 'heat', 'hid' and 'hit', the vowels are progressively shorter in duration. The first two words have phonologically long vowels, but the vowel of 'heed', coming before voiced [d], is longer in duration than that of 'heat'. The vowels of the last two words are phonologically short; but the vowel of 'hid' is longer in duration than the vowel of 'hit'. In a systematic transcription, we need only capture the length distinction: [hiːd, hiːt, hɪd, hɪt]. We can transcribe the duration differences more impressionistically as [hiːd, hiˑt, hɪd, hɪ̆t], where [ˑ] marks a duration somewhere between long [ː] and (unmarked) short, and [˘] marks the shortest one of the series.

Another systemic variable is **rhotics** (r-sounds). Some varieties (such as most of Anglo-English, Australia, New Zealand, South Africa and parts of the USA) only permit [r] sounds before vowels – they are **non-rhotic** – while others (such as most of North America, parts of England, Ireland and Scotland) permit [r] after vowels and before consonants and are called rhotic.

Non-rhotic varieties typically have a larger number of diphthongs (vowel + vowel combinations) than do rhotic varieties. For example, in RP, the word 'care' in isolation is pronounced [kɛə]. When a consonant comes after it, as in 'I don't care for that', the word is also pronounced [kɛə]. But if a vowel follows, then [r] is inserted, as in 'care [kɛər] in the community'. In rhotic varieties, the word 'care' is always pronounced with [r], e.g. [keːr].

Distinctions made in one variety are not always made elsewhere: for instance, for many Anglo-English speakers, 'paw', 'poor', 'pore' have identical vowels (such as [ɔː]), while other English speakers do distinguish these (e.g. as [ɑ, ur, ɔr]) (Table 5.1); some American speakers do not distinguish 'merry', 'Mary' and 'marry', [meri], which are all distinct in e.g. RP, [mɛri, mɛəri, mæri]. While northern and southern varieties of Anglo-English both have a short [a] vowel and a long [ɑː] or [aː] vowel, there are **distributional** differences, so that words like 'grass', 'bath', 'after' have the short vowel [a] in the north, but the long one, [ɑː] or [aː], in the south.

Finally, varieties vary in realisation; that is, in the way phonologically equivalent vowels are produced. Australian English has virtually the same vowel system as southern Anglo-English; but as we will see in Section 5.5.3, their realisations in these varieties are different. So we cannot state what 'the vowels of English' are, because they vary so much, and along many dimensions. In this book, we will adopt the system of so-called 'keywords'. The concept comes from John Wells's work (1982), and it makes use of English spelling, which is independent of dialect.

Keywords exploit the fact that the spelling often captures potential (or English-wide) differences which are not exploited in all varieties of English. Referring to vowels by keyword makes it easier to compare across dialects. If we referred to 'the phonemes of American English' and 'the phonemes of RP', there would be different sets, and the phonemes would not be distributed in the same way through the lexicon. Keywords make it easier to see what the distribution is and provide a way to refer to classes of vowels without using phonemes.

Table 5.1 Anglo-English vs. American homophones.

	Anglo-English	*General American*
paw		pɑː
pore	pɔː	por
poor		pur

Table 5.2 shows keywords in English orthography, and then gives phonetic values for the vowels of those words, as can be found in 'Illustrations of the IPA' (see Further Reading, p. 79). The transcriptions reflect roughly where the vowels lie in the cardinal vowel system. The qualities of vowels are more precisely specified for some of these varieties by plotting them on the vowel quadrilateral as in Section 5.5.3.

5.5.1 Transcribing vowels

We shall now discuss a few of the main issues in transcribing English vowels. In the examples here, we use the same conventions as the original researchers.

First, it must be decided whether to transcribe vowel quality, vowel length (quantity) or both. RP, for example, has short [ɪ] (as in KIT) and long [i] (as in FLEECE). We could transcribe them as [i–iː], which captures the contrasting length ([ː] is the diacritic for long) but not quality; or as [ɪ–i], which captures quality but not quantity; or as [ɪ–iː], which captures both quality and quantity. Representing either quality or quantity (but not both) makes the transcription simpler.

Table 5.2 Vowels in English keywords.

Keyword	RP (Roach 2004)	Tyneside (Tyn) (Watt & Allen 2003)	General American (US) (Ladefoged 1999)	Australian (Aus) (Cox and Palethorpe 2007)	New Zealand (NZ) (Bauer et al. 2007)
KIT	ɪ	ɪ	ɪ	ɪ	ə
DRESS	e	ɛ	ɛ	e	e
TRAP	æ	a	æ	æ	ɛ
LOT	ɒ	ɒ	ɑ	ɔ	ɒ
STRUT	ʌ	ʊ	ʌ	ɐ	ɐ
FOOT	ʊ	ʊ	ʊ	ʊ	ʊ
BATH	ɑː	a	æ	ɐː	ɐː
CLOTH	ɒ	ɒ	ɑ	ɔ	ɒ
NURSE	ɜː	øː	ɚː	ɜː	ɵː
FLEECE	iː	iː	iː	iː	iː
FACE	eɪ	eː	eː	æɪ	æe
PALM	ɑː	ɒː	ɑ	ɐː	ɐː
THOUGHT	ɔː	ɔː	ɑ	oː	oː
GOAT	əʊ	oː	oː	əʉ	ɐʉ
GOOSE	uː	uː	uː	ʉː	ʉː
PRICE	aɪ	ai	aɪ	ɑe	ɑe
CHOICE	ɔɪ	oe	ɔɪ	oɪ	oe
MOUTH	aʊ	æu	aʊ	æɔ	æo
NEAR	ɪə	iɐ	iːr	ɪə	iə
SQUARE	eə	ɛː	eːr	eː	eə
START	ɑː	ɒː	ɑr	ɐː	ɐː
NORTH	ɔː	ɔː	or	oː	oː
FORCE	ɔː	ɔː	or	oː	oː
CURE	ʊə	uɐ	ur	ʉ.ə or oː	ʉə
HAPPY	i	i	i	iː	i
LETTER	ə	ə	ɚ	ə	ə
COMMA	ə	ə	ə	ə	ə

Secondly, we have to decide whether to use simple, Roman-shaped vowel symbols, or to use other shapes. For example, most varieties of English have in words like GOOSE a vowel that is much fronter than CV8; [ʉ] is a more accurate representation of it than [u]. But it could also be argued that [u] should be preferred because it is a simpler shape, and is more familiar to English speakers. The symbol [ʉ] highlights the fact that the sound it stands for is not the same as for instance in German 'Kuh', 'cow', which is closer to CV8; but [ʉ] is a less familiar symbol. In making any transcription, the conventions should be stated: if [u] is used, the accompanying conventions should say that [u] stands for a vowel with a quality like [ʉ].

A third issue in transcription is how to handle the final parts of diphthongs, and (in rhotic varieties) r-coloured vowels. There is a tradition of using vowel symbols like [aɪ] and [aʊ] for PRICE and MOUTH, but there is also a strong (mostly American) tradition of representing these vowels as [aj aw], so that [j w] are parallel with [r] – that is, START is transcribed with [ar], parallel with [aw] and [aj].

5.5.2 More on the keyword transcriptions

The varieties represented in Table 5.2 and subsequent vowel charts are all taken from 'Illustrations of the IPA' (see Further Reading, p. 79), showing how the principles of the IPA can be adopted to transcribe and describe languages. The 'Illustrations' are short and easy to read, and they contain a variety of transcription choices.

The RP transcription uses symbols which reflect the preferences of teachers of English as a Foreign Language; simple symbols are used (such as [e] rather than [ɛ]) but the symbol [æ] is used (rather than simpler [a]) because it reminds students that the front open vowel in RP is closer than [a] in e.g. many European languages. The Tyneside transcription makes for an interesting contrast with RP: note the different distribution of vowels shown up by the keyword system, such as the vowels of STRUT and BATH, of FACE and GOAT, and of words like NEAR and CURE.

The system used for American English here is one of four presented in the *Handbook of the International Phonetic Association* (IPA 1999). This system marks both vowel quality and vowel length, so it is more detailed and less simple than it need be. For instance, the pair 'bead' – 'bid' is transcribed [iː ɪ], rather than e.g. [iː i] or [i ɪ], which also capture the distinction.

Transcriptions of Australian English were traditionally based on transcriptions of RP. The one presented here attempts to capture the quality of Australian vowels rather than using RP as a model. New Zealand English is subtly different from Australian English, and this can be seen in the choice of transcription symbols for New Zealand, which are rather faithful to the phonetic detail.

5.5.3 Comparison of vowels across dialects

In order to see some of the differences and similarities between varieties of English, we will plot some of the vowels represented in Table 5.2 on the vowel quadrilateral, and then look more closely at a few keywords. This will let us see two things:

1. The symbols used to transcribe vowels represent an abstraction over the data: for example, sometimes vowels with roughly the same vowel qualities in two different varieties are transcribed with different symbols. Likewise, identical symbols are sometimes used to represent different vowel qualities.
2. The IPA cardinal vowel system can be applied to real data, although the vowels of spoken language are not the same as cardinal vowels.

The monophthongs of RP, Australian and American are shown in Figures 5.3–5.5. Figures 5.6–5.9 show the diphthongs from the same varieties. The vowels plotted on these graphs should be cross-referred to the keywords in Table 5.2. These plots show where the vowels lie in the CV space, so we can interpret the symbols used more accurately.

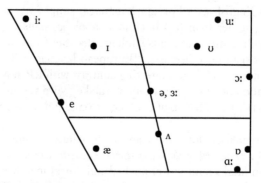

Figure 5.3 RP monophthongs.

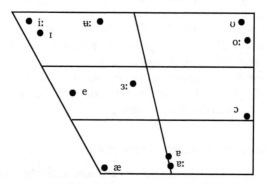

Figure 5.4 Australian monophthongs.

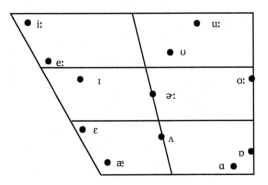

Figure 5.5 American English monophthongs.

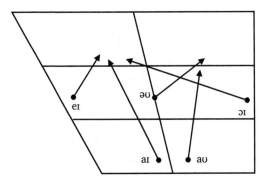

Figure 5.6 RP closing diphthongs.

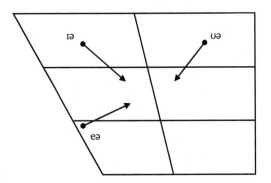

Figure 5.7 RP centring diphthongs.

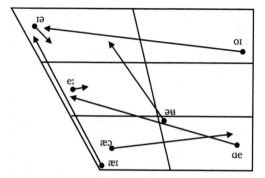

Figure 5.8 Australian diphthongs.

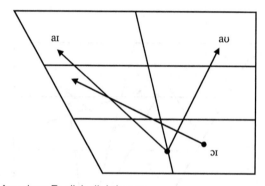

Figure 5.9 American English diphthongs.

The trap vowel

The TRAP vowel varies along the front–back and open–close dimensions and is variously transcribed as [a æ ɛ]. What cannot be shown from the vowel quadrilateral so easily is the differences in duration. In the USA, this vowel is regularly long in duration in comparison with other varieties of English.

The symbol [æ] stands for three different qualities: most open in Australia, closest and frontest in RP and most central in American English. If we wanted to distinguish these qualities while using the same symbol, we could elaborate the transcriptions with diacritics. 'Closer' and 'more open' are handled with [˔], [˕] respectively; 'fronter' and 'backer' with [˖], [˗]. Vowels shifted to the centre of the quadrilateral can be marked with [¨]. So we could write [æ̝] for RP, [æ̞] for Australian and [æ̈] for American. This transcription style is comparative. Another strategy would be to refer the qualities directly to CVs, in which case we might transcribe RP as [ɛ̞] (i.e. more open than CV3, [ɛ]), Australian as [a] (close to CV4) and American as [ä] (more centralised than CV4, [a]). This transcription style is more impressionistic. It is precisely because of the problems of deciding which symbol to use that phoneticians use graphs to plot where vowels lie, even if this is just an approximation.

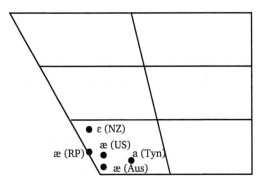

Figure 5.10 TRAP vowels.

The strut vowel

The STRUT vowel has an interesting history in English. In northern Anglo-English varieties, it is the same vowel as in FOOT, which is historically how this vowel was pronounced; the vowel [ʌ] is an innovation. This historical split of [ʊ] into both [ʌ] and [ʊ] leaves its mark on the wide variety of sounds that represent the STRUT set: it varies on both the open–close dimension and the rounded–unrounded dimension. In Australia and New Zealand, the STRUT vowel is even more open, and is transcribed with [ɐ], an open central vowel.

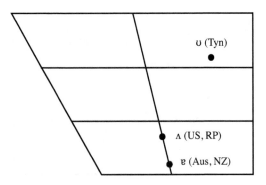

Figure 5.11 STRUT vowels.

The face vowel

The FACE vowel is very variable in English, ranging through diphthongs (mostly rising towards [i] or [e] from open vowels like [æ] or [a]) to monophthongs in the [e] region. Again, this diversity partly reflects the history of the vowel. In Figure 5.12, diphthongs are marked with an arrow; the dot marks the start of a diphthong and the arrow-head marks the end.

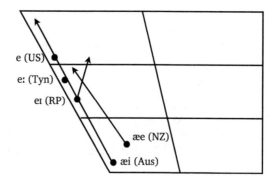

Figure 5.12 FACE vowels.

The goose vowel

The GOOSE vowel is often very front in modern English, especially following alveolar consonants like [s t]; some transcription systems represent this through use of the symbol [ʉ]. However, in older, more conservative varieties of both RP and General American, the GOOSE vowel was much backer, which partly explains the use of [u] to represent it. This vowel can also be unrounded, in which case a more accurate transcription might be [ɨ]; it is often produced this way in the south east of

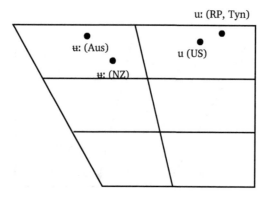

Figure 5.13 GOOSE vowels.

England in phrases like 'it's really good', [gɨːːd]. This pronunciation is not, as one might think, new: it is found in phonetic descriptions of English at least from the 1920s.

5.6 Reduced vowels

In unstressed syllables, English permits a narrower range of vowels than in stressed syllables; and there are a number of vowels which are particular to unstressed syllables, often known as **reduced vowels**. The main ones are the unstressed vowels of HAPPY, COMMA and WANTED.

The HAPPY vowel is usually a close front vowel such as [i] or [ɪ]. In some varieties it may be much more open, as in north west England or some parts of the Southern USA, where it can be close to [e] or [ɛ].

The COMMA vowel is canonically a mid central vowel in the region of [ə] (though see notes on individual varieties above), but it is particularly susceptible to its surrounding context. For example, in the phrases 'to the [tə ðə] park' vs. 'to the [tə̈ ðə̈] hill', there are backer vs. fronter qualities respectively, reflecting the vowels of the words 'park' and 'hill'. This is a form of 'vowel harmony', where the vowels in a stretch of speech share some phonetic property (here, frontness or backness).

The vowel of WANTED varies along the front–back dimension, with some varieties having [ɪ], others having backer vowels such as [ɨ], or indeed the same vowel as COMMA.

Many function words (prepositions, auxiliary verbs, pronouns and determiners) in English have 'strong' and 'weak' forms, where the 'strong' form contains a 'full' vowel and the 'weak' form (which is always unstressed) contains a 'reduced' vowel. Weak forms are generally pronounced without [h]. Compare the vowels in the underlined words in the following sentences (stress is marked [']):

(1)   I didn't 'want to [tə] 'walk there, but [bət] I 'had to [tuː].
(2)   'Chris had [əd] never 'seen the [ðə] 'film but 'Pat 'had [had].
(3)   'Chris 'told her [ə/ɚˑ] she'd 'seen him [ɪm]; 'Pat said he'd [id] 'seen 'her [hɜː/hɚˑ] but not 'him [hɪm].
(4)   We 'thought it was [wəz] 'raining, but it 'wasn't [wɒzənt].

5.7 Voiceless vowels

A common feature of conversational speech is the devoicing of vowels in unstressed syllables, especially adjacent to voiceless consonants. The IPA marks voiceless vowels with the diacritic [̥].

The commonest environment for devoicing is where there is an unstressed vowel with voiceless consonants on either side. Words like 'potato' and 'suppose', which have unstressed first syllables and voiceless consonants on either side of the vowel, frequently have voiceless vowels in the first syllable: [pə̥tʰ-], [sə̥pʰ-].

(5)   get t[ə̥] p[ə̥]sitions of power
        yeah, this [i̥]s Marcia
        I am going t[ə̥] cook t[ə̥]day . . .
        what I'm having to do f[ə̥] people I know . . .
        s[ə̥] sh[i̥]s came in asking me if I'd seen Gary

In a few cases, devoicing can give rise to pairs of words which are only slightly different such as: 'sport' –'support', [sp-, sə̥pʰ-]; 'please' – 'police', [pl̥ -, pə̥l-]. The main differences in these pairs are in the co-ordination of voicing with other articulatory events and the duration of the surrounding sounds. For example, in 'sport' vs. 'support', the main difference is in the immediate start of voicing on release of the plosive in 'sport', and the rounding starting earlier in 'sport' than in 'support'. In the 'please' – 'police' example, the main difference is in whether there is voicing co-ordinated with lateral airflow or not (Section 7.3).

Summary

In this chapter we have looked at the theory of cardinal vowels as a framework for describing vowels, and then seen it applied to a small number of varieties of English. Vowels are an important starting point in the phonetic analysis of any variety of English, since they are highly variable sociolinguistically

Exercises

1. Try to complete the chart of keywords with vowels appropriate for your own variety of English. (You could use one of the dialects as a model, and adjust as necessary.) For diphthongs, remember to locate the start and end points of the vowel.

2. Plot your vowels on a series of vowel quadrilaterals. It might be easier to separate e.g. short from long vowels; monophthongs from diphthongs; closing vs. centring diphthongs. Use the table of keywords as a reference point.

3. In English, vowel quality depends somewhat on stress. Some ortho-graphically identical words have different stress patterns depend-ing on whether they are a noun, verb or adjective. Transcribe your productions of the following words (the first is done for you as an illustration):

record	'rɛkɔːd	rɪ'kɔːd
alternate		
object		
minute		
permit		
present		
produce		
frequent		
invalid		

4. Find an English text and (a) identify those words which have strong and weak forms, then (b) transcribe the strong and weak forms using symbols appropriate for your own variety.

Further reading

The history and theory of cardinal vowels is discussed in Abercrombie (1967), Catford (2001), Jones (1975), Ladefoged (2006), Laver (1994) and IPA (1999). Laver (1994) also discusses problems in the defini-tion of vowels. Overviews of the acoustics of vowels can be found in e.g. Johnson (2002), Ladefoged and Maddieson (1996) and Ladefoged (2005).

Most of the material in this chapter is taken from 'Illustrations of the IPA', applications of the cardinal vowel scheme regularly published in the *Journal of the IPA* (Bauer et al. 2007; Cox and Palethorpe 2007; Hillenbrand 2003; Ladefoged 1999; Roach 2004; Watson 2007; Watt and Allen 2003). Other varieties are discussed in, e.g. Wells (1982), Foulkes and Docherty (1999), Giegerich (1992) and Rogers (2000). More on the duration of American English vowels can be found in Jacewicz et al. (2007); more on American English triphthongs can be found in Thomas (2003).

For more on the Scottish Vowel Length Rule, see Rathcke and Stuart-Smith (2015) and references in there.

An interesting historical discussion of rhoticity in Australian English can be found in Trudgill and Gordon (2006).

6 Approximants

6.1 Introduction

As we have seen, the IPA distinguishes between consonants and vowels as two different kinds of segment. The distinction seems real enough if we consider obvious vowels like [ɑui], or obvious consonants like [pfm]. In fact, the distinction between vowel and consonant is not so straightforward, and this point is most clearly seen with the approximants.

Table 6.1 Approximants in English at the systematic level.

	Alveolar	Alveolar lateral	Palatal	Labiovelar
Approximants	r	l	j	w

Approximants are formed when two articulators are brought together ('approximated': 'ad-', 'to', 'prox-', 'near', in Latin) so that air passes through the vocal tract without generating any friction noise, and the velum is raised, sealing off the nasal cavities. In this respect, approximants are like vowels: in fact, the definition just given fits vowels as well as approximants. The theoretical distinction between consonants and vowels is difficult to make. In common with the IPA, we will treat vowels as sounds which form a syllable, and approximants as vocalic sounds which function as consonants.

Approximants can have airflow down the mid-line of the oral tract, or down one (or both) sides. In English, the approximants at the systematic level are [j w r l]. We will start by looking at [j] and [w], because these closely resemble cardinal vowels [i] and [u], and are the most straightforward to describe. We will then move on to look at [l] and [r], which are phonetically complex and highly variable across varieties of English.

6.2 The palatal approximant [j]

6.2.1 Phonetic description of [j]

The palatal approximant [j] is closely related to the cardinal vowel [i]. Many phoneticians and phonologists treat [j] as the consonantal equivalent of [i]. In English spelling it is usually represented by the letter <y>, as in 'you', 'yet' and 'York', and is often part of the value of the letter <u> in words like 'use', 'computer', 'cue'.

The palatal approximant [j] is made by raising the tongue body up to the hard palate. At the same time, the lips are spread. The velum is raised, so air does not escape through the nose. The vocal folds are vibrating, so there is voicing.

The palatal approximant shares its articulatory features with cardinal vowel 1, [i]. Produce CV1 and hold it: [iːːː]. Now make another vowel sound such as [ɑːːː], and alternate the two sounds. Gradually make the [i] sound shorter, until it is extremely short, and you will end up with something like [jɑːːːjɑːːː]. The palatal approximant can be thought of as a very short, non-syllabic version of [i]. The difference is that the vocalic version is syllabic, and the consonantal version is not. As a consequence, the approximant [j] does not really have a steady state where it is held, but consists mostly of a movement into palatal approximation and, once that has been achieved, a movement out of it.

6.2.2 The distribution of palatal approximation

[j] in English only occurs before vowels. Many speakers will be able to form pairs with 'beauty' – 'pewter', [bj-, pj], and 'duty' – 'tutor', [dj-, tj-], because the words that have alveolar sounds initially are followed by the sequence [ju]. For speakers of many other varieties of English (including most of the USA, but also some British varieties), the words 'duty', 'tutor' and others which start with alveolars do not have the sequence [ju], but just the vowel [u]. So the transcription would be [bj-, pj-, d-, t-] (rather than [dj-, tj-]). This feature is sometimes known as **yod-dropping**.

6.2.3 Voicelessness and palatality

Palatal approximation in English is generally accompanied by vocal fold vibration: [j] is normally voiced. However, it can also be accompanied by voicelessness in clusters with voiceless consonants. For instance, in 'beauty' it is voiced, but in 'pewter' it is voiceless. When voiceless, there is greater airflow across the glottis because it is open. A greater quantity of air means that the pressure behind a constriction can build up more quickly; and in turn, this means that it is easier to generate noisy turbulent airflow with voiceless sounds than with voiced sounds. So strictly speaking, most of the sounds that result from the combination of voicelessness + palatality + open approximation are in fact not approximants but fricatives.

There are several possible ways to transcribe the combination voicelessness + palatality + friction. An allophonic transcription could modify [j] by marking voicelessness using the diacritic [°] or [̥]. Words like 'pewter', 'few', 'cue' and so on can be transcribed with [j̊]: [pj̊uːtə, fj̊uː, kj̊uː]. This captures the structural similarity between the voiced and the voiceless pairs, so for instance for 'beauty' we would have [bju-] and for 'pewter' we would have [pj̊u-], and it makes it obvious in a visual way that there is a relationship between the sequences in both cases.

In an impressionistic transcription, we could use the symbol for a voiceless palatal fricative, [ç], so we would have [pçu-] for the start of 'pewter'. This makes it more obvious that as well as palatality there is voicelessness and friction; in the transcription [j̊], friction is more implicit than explicit, and the transcription reflects the phonological system of English better.

6.2.4 The acoustics of the palatal approximant

Figure 6.1 shows a spectrogram of the phrase 'a yacht', [ə jɒt].

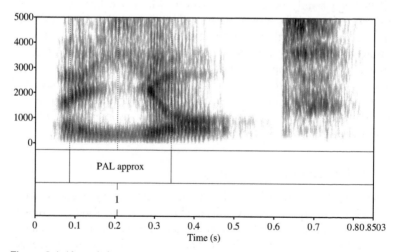

Figure 6.1 'A yacht'.

For [j], as for [i], there is a low F1, because the tongue body is close (i.e. raised), and a high F2, because the tongue body is front in the mouth. The portion labelled 'PAL approx' is part of the spectrogram where the palatal approximation is clearly visible on the spectrogram. Notice the voicing throughout, seen in the vertical striations that continue throughout the marked segment.

6.3 A doubly articulated sound: the labiovelar approximant [w]

The labiovelar approximant [w] is closely related to the cardinal vowel [u]. Just as many phoneticians and phonologists treat [j] as the consonantal equivalent of [i], so they also treat [w] as the consonantal equivalent of [u].

For [w], there were two articulations with the same degree of stricture, and we say that [w] is a **double articulation**: open approximation at (1) the lips, (2) the tongue back at the velum. The tongue back is raised up to the soft palate (i.e. the velum) in a stricture of open approximation. At the same time, the lips are closely rounded, but not so close as to produce friction noise: in other words, there is a second stricture of open approximation, at the lips. The velum is raised, so air does not escape through the nose. The vocal folds are vibrating, so there is voicing.

The labiovelar approximant shares its articulatory features with cardinal vowel 8, [u]. Produce CV8 and hold it: [uːːː]. Now make another vowel sound such as [ɑːːː], and alternate the two sounds. Gradually make the [u] sound shorter, until it is extremely short, and you will end up with something like [wɑːːːwɑːːː]. The labiovelar approximant can be thought of as a very short, non-syllabic version of [u].

If you look at the 'approximants' row on the IPA chart, you will see that there is no place for [w], unlike [j]. This is because [j] has only one constriction, which is the tongue body at the soft palate, so [j] appears in the column headed 'palatal', but [w], as a **doubly articulated** sound, has two places of articulation, a circumstance that does not fit neatly on the IPA chart.

6.3.1 Labiovelarity and voicelessness

Just as [j] has a voiceless counterpart, so does [w]. This sound can be transcribed as [w̥] or [ʍ]. As with [j̊], there is friction for this sound, but the audible friction is generated at the lips.

The combination of tongue-back raising + lip-rounding + voicelessness occurs in two main places in English. The first is parallel to the places where voicelessness + palatality + approximation occur in clusters with voiceless consonants (words like 'pewter', 'cue', 'few', as we saw in 6.2.3).

So for instance, words like 'twin' and 'twenty' have a period of labiovelar approximation + voicelessness once the plosive has been released, [tw̥].

The other place where it occurs depends on the speaker's dialect. For many speakers of English, words like 'witch' – 'which', 'wail' – 'whale' are homophones, i.e. they sound identical. But for some speakers, including many Scots and North Americans, there is a lexical distinction maintained between [w] and [ʍ], with [ʍ] being used in words spelt <wh>. So these speakers have phonologically contrastive pairs like [wɪtʃ] vs. [ʍɪtʃ], [weːl] vs. [ʍeːl]. To represent this lexical contrast, it is preferable to use a separate symbol, [ʍ], rather than a composite one with a diacritic, [w̥], on the principle that each distinctive sound of a language should be represented by a distinctive symbol (the principle of 'one sound, one symbol').

6.3.2 The acoustics of labiovelar approximants

Figure 6.2 shows a spectrogram of the phrase 'a win'.

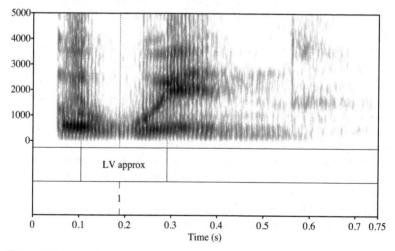

Figure 6.2 'A win'.

The portion labelled 'LV approx' is the portion where there are clear signs of labiovelar approximation. As the lips are rounded and the tongue back is raised towards the velum, the first formant moves downwards ([u], like [i], has a low F1), while F2 gets much lower, because of both tongue backing and lip-rounding. As the approximations are made, the vocal tract narrows, and the amplitude diminishes: it can be seen from the spectrogram that there is almost no visible information much above 1000 Hz.

Notice that for both [j] and [w] the formants are moving throughout the labelled portions. The point labelled 'l' for [j] is where F2 is highest and F1 is lowest: this is the most '[j]-like' part of the portion. The point labelled 'l' for [w] is where F1 and F2 are lowest: the most '[w]-like' part of the portion.

Auditorily, as visually, the phonetics associated with [j] and [w] is distributed over a long stretch of time: this is a recurrent property of approximants, and it is most clearly visible when we look at spectrograms, or listen to very short stretches of speech where the 'blending' of sounds into one another is very obvious. Notice that the formants are constantly moving: there is no 'steady state', because in making an approximant, the articulators are gliding into and out of a kind of articulatory target.

6.4 Laterals

Lateral approximants, more frequently called just 'laterals', occur in English. Laterals are represented in English orthography with the letter <l>. Phonetically they are very variable sounds both for individual speakers and across varieties of English.

Laterals are made with a complete closure of the tongue front (either the tip or the blade) against the alveolar ridge, which makes this part of the tongue gesture the same as that for [t d n]. But for laterals, one or both sides of the tongue is kept down, allowing air to escape. If you say the word 'leaf', and isolate the first consonantal sound, then suck air in, you should feel that one or both sides of the mouth go cold and dry. Just as some people are left-handed and some are right-handed (and some are ambidextrous), so some predominantly produce laterals with one or the other side of their tongue.

Lateral approximants are a little different from the other approximants in terms of their overall gesture: they do not have a stricture of open approximation. On the other hand, the acoustic effect of open approximation is that it produces frictionless airflow, and laterals in English do not have friction, so they are classified as approximants.

Laterals vary in several ways: voicing, place of articulation, secondary articulation and syllabicity. In the next sections, we will look these features one by one.

6.4.1 Voicing

Laterals are generally voiced throughout, i.e. they are accompanied by vocal fold vibration: the laterals in 'loose' (a simple syllable initial), 'hollow' (between vowels after a stressed syllable), 'allow' (between vowels before a stressed syllable) and 'fall' (syllable final) are all fully voiced.

Laterals may be produced with voicelessness. This happens after voiceless plosives in a cluster syllable initially, as in 'play', 'plum', 'clay', 'clunk'. The combination of voicelessness + laterality without friction has no IPA symbol of its own, so a composite one has to be made from a lateral approximant symbol together with a diacritic for voicelessness: [l̥]. This is how clusters such as those we have just mentioned are usually transcribed: '[pl̥]ay', '[kl̥]ay', etc. As with [j] and [w], it is hard to produce frictionless sounds in combination with voicelessness, so these sounds typically have some degree of friction. (See Section 8.2 for more on lateral fricatives.)

6.4.2 Place of articulation

For English laterals the active articulator is the tongue tip or the tongue blade, which makes a closure at the alveolar ridge.

Laterals are produced with a dental place of articulation when the next sound is also dental. Laterals combined with [θ] regularly have a dental articulation: 'hea[l̪]th', 'wea[l̪]th', 'stea[l̪]th'. Across word boundaries, too, laterals can be produced with a dental place of articulation as in 'all the people', [-l̪ ð-, -l̪ː-].

There is another variant of [l] which it is a bit counterintuitive to call 'lateral', because it has no lateral airflow; but it turns up as a variant of [l], so it makes sense to think of it as belonging in the same family of sounds, i.e. as an allophone of /l/. Many varieties of English, including many southern Anglo-English, African American, Scottish and Australian ones, use a vocalic articulation for laterals which involves no constriction of the front part of the tongue at all. For example, a word like 'hill' can be produced as something like [hɪw, hɪɤ, hɪö]. Phonetically, these sounds are not laterals, but vowels; but they function just like [l] in the same position. They are said to be 'vocalised'. As linguists, one of our jobs is to explain how it comes to be that 'laterals' can turn out not to be laterals at all; we will do this in the next section.

6.4.3 Laterals: primary and secondary articulations

In considering how lateral approximants are made, we have looked only at the front of the tongue. This is not, however, the whole story. Making a closure with the tip or blade of the tongue leaves the tongue body and tongue back free, as well as the lips, to be placed into a range of configurations. You can try this for yourself. Make a [l]-sound, and concentrate on your tongue tip. As you make this sound, move your tongue body backwards and forwards, and round and spread your lips as if trying to make a range of vowel sounds at the same time as making a [l] sound. What you should hear is that the 'tone' of the sound changes constantly with the changes in the shape and size of the vocal tract caused by the movement of the tongue body. All of these different sounds are voiced alveolar lateral approximants.

In making [l], there are actually two (or three) different articulations. The **primary articulation** is the closure of the tongue tip against the alveolar ridge. The other articulations are called **secondary articulations** – so called because they are more open articulations than the primary one.

Secondary articulations are very similar to vocalic articulations. To make a secondary [i] articulation, spread the lips and push the tongue body forward and high in the mouth; to make a secondary [ɯ] articulation (like [u] without the rounding), raise the tongue back up towards the velum while keeping the tongue tip fixed to the alveolar ridge. These two secondary articulations are called **palatalisation** and **velarisation** respectively, and are transcribed as [ʲ] and [ˠ] respectively. Velarisation is often accompanied by **labialisation** (i.e. lip-rounding; symbolised with the diacritic [ʷ]), giving **labiovelarisation**, which can be transcribed as [ˠʷ]. Phoneticians often refer to the auditory impression of these qualities: palatalised laterals are often called 'clear' (often also 'light', by American linguists) and velarised laterals are often called 'dark'.

Palatalisation and velarisation are at opposite ends of a scale. Palatalisation involves tongue-body fronting and raising, while velarisation involves tongue-body backing and raising. In between, as you will have observed, there are many shades of difference.

Now say a few pairs of words: 'leaf' – 'feel', 'loaf' – 'foal', 'lot' – 'toll'. If you compare the laterals at the start and the end of these words, you will notice that they sound different. If you hold the articulation, you will feel a different tongue shape and posture. Syllable-final laterals are backer, more velarised, or 'darker' than syllable-initial ones. They are also longer in duration. Conversely, syllable-initial laterals are usually more palatalised, or 'clearer', than syllable-final ones. It is important to note that these are terms are relative. In some varieties of English, all laterals are dark, even when syllable initial. This is the case for e.g. many varieties of North American English (but perhaps especially New York), Manchester and Leeds (both in northern England). However, there are still relativities within these varieties, so while the initial laterals are dark, the final ones are even darker. Conversely, some varieties have clear laterals in all positions, such as many varieties of Irish English and Newcastle (England). Likewise, although these varieties have clear laterals finally, the final laterals are still darker than the initial laterals, without actually being dark.

For many varieties of English, syllable-final laterals are regularly heavily velarised, or labiovelarised.

In many cases, there is a vocalic **on-glide**. As the articulators move out of the vowel into the lateral, they produce what sounds like a distinct sound. Compare, for instance, the words 'feed' and 'feel'; you may well notice that the [i] vowels end differently. Speakers who have a strong on-glide into the lateral will be tempted to transcribe 'feel' as something like [fiəlˠ], but 'feed' as [fiːd]. This on-glide is very distinctive for combinations of vowel + dark lateral in many varieties, and it highlights the auditory significance of the secondary articulation. It may also explain how it comes to be that in so many varieties of English, syllable-final laterals can be vocalised. Vocalisation means that the consonantal articulation from [lˠʷ] (i.e. the tongue tip at the alveolar ridge) is lost, but the 'secondary' articulations are retained – we use the scare quotes because now, of course, this is not a secondary articulation but the primary articulation. Remember the earlier transcriptions of 'hill' as [hɪw, hɪɣ, hɪö]. These all capture some kind of (labio)velar approximation at the end of the word. In these varieties, it seems that the most salient feature of syllable-final 'laterals' is not laterality but velarisation, or labiovelarisation.

Another phenomenon associated with dark syllable-final laterals is that in some British English and Australian varieties, the vowel of goat has a backer and more rounded beginning when before a dark lateral: in these varieties, we get something like [əʊ] for 'goat', but something more like [ɔʊ] for 'goal'. In Melbourne (Australia), for some speakers 'gulf' and 'golf' are homophones, [gɔʊf]: there is rounding syllable finally (resulting in [ɔʊ] instead of [ʌlˠ]) and the lateral is vocalised, resulting in [ʊ]. What is achieved by these kinds of articulations is that labiovelarisation is audible (and probably also visible in a face-to-face setting) quite a long time before laterality starts; in turn, this may enhance the percept of the dark lateral.

6.4.4 Syllabic laterals

Laterals can form syllables by themselves, usually as an alternative to the sequence [əl]. **Syllabic** consonants are transcribed with the diacritic [ˌ] placed below the relevant symbol. The clearest cases are those where the consonant at the start of the same syllable is one which can be released laterally (i.e. [t d]; see Chapter 7), which involves releasing not the front of the tongue, but the side of the tongue. Compare, for instance, 'bottle' with and without a syllabic lateral: [-təlˠ, -tl̩ˠ]. To make the version with [-təlˠ], make sure the tongue releases from the alveolar ridge, allowing a short period of vocalicity before it is raised again to make [l]. To make the syllabic version, [-tl̩ˠ], keep the tongue on the alveolar ridge and lower the tongue on one side, allowing air to pass out laterally.

Syllabic laterals are generally found word finally: 'bottle', 'little', 'handle', 'facial', etc. For many verbs, the syllabic is possible even when a suffix is attached, as in 'pickle', 'pickling', which can be [pɪk.l̩ɪŋ] rather than [pɪk.lɪŋ] or [pɪ.klɪŋ]. But they can also, in some varieties, occur word medially, as in 'Italy', [ɪt.l̩.i].

The distribution of syllabic laterals is similar to that of syllabic nasals, which are discussed in Section 9.4.

6.4.5 Acoustics

The articulatory variability is reflected acoustically. Figure 6.3 shows the effect of secondary articulations on the acoustics of laterals. This is a spectrogram of a production of [l] whose secondary articulation is shifted from palatalised to velarised. Notice that F2 – associated with frontness and backness – changes, moving from rather high, at around 2100 Hz, to low, at under 1000 Hz.

Figure 6.4 shows a spectrogram of an utterance of the word 'leaf'.

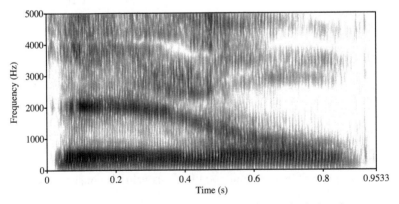

Figure 6.3 An alveolar lateral with varying secondary articulation, from palatalised to velarised.

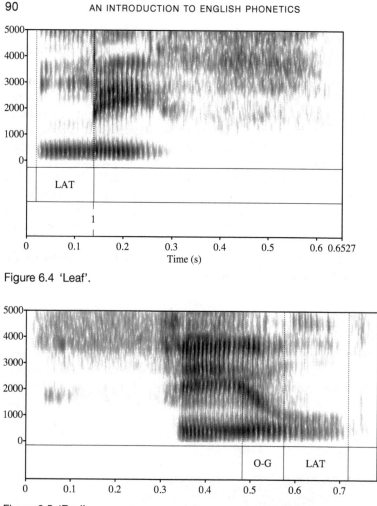

Figure 6.4 'Leaf'.

Figure 6.5 'Feel'.

The lateral portion is labelled 'LAT'. At the very end of it, at the point marked 1, there is a spike; this corresponds to the release of the tongue tip from the alveolar ridge and the switch from central to lateral airflow. This change in airflow has an acoustic effect too: notice that the lateral portion is lighter in colour (which means that it is lower in amplitude) than the following vocalic portion. F2 during the lateral portion is just about visible at around 1600 Hz; this value is consistent with a relatively clear lateral.

Figure 6.5 is a spectrogram of an utterance of the word 'feel'. The portion labelled 'O-G' (on-glide) shows the formants moving from the values for the vocalic portion – note in particular the high F2 associated with a close front spread vowel – to the values for a velarised lateral. This implies a low F2; and in the portion labelled 'LAT', it can be seen that F2 is at around 1000 Hz. This utterance is by the same speaker as the previous example, so the lateral here is darker than the lateral in 'leaf'. The on-glide, it can be noticed, is almost as long as the period of only lateral airflow. Notice that as with 'leaf', lateral airflow induces lower amplitude, seen in the overall lighter spectrogram for the LAT portion.

It should be clear from Figures 6.4 and 6.5 that syllable-initial and syllable-final laterals are far from mirror images of one another. There are two main differences. First, the syllable-initial lateral is clearer, and has a higher F2 than the syllable-final lateral. Secondly, the syllable-initial lateral has a more abrupt ending than the beginning of the syllable-final one: while the transition out of the lateral portion is rapid, in the syllable-final case, the transition into the lateral portion is slow.

6.5 'Rhotics'

The last set of approximants we will look at is not one that appears on the IPA chart. The term 'rhotics' comes from the name for the Greek letter rho, <ρ>, and has been the topic of quite considerable discussion. There are many symbols on the IPA chart which are based on the letter <r>: [ɹ ɾ ʀ ʁ ɽ ɻ]. Many of these represent the phonetic values of the letter <r> in many European languages. For instance, English has [ɹ], French has [ʀ ʁ], Finnish and Spanish have [ɾ r] and so on. If you look these symbols up on the IPA charts, however, you will see that they do not fit under a single heading for either place or manner of articulation. The term 'rhotic' has been coined to cover this set of sounds, and when it comes to English, we need to consider some extra sounds which are not part of the set just given.

The second thing to say is that not all rhotics are in fact approximants. For example, the trill [r] involves several short periods of closure of the tongue tip against the alveolar ridge, while the tap [ɾ] has just one. In English, most rhotics are approximants and they have a similar distribution in words to laterals: for example, they occur in similar environments in consonant clusters, and behave similarly with respect to voicing in such clusters. So in this chapter, we will group rhotics together on functional grounds.

At the systematic phonetic level, we transcribe rhotics broadly with [r], since there is rarely any ambiguity about its value, and the letter <r> is familiar; narrower transcriptions are used below so that different types of [r] can be compared across varieties and to convey more of the phonetic detail. /r/ is used to refer to the term in the phonological system, whose phonetic realisation is variable; and it may also not be realised.

6.5.1 Linking- and intrusive-r

As we saw in Chapter 5, English dialects are classed as either rhotic or non-rhotic. Rhotic dialects are those where /r/ is pronounced after vowels: so words like 'car', 'weird', 'born' are pronounced with [r]. In these dialects, word pairs like 'sauce' – 'source' and 'law' – 'lore' are not homophones; the second item of the pair is pronounced with [r], while the first one is not; and the two words might have different vowel qualities too.

Non-rhotic dialects are ones where /r/ is pronounced only before a vowel. [r] does not occur before consonants in non-rhotic varieties; vowel + /r/ sequences in this context have developed so that the vowel has a centring **off-glide**, producing diphthongs like [iə uə ɛə], or is long, as in [ɪː ɛː ɔː ɑː]. Non-rhotic varieties include much of England, Wales, Australia, New Zealand and South Africa, and some parts of North America. In these varieties, pairs like 'sauce' – 'source' and 'law' – 'lore' are frequently homophones (check the north and thought vowels in Table 5.2). But these varieties usually have [r] as a linking sound between vowels. When r-final words join with vowel-initial words, [r] is inserted. So while 'I fear nothing' has no [r], 'I fear evil' usually does. This is often called **linking-r**.

This principle is often overgeneralised by non-rhotic speakers. If we take two verbs, 'saw' and 'soar', both pronounced [sɔː] by non-rhotic Anglo-English speakers, and add the suffix <-ing>, we get 'sawing' and 'soaring'. While 'sawing' can be pronounced [sɔːɪŋ], it can also be pronounced [sɔːɹɪŋ], homophonous with 'soaring'. This is often called **intrusive-r**, because in these cases /r/ is pronounced where historically there is no warrant for it. It happens between words too, as in 'law[r] and order', 'Pizza[r] Express', 'vodka[r] and lime'. On the other hand, African American Vernacular English, which is reported by Labov (1972) as being mostly non-rhotic, sometimes drops /r/ where rhotic speakers have it, e.g. 'story', [stɔɪ]; 'Paris', [pæs]; 'Carol', [kal].

From the point of view of modern speakers, linking- and intrusive-r are the same phenomenon: a way to join two vowels together by using an alveolar approximant. The term 'intrusive-r' has its basis in the spelling system of English, and carries somewhat prescriptive (and negative) overtones: the only difference between linking-r and intrusive-r is that intrusive-r refers to a linking-r when there is no <r> in the spelling.

6.5.2 Rhotics in English

The starting point for our discussion of rhotics is the voiced alveolar approximant [ɹ]. This is the commonest variety of rhotic in English, and is used in Britain, Ireland, North America and most parts of the Southern Hemisphere. To produce this sound, the tongue tip or blade is raised up towards the alveolar ridge in a stricture of open approximation, the velum is raised and the vocal folds vibrate.

However, this is a simplified description. [ɹ] is frequently accompanied by other articulations. If you compare 'red' and 'led' and watch your lips, you may well see that for 'red' there is lip movement, whereas for 'led' there is not. This could be more accurately transcribed as [ɹʷ]. The movement is often protrusion or rounding, and the rounding can, in more extreme cases, involve puckering of the lips or contact between the upper teeth and lower lip. These more extreme cases could be transcribed as [ɹʋ, ɹʋ͡]. [ʋ] is the IPA symbol for a labiodental approximant, i.e. a sound made between the lips and the teeth which is made with open approximation and no friction noise generated. Some speakers actually do produce friction: this could be transcribed as [ɹṽ]. The symbol [͡] represents the fact that the two articulations are produced at the same time, rather than one after the other in sequence, as implied by [ɹʋ]. This is another example of a double articulation, which we saw in Section 6.3.

Alveolar approximants often have another secondary articulation. Recall that for laterals, the main place of constriction is at the tongue tip, leaving the body and back of the tongue free to form other articulations. The same is equally true for [ɹ]. [ɹ] is frequently dark, or velarised. This is marked in transcription as [ɹˠ]. As with laterals, the degree of velarisation is variable. Typically, speakers with clear initial laterals have darker initial rhotics; and speakers with darker initial laterals have clearer initial rhotics.

Commonly, [i] is both labialised and velarised: [ɹˠʷ]. Just as [l] often loses its primary articulation at the tongue tip and instead the 'secondary' articulations are retained (so-called vocalisation), so also [ɹ] sometimes loses its primary articulation at the tongue tip, but the secondary articulation of labialisation is retained. Many speakers produce /r/ as a labiodental approximant, [ʋ]; or as a velarised labiodental approximant, [ʋˠ].

One way to understand non-rhotic accents is as varieties which have lost the tongue-tip articulation of [ɹ] syllable finally, leaving just vowel colouring. This is parallel with loss of tongue-tip articulation in the case of vocalised [l].

6.5.3 Non-approximant articulations

Although approximation is the most common articulation type, rhotics can be produced in a variety of other ways.

In South African English, alveolar approximants occur, and are usually clear; but other articulations are found too, such as alveolar fricatives. These are not like [z], because the tongue shape is not right to produce the narrow channel needed for this. The friction is generated with the tongue tip at the alveolar ridge, and the articulation is the same as that for [ɹ] except that there is close instead of open approximation. There is no specific symbol for this sound, but one can be composed from the symbol [ɹ] with the diacritic [˔], which stands for a closer articulation, giving [ɹ̝].

Another common variant of [r] in South Africa is a tap, [ɾ]. Taps are produced with a short movement of the tongue tip towards the alveolar ridge which makes a closure of short duration. Taps are therefore not approximants, but stops. Taps occur in very conservative varieties of RP especially between vowels, and can be commonly heard in old British films. Nowadays, taps for rhotics most commonly occur in Anglo-English only after [θ], where they tend also to be voiceless, as in 'three', [θɾ̥i]. Taps are also common realisations of /r/ in Liverpool (England) and Scotland. They may be voiced or voiceless, and when voiceless they often have a lot of friction accompanying them. The voiceless taps seem to come utterance finally or next to a voiceless consonant, as in 'winter time' and 'shirt', which can both have the cluster [ɾ̥t]. Taps are also variants of [t] and [d] and are discussed in more detail in Chapter 7.

6.5.4 Non-alveolar articulations

Rhotics need not be alveolar, as we have seen. They may also be labio-dental (usually with some kind of velarisation), though this is most often a feature of an individual's speech rather than of a whole community.

Rhotics can also be produced at places of articulation further back than alveolar. One such type of rhotic is produced by combining retro-flexion (i.e. backward curling of the tongue) and approximation, giving the sound [ɻ], often known as 'curled-r' in the USA. This kind of articu-lation is also generally accompanied by labiovelarisation, and is found in many parts of the Western USA and in some parts of England.

A similar sound to this is known as 'bunched-r' or 'molar-r'. It is described by Laver (1994: 302) as made not with the tongue tip (which is retracted), but with the tongue body, which is raised up to the back of the hard palate and the front of the soft palate (velum), roughly the same location as the first molar teeth (hence the name 'molar-r'). For retroflex sounds, the surface of the tongue behind the tip is concave; but for molar-r the tongue shape is domed, or convex. These two sounds are very alike auditorily, and they are both found in the Western USA. Other kinds of rhotics that are frequently mentioned involve some kind of constriction further back than the velum, such as at the uvula or in the pharynx. These are common articulations in related European languages, such as German, Dutch or Danish, but they are very unusual in English. Uvular approximants did occur in Northumberland (north east England), and can be heard in some of the recordings of the older speakers of the Survey of English Dialects, e.g. 'tree', [tʁəɪ], and 'straight', [stʁerɪ]. (These recordings are accessible online from the British Library.) This feature, if it persists among modern speakers, is rare. The symbol used to transcribe this sound, [ʁ̞], combines the symbol for a voiced uvular fricative, [ʁ] with the diacritic [̞], which marks a more open articulation, i.e. it opens close approximation resulting in friction to open approximation.

6.5.5 Acoustics

A common property of rhotics is that they have a low F3 (around 1800 Hz). Because most versions of rhotics involve movement of the tongue body, which is relatively massive and slow to move, their acoustic properties tend to be very extensive in the time domain.

We illustrate this with the approximants [i] and [l]. Figure 6.6 shows two utterances: 'to lead', [tə liːd], and 'to read', [tə ɹiːd]. The portion of

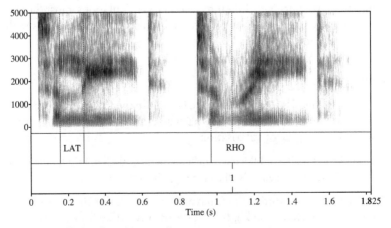

Figure 6.6 'To lead' and 'to read'.

laterality is labelled 'LAT'. Notice that it has more or less clear boundaries on the spectrogram, corresponding to the fairly abrupt onset and
offset of lateral airflow. [ɹ], like [j] and [w], has no clear beginning or
end. The portion labelled 'RHO' surrounds obvious formant transitions
where F3 moves downwards, and the point marked 'l' is the place where
F3 is lowest on the spectrogram.

Without either labialisation or velarisation, [ɹ] has a low F3. With
these secondary articulations, F3 is lowered still further. So one explanation for the secondary articulations is that they enhance the low F3 of
[ɹ] and so make it more perceptually salient.

Summary

In this chapter, we have looked at approximants, which have similarities with vowels but which function as consonants in English. We have
seen that two approximants, [j] and [w], are close to cardinal vowels.
The other two approximants, [r] and [l], are very complex in their
articulations, and in the range of possible articulations across varieties
of English.

We have also discussed primary, secondary and double articulations.
We have seen that approximants combine consonantal and vocalic elements in their articulation, and the vocalic elements are a property of
the sounds in English: [j] always has palatalisation; [w] always has labiovelarisation; [l] is darker or more velarised syllable finally than syllable
initially; [r] typically has labialisation and/or velarisation as part of its
phonetic make-up. In later chapters, we will see that secondary articulations are an important factor in the make-up of English sounds; but
while approximants have inherent secondary articulations, most (but by
no means all) other consonants share their secondary articulations with
adjacent vowels.

Exercises

1. Give a phonetic description of the laterals in the following words and
phrases as you produce them. Pay particular attention to voicing, duration, and the degree of velarisation.

> I like it; I'll hike it; I'll wipe it; he'd fill them; he'd fill it; he'd fill ink pens;
> all those; all of them; it's all a memory; it's all the memory

2. Make a list of words which have <r> (a) initially (like 'read'), (b)
after a plosive (like 'creak'), (c) after a fricative (like 'three'), (d) after
a vowel (like 'star'). Describe in as much detail as you can how you

produce these words, paying attention to secondary articulations. Can you extend any words in (d) (e.g. 'star/starry')? What happens to rhoticity in that case?

Further reading

For more on primary, secondary and double articulations, see Ladefoged and Maddieson (1996), and Laver (1994). Jones (1975) and Cruttenden (2001) give classic descriptions of English approximants. Kelly and Local (1989) and Wells (1982) make observations on yod-dropping in a range of English varieties.

Laterals and rhotics have been the source of much phonetic research. One of the original papers on this topic is Lindau (1985). For an interesting study of the sociolinguistic significance of laterals, read Slomanson and Newman (2004), a study of laterals in New York Latino speech; Stuart-Smith (2007) discusses rhotics in Glasgow.

7 Plosives

7.1 Introduction

Plosives are among the most variable and complex sounds in English. The aim of this chapter is to demonstrate and explore some of this complexity.

Table 7.1 Plosives in English.

Voicing	Place of articulation			
	Bilabial	Alveolar (coronal)	Velar (dorsal)	Glottal
Voiced	p	t	k	
Voiceless	b	d	g	?

The precise place of articulation for plosives is highly dependent on the context. Table 7.1 uses the terms labial, coronal and **dorsal** to reflect this variability in place of articulation. These terms are commonly used in phonology, and they refer to active articulators: lips, tongue tip/blade and tongue back. Glottal stops are common in English and so are included in Table 7.1.

By the end of the chapter, you will understand how it comes to be that the apparently simple plosive system of English is phonetically very rich.

7.2 Overview of the production of plosives

Throughout the articulation of plosives, the velum is raised, sealing off the nasal cavities so air cannot escape through the nose.

Plosives have three main phases: closing (C), hold (H) and release (R). In this section, we will look at these phases in more detail.

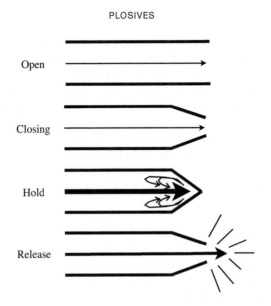

Figure 7.1 The phases of a plosive. During the hold phase, the pressure
behind the closure builds up. The greater pressure behind the
closure produces a burst of noise, plosion, on release.

7.2.1 Closing phase

During the closing phase, two articulators are brought together to form
a complete closure behind which air will be trapped. The action of
forming a closure does not last long: typically no more than a few tens
of milliseconds.

As the articulators move to form the closure, the shape of the vocal
tract is changed. Acoustically, changes in shape of the vocal tract lead to
changes in its natural resonances, and so it is possible to hear both that a
closure is being made and where the closure is being made.

These movements into closure can be heard if you produce sequences
of vowel + plosive, but hold the closure and do not release it. Try saying
'nab' but once the lips are together, do not separate them. Try the same
with 'had' and 'hag'. You should be able to hear that the vowels end differently for each place of articulation. The difference is slight, so you
will need to listen carefully.

7.2.2 Hold phase

During the hold phase time, the vocal tract is completely closed. Air
cannot escape through the nose because the velum is raised; air is

trapped behind the closure. However, the lungs are still forcing air out of the vocal tract, so the pressure behind the closure builds up. You can feel the build-up of pressure behind a closure if you make a closure at the lips (as for [p] or [b]), and then make a conscious effort to breathe out. This is an exaggerated version of what happens in speech, but the mechanism is essentially the same.

The duration of the hold phase depends on many factors. In citation form and when before a pause, the hold phase is longer for [p t k] than for [b d g]. In other conditions (such as connected speech, like conversation), the average hold duration for all kinds of plosive is somewhere around 50 ms.

7.2.3 The release (plosion)

Finally, the two articulators are released, letting out the air trapped behind the closure. Because this air is at a higher pressure than the air on the other side of the closure, the release generates a transient burst of noise. This part of a plosive is often called the '(plosive) burst'; the word 'plosive' is related to the word 'explode'. It lasts no more than a few milliseconds.

If you say [apa ata aka aba ada aga] and you hold the back of your hand 2–3 cm away from your lips, you will feel this burst on your hand – more strongly for [p t k] than [b d g], and probably most strongly for [p b] because the volume of air behind the closure is greatest for bilabials, and the hand is close to the source of the noise.

If a complete closure is made by raising the tongue tip to the alveolar ridge, then it is usually released by lowering the tongue tip from there, with the sides of the tongue moving symmetrically. The same is true for labials and dorsals. Such plosives are **centrally released**, with oral escape. Central release is the normal release for English plosives. We will look at other types of release later.

7.2.4 Simple acoustics of plosives

The three phases of a typical plosive can be seen in a waveform and spectrogram as in Figure 7.2, which shows a voiced velar plosive between two vowels, in 'a good (hobby)'.

During the closing phase, the formants move slightly. These movements are called transitions. They correspond to movements of the articulators into the closure. During the hold phase, the amplitude drops significantly because there is no airflow through the vocal tract. On release, there is a transient burst, seen as a sudden increase in energy, in the waveform and the spectrogram.

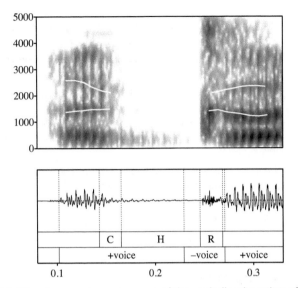

Figure 7.2 Waveform and spectrogram of the underlined portion of 'a good (hobby)', [ə gʊd hɒbi].

Although there is some voicing during the closure (notice the regular peaks in the waveform), it is quiet and its amplitude diminishes until eventually it stops. Voicing starts again very soon after the release of the closure.

7.3 Voicing and plosives in English

English phonology recognises two sets of plosives, 'voiced' /b d g/ and 'voiceless' /p t k/, as in pairs such as 'pit' – 'bit', 'rapid' – 'rabid', 'locking' – 'logging', 'hat' – 'had'. These labels are not so helpful from a phonetic perspective, because they hide the complexity of the relationship between voicing, closure and release.

Vowels before [p t k] are regularly shorter than vowels before [b d g]: compare the vowels of 'lock' and 'log' (e.g. [lɒk, lɒˑg]) or 'heat' and 'heed' ([hiˑt, hiːd]).

There are many permutations of voicing and closure. There can be voicing throughout the hold phase, within constraints. Voicing can stop before, at or after the closure is achieved; and start again at or after release. Some possible arrangements are illustrated in Figure 7.3.

The time between the release and the onset of voicing is called **voice onset time** (VOT). It is measured in milliseconds (ms). If the voicing

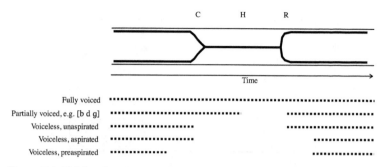

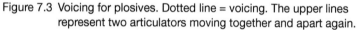

Figure 7.3 Voicing for plosives. Dotted line = voicing. The upper lines
represent two articulators moving together and apart again.

starts after release, VOT is said to be positive, while if it starts before
release, it is said to be negative.

7.3.1 Fully voiced plosives

In fully voiced plosives, modal vocal fold vibration continues through
all phases of the plosive.

Make a fully voiced plosive by producing a vowel, e.g. [ɑ], and then
make a closure at the lips while continuing to say the vowel. This results
in a closure with a low-pitched (and quiet) buzzing sound. For the vocal
folds to vibrate, there needs to be a difference in pressure above and
below the glottis. With a complete oral closure, eventually the pressure
above and below the glottis equalises, because the air above the glottis
has no means of escape. Therefore the duration of a fully voiced closure
is constrained by how long a pressure difference across the glottis can
be maintained. If the closure is released as soon as the voicing stops, a
fully voiced plosive is produced. Fully voiced plosives commonly occur
between two voiced sounds, as in 'hobby', 'under', 'hunger', and in some
(but by no means all) varieties they are normal productions of [b d g].

7.3.2 Partially voiced plosives

If preceded by a voiced sound, the sounds [b d g] in English are generally partially voiced: voicing continues during the early part of the
closure but then ceases part way through the hold phase. On release,
voicing starts again almost immediately.

An example of this is shown in Figure 7.5, which contains [b] between
two vowels. Voicing stops half way through the hold phase, and starts
again immediately after the release of the closure.

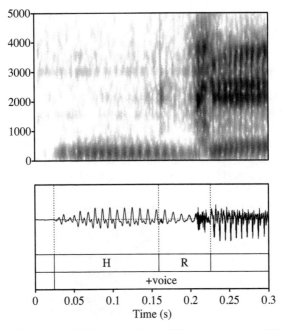

Figure 7.4 Fully voiced [g], in 'gig', [ɡɪɡ]. (After a pause; no visible C phase.)

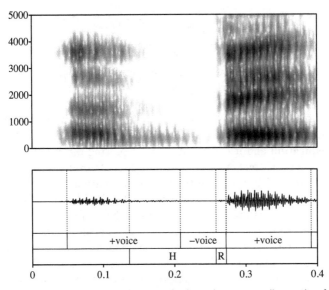

Figure 7.5 Vocalic portion, closure, plosive release, vocalic portion from 'a bit', [ə bɪt].

Utterance-final [b d g] are often partially voiced, and have no voicing, or whispery voice, on release; this can be transcribed as [b̥ d̥ g̥].

7.3.3 Voiceless aspirated plosives

Voiceless aspirated plosives are the commonest productions of the sounds [p t k] in English. In this arrangement, voicing stops at about the same time as the closure is made. Throughout the closure, the vocal folds are held open, so that the hold phase is voiceless. Vocal fold vibration starts after a delay of approximately 20–50 ms after the release of the closure. For voiceless aspirated plosives, VOT is typically 20–50 ms.

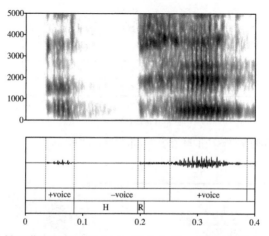

Figure 7.6 Vocalic portion, closure, plosive release, aspiration, vocalic portion from 'a pit', [ə pʰɪt].

Figure 7.6 shows the lag between release and onset of voicing. After the release, there is a period of noise before voicing begins. This is called **aspiration** and it is generated by air passing through the glottis and then the vocal tract. Aspiration is a product of turbulent airflow, and sometimes it persists even after the voicing has started.

If you say the phrases 'a pick, a tick, a kick' with the back of the hand just in front of the mouth, you will probably feel aspiration as a puff of air. Aspiration is transcribed with a superscript [h]: [ə pʰɪk, ə tʰɪk, ə kʰɪk]. The quality of this aspiration depends on the accompanying vocalic articulation: with front, close vowels (in words like 'peat', 'tick', 'king', 'cute' in most varieties), the aspiration has qualities of palatalisation; with back, close vowels, the aspiration has qualities of labiovelarisation (in words like 'port', 'took', 'queen' in most varieties);

with [r]-sounds, there is accompanying retroflexion, and possibly also labiovelarisation, as in 'prey', 'treat', 'creep'.

The degree and duration of aspiration depend on word and sentence stress. The more prominent a word is, the more aspiration with any voiceless plosive in it it is likely to have.

7.3.4 Voiceless unaspirated plosives

For voiceless unaspirated plosives, there is no voicing during the closure. Vocal fold vibration starts very soon (about 5–20 ms) after the release of the closure.

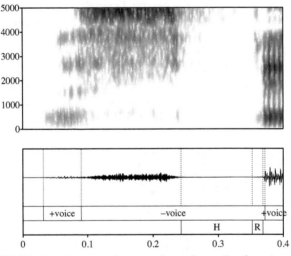

Figure 7.7 Friction, closure, release and vocalic portion from 'a spit', [ə spɪt].

Unaspirated plosives are regularly found in English in the syllable-initial clusters [sp st sk]. If you say 'a pie' and 'a spy' with your hand just in front of your mouth, you will feel a noticeable difference: for 'a pie', you will feel a stronger puff of air than for 'a spy'. This corresponds to the difference in aspiration, and a shorter VOT for these plosives. If you can produce 'a spy', but remove the [s] and keep an unaspirated plosive, the resulting sound will probably be closer to the English sound [b] than the [p] sound. This is because when preceded by a voiceless sound or when utterance initial, the closure for [b d g] is usually voiceless. On release into a following vowel, voicing starts almost immediately.

7.3.5 Voiceless preaspirated plosives

If voicing stops before a complete closure is achieved, i.e. the vocal folds allow air to pass through while the closure is still being made, this results in a short period of voicelessness and friction as the closure is being made, and is commonly known as preaspiration, though there are two types.

Voiceless friction can be generated as the articulators approximate one another. This can be transcribed using the appropriate fricative symbol, e.g. [ᶲp, ˢt, ˣk]. Shortness is indicated by a superscript.

The other source of noise is turbulence at the glottis. This source of noise is transcribed as e.g. [hp ht hk] and is known as **preaspiration**.

Preaspiration is not common in English, but has been reported for word- and utterance-final plosives in Tyneside, north east England (Watt and Allen 2003), and Hull (Williams and Kerswill, in Foulkes and Docherty 1999: 147).

Figure 7.8 shows a spectrogram and waveform of part of the word 'loop', [luːᶲpʰ], as spoken by a young female speaker from Tyneside. In this production, voicing stops before the closure is made, resulting in a short period of voiceless friction at the lips. This is represented in the transcription by [ᶲ], the symbol for a voiceless bilabial fricative, with

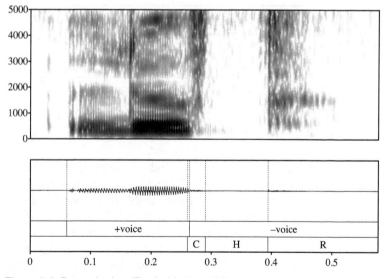

Figure 7.8 Preaspiration. The hold phase (H) starts after the offset of voicing, producing a short portion of voiceless friction while the closure is made.

the superscript indicating its short duration. The friction could also be transcribed as [ʍ], [luːᵘ̥pʰ], to capture the combination of voicelessness + labiovelarity, or [ʰ], [luːʰpʰ], to capture voicelessness which matches the preceding vowel, and to mirror the way we transcribe aspiration as [ʰ] after the release of a plosive. As is common, there is more than one way to transcribe preaspiration.

7.4 Glottalisation

Closures of voiceless plosives [p t k] and the affricate [tʃ] are often accompanied by **glottalisation**. This involves the adduction of the vocal folds usually before the oral closure is made. If complete, the adduction results in a glottal stop; if incomplete, there is a portion of creaky voice. Both of these give an auditory impression of the vowel being cut short. This is often called 'glottal reinforcement'.

Glottalisation is limited to syllable-final voiceless plosives.

Figure 7.9 shows a New Zealand speaker's production of the vowel + plosive portion the word 'kit', [kʰɪʔtʰ] with glottal reinforcement. There is a short portion between the segments labelled '+voice' and '−voice' where there is a glottal stop (labelled 'ʔ'): in the spectrogram, it shows up as an irregular and distinct vertical striation. On the waveform, notice

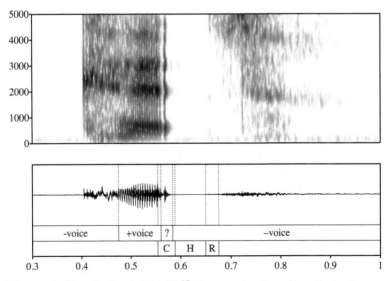

Figure 7.9 Glottalisation in 'kit', [kʰɪʔtʰ], as spoken by a New Zealand speaker (IPA).

the similarly abrupt pulse during that segment; the amplitude drops away more abruptly than in other vowel-to-plosive transitions that we have seen. This abrupt ending to the vowel gives the impression of it having been cut short: voiceless plosives in English are regularly preceded by shorter vowels than voiced plosives, so glottalisation enhances the percept of 'shortness'.

Glottalisation is especially common with alveolar closure, and sometimes even replaces alveolar closure, when it is known as 'glottal replacement'. It is less common in conjunction with bilabial or dorsal closure, though there are varieties of English where bilabial and dorsal closure can be replaced by just glottal closure, as in Cockney [ə kʰaʔ ə tʰi] for 'a cup of tea'.

7.5 Long closure

Plosives are sometimes called maintainable stops because they can be held for varying periods of time. For instance, in a sequence of two plosives of the same kind, it is possible to produce a long closure, as if for two plosives: 'coo[k] + [k]arrots', 'if I ha[d] + [d]one it'. The closure is made as for the end of the first word, but then held approximately twice as long before being released. There is only one release in such sequences, although of course it is possible to produce a sequence of two plosives. Long closures can be transcribed with the symbol [ː] to mark length: [kʊkːarəts], [hadːʌn]; or as two plosives, but perhaps with the first marked as unreleased: [-k˥ k-]. This is useful to make it easier to mark stress and word breaks: 'cook carrots', [kʊk˥ 'karəts].

7.6 Place of articulation

As well as labial, coronal and dorsal plosives, English has a plosive at a fourth place of articulation: the glottal stop. Because glottal stops are frequent in English, we include a discussion of them in this section.

Place of articulation for plosives in English varies in part because of a process called **assimilation**, where the place of articulation for the plosive adapts to the place of articulation for a following sound.

7.6.1 Labial

Most labial plosives in English are bilabial, [p b]. Occasionally they may be labiodental. This might not be a straightforward labiodental closure, but rather a bilabial closure during which time the upper teeth are resting on the inside of the lower lip. This kind of production can come in sequences such as [b] + [v], e.g. 'obvious'. These plosives take longer to release, since there is more contact between the upper and lower articulators than if the closure were purely bilabial. There is no separate IPA symbol for labiodental plosives, but the symbols [p b] can be modified with the 'dental' diacritic [̪], giving [b̪p̪], or perhaps [b̪b̪, p̪p̪].

7.6.2 Coronal

Coronal plosives can be made with either the tongue tip or the tongue blade. This seems to be a matter of individual habit. In using the word coronal, we are recognising that the tip or the blade of the tongue can be used to make closures at a number of different places. The main ones are dental, alveolar and postalveolar.

Dental plosives occur in a number of places in English: before the sounds [θ] and [ð], as in 'width', 'breadth'; and often as an alternative production of [ð] in utterance-initial position. The IPA does not provide special symbols for dental plosives, so the diacritic [̪] is added below the symbol to mark a dental place of articulation, as in [d̪θ] for 'breadth' or [t̪θ] for 'eighth'.

The voiceless alveolar plosive and the voiced alveolar plosive ([t d] respectively) have slightly different tongue shapes in many varieties. For [t], the tongue tip tends to have a little slit in it, so that on release, there is often a short period of friction (affrication), which we could transcribe as [ts]. [d] on the other hand usually does not have this tongue shape, so its release is less affricated and sounds 'flatter'.

Postalveolar plosives occur as part of affricates [tʃ dʒ] (which we will discuss in Chapter 8), and in clusters before [ɹ], as in 'train', 'drain'. If you compare the tongue postures for the initial plosives of 'tie' and 'try', you will notice that for 'try' the tongue tip or blade is making contact a bit behind the alveolar ridge; you may also notice that the sides of the tongue are curled up a little and the part of the tongue that makes contact with the roof of the mouth might be different from the part for 'tie': in my own production, the frontmost underside of the tongue makes contact for the postalveolar plosive. Postalveolar plosives can be transcribed [t d]; the diacritic [-] means 'retracted' (i.e. further back).

7.6.3 Dorsal

The back of the tongue (dorsum) and the roof of the mouth both have large surface areas compared with e.g. the lips. In English, dorsovelar plosives can be made at a number of places along the roof of the mouth, and this is especially so for combinations of [k] + vowel.

If you say the words 'key', 'cat', 'court' (or words with vowels close to CV1, CV4 and CV7 or CV8), and isolate the initial consonant articulation, you should be able to feel that the back of the tongue makes contact with the roof of the mouth in different places. For 'key', the articulation is quite far forward (**advanced**), which can be transcribed with the diacritic [˖]: [k̟]. For 'court', the articulation is much further back (retracted), and if you compare this [k] sound with that of 'key', you will hear that it has a lower-pitched ring to it. This is partly because the lips are rounded (the vocalic articulation includes a high tongue back and lip-rounding); but even if you unround your lips, the sound is still different. The diacritic for this is [-]: [k̠]. The sound in 'cat' is 'neutral': neither particularly front nor back when compared with the others.

This variability arises because the plosive consonant is **co-articulated** with vocalic articulations which differ in tongue frontness and backness and in lip posture. Already in hearing the [k] sound in 'key', some secondary articulations associated with the vowel are audible. Because they anticipate the next sound, this is often called 'anticipatory co-articulation'. At a narrower, more detailed phonetic level, then, we have as many 'kinds of [k]' as we have kinds of vocalic articulation.

We have talked about 'vocalic articulation' and not 'vowel'. This is because velars do not depend on vowels for their place of articulation: they depend on the subsequent approximant or vowel, whichever is closer. In the word 'screen', there is a retracted [k̠], not the advanced [k̟] of 'keen' or 'ski'. In this case, [k] is co-articulated with [ɹ], which for many speakers of English has a secondary articulation of velarisation and/or lip-rounding. Likewise, in 'queen', the velar articulation is co-ordinated with the labiovelarity of [w] and not the frontness and spread lips of [i].

Note that this relationship between vocalic and dorsal articulations is not reciprocal: in sequences of vowel + [k g], the place of articulation of the dorsal is less adapted to the vocalic articulation than in [k g] + vowel: compare 'keep' and 'peak', and 'caught' and 'talk'; you will probably find that when the velar comes after a vowel, its place of articulation is neither particularly front nor back compared with when it precedes a vowel.

7.6.4 Glottal

Glottal stops occur in English, although they are not used to distinguish one word from another. For this reason, they find no place in a phonemic analysis of English except as free variants of other sounds, or as predictable sounds. For instance, if we compare e.g. [ɪl] and [ʔɪl], these are just different productions of the word 'ill'.

Phonetically, glottal stops are very common in spoken English. They occur in a number of locations. These are all illustrated in the transcription in (1) below, which is taken from a conservative RP speaker:

1. Simultaneously with, or instead of, voiceless alveolar plosives, ('salt', line 4; 'important', line 5) – glottal reinforcement and glottal replacement respectively.
2. Word initially, as markers of phrase beginnings or to mark vowel-initial words which carry stress ('all', line 9).
3. As a way to mark repair ('that is the- . . .', line 3).
4. Occasionally instead of [ð] word initially ('that's', line 5).

(1)   VT 020104

1	M	now brining is salting them
2	P	yeap
3	M	and that is the? ⌐ ?ap not just to give
4		a sal? flavour
5		?at's not the impor[tan? thing
6	P	[it's to draw
7		the moisture ou[t
8	M	[and
9		to get [?all the [moisture [out
10	P	[yeap [yeap [yeap

7.7 Release features of plosives

There are four main ways to release plosives in English: centrally (along the middle of the vocal tract), centrally into friction (as is the case with affricates [tʃ dʒ]), nasally (through the nose) and laterally (down one or both sides of the tongue). Another possibility is inaudible release.

The type of release is often predictable from context. The direction and type of airflow on release usually match those of the subsequent sound: so in sequences of plosive + vowel, plosives are released centrally, because vowels require airflow down the mid-line of the vocal tract. In a sequence of plosive + nasal, however, the plosive may be released nasally, because nasals require nasal airflow.

7.7.1 Central release

We have already discussed central release. Central release of plosives always occurs when plosives are released into fricatives, approximants (except lateral approximants), vowels and other plosives. It may also occur before nasals and laterals, though other kinds of release into these consonants are possible.

7.7.2 Fricative release

Plosives can be released into friction which is generated immediately on release. In this case, the two articulators are separated only so far as to generate a stricture of close approximation, causing friction on release. This friction is **homorganic** with the plosive, i.e. it is made at the same place of articulation. The friction can be long or short in duration.

Combinations of plosive + long **fricative release** are commonly known as 'affricates'. English has two clear instances of affricates, [tʃ] and [dʒ]. These are clear cases because they both pattern phonologically as one unit. They occur both syllable initially and syllable finally. For both, the coronal closure is postalveolar, and the tongue shape is the one required for [ʃ] and [ʒ]. (See Chapter 8 for more details on the production of fricatives.) More narrowly, then, they can be transcribed as [tʃ dʒ].

The release of the plosive portion is immediately into friction. The best way to realise the difference is to take a pair where there is a sequence of [t] + [ʃ] vs. an affricate [tʃ], such as 'why choose/white shoes', 'to buy chews/to bite shoes'. In the cases with affricate [tʃ], the first word ends with an open articulation, and the second begins with an affricate; in cases with [t + ʃ], the first word ends with an alveolar closure and the second starts with a fricative. The closure is longer in the [t + ʃ] sequences than in the [-tʃ-] cases. The tongue shape on release is flatter in the [t + ʃ] sequences, whereas in the [-tʃ-] cases it has the appropriate shape for generating postalveolar friction. The closure is also a little further back for the affricate [tʃ]. These many small details reveal some of the subtle phonetic distinctions that can be made to differentiate what on paper at least look like potentially homophonous sequences.

Other common affricate sequences in English are [tɹ̝ dɹ]. [tɹ̝] occurs syllable initially, e.g. in 'tree', 'tram', 'true'. The plosive part, [t], involves a postalveolar closure with a tongue shape appropriate for a [ɹ] sound: the tongue is somewhat curled back, the sides make a tight contact with the teeth, and the tongue back is raised. It can be classed as an affricate because the release part, [ɹ̥], involves friction caused by the curling back of the tongue. There may also be a narrow channel down the tongue, causing some degree of whistling on release.

[dɹ] is the voiced equivalent of [tɹ̝]. As a voiced sound, it has weaker friction than [tɹ̝].

[tɹ̝] and [dɹ] are distinguishable from sequences of [t + r] and [d + r] because they only occur syllable initially. If you compare pairs such as 'a tree', [ə 'tɹiː] vs. 'at Reeth', [ət 'ɹiːθ], then you should notice several differences between them (Table 7.2).

Table 7.2 Differences between [t + r] and [t̪ɹ̥].

[t + r]	[t̪ɹ̥]
Possibility of glottalisation in preceding vowel	Impossibility of glottalisation in preceding vowel
Voicing combined with rhoticity	Voicelessness combined with rhoticity
Lip-rounding starts late	Lip-rounding during closure

We turn now to plosives with short periods of friction on release. We will transcribe these with a small superscript symbol for the frication portion.

Initial [ð] can often be pronounced as [d̪ð], especially when utterance initial. Many function words (which are commonly phrase initial), such as 'the', 'this', 'that', 'those', 'they', start with this sound.

Below are three examples of [d̪ð]. G speaks a dialect from the West Midlands of England (around Birmingham); W's variety is from the north west of England.

(2) jdc 123.04

1 G →   d̪ðat's (.) [totally perfect
2 W   [ʔs genius

(3) jdc 174 bar crawl

1 W →   we're- d̪ðey're starting in (.) ((Placename))
2   (0.3)
3 G →   who's (.)d̪ðey

Plosives released with short periods of friction are common in English. Most speakers have some degree of frication in their release of the closure for [t], giving a sound which is sometimes transcribed as [ts]. In Edinburgh (Chirrey, in Foulkes and Docherty 1999: 227), fricated releases for word-final plosives are reported, as in [tʰeːʔkxh, fʉdzh], 'take, food', respectively.

7.7.3 Nasal release

In order for the pressure to build up for a plosive release, air is trapped in the oral tract, and for this the velum must be raised. It is possible for

the air to be released through the nose, i.e. nasal release. This is produced by lowering the velum while keeping the oral closure. The IPA
transcription for **nasal release** is a superscript [n]: [tⁿ].

Nasal release is used in English as a way to join a sequence of
plosive + nasal consonant, as in the word 'button'. One way that the
plosive [t] can be released in this word is with an oral, central release,
as in [bʌtən]. The second is a nasal release, as in [bʌtⁿn̩]. You might be
able to isolate the [tⁿ] sequence and produce a chain of alveolar plosives with voiceless nasal release, [tⁿn̥]. When you do this the tongue
is kept in place against the alveolar ridge. If you pinch your nose, you
will not be able to produce it because the air will remain trapped in the
nasal cavities.

Note that the place of articulation for the nasal and the plosive are
the same, and this is the regular pattern: 'happen', [hapnm], and 'bacon',
[beɪknŋ], exhibit the same pattern. One 'weak' form of the word 'can'
(whose 'strong' form is [kan]) is with a syllabic nasal: 'I [knŋ'] buy
them'. The place of articulation is the same across the plosive + nasal
sequence, but the nasal could also have the same place of articulation as
the bilabial plosive in 'buy', giving e.g. [kəm baɪ]; this is the pattern we
regularly find when the nasal is not syllabic.

7.7.4 Lateral release

Lateral release involves letting air out down the sides of the vocal tract
rather than down the mid-line. This occurs in English only in sequences
of [t + l] and [d + l], with the sides of the tongue being lowered while
the tip or blade of the tongue makes a complete closure against the
alveolar ridge, as in 'immediately', 'rapidly', 'little', 'handle'. Lateral
release is transcribed with a superscript [l]: [tˡl dˡl].

Lateral release is just one possibility for joining the elements of
plosive + lateral sequences, because it is also possible to release the
plosives centrally, into a vowel articulation.

Lateral release is generally optional in English, and its distribution a
little complex. It is common in unstressed syllables at the ends of words
where the final vowel is (or would be) [ə], like 'handle', 'little', 'bottle',
'puddle' (which end in [-dəl -təl] or [-tˡl̩, -dˡl̩]), but can sometimes also
be heard in the middle of words, as in 'Italy', ['ɪtəli 'tˡli].

Some dialects (notably in northern England) also have laterally released [t d] sounds in some initial clusters, in words such as
'clothes', 'clean', 'gloves': i.e. in clusters which in other varieties have
velar + lateral articulations, pronounced with [tˡl- dll-] in those
dialects.

7.7.5 Inaudible release

Sometimes plosives have no audible plosion. **Inaudible release** is marked with the diacritic [˥].

This can arise when one stop closure is made, then another: the second one masks the release of the first, while the hold of the first masks the transition into the closure of the second.

This is well illustrated in words with plosive + plosive clusters, such as 'tact' and 'apt'. There are two possibilities for the first of the plosives in the [kt] and [pt] clusters. The first is that the plosive is released, so that two distinct plosive portions are heard: [takt apt] (Figure 7.10).

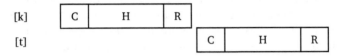

Figure 7.10 A sequence of [kt], with two audible releases.

The second possibility is that the first plosive of the cluster is inaudibly released; in this case, closure into velarity or labiality is heard in the vowel. Once the dorsal or labial closure is achieved, the alveolar one is made; and when the alveolar closure is achieved, the first closure is released (Figure 7.11). In the case of a velar + alveolar sequence, the velar closure is behind the alveolar one, so nothing will be heard. In the case of a labial + coronal sequence, the amount of air between the two closures is very small, and release of the labial closure may generate a percussive sound (i.e. just the sound of the articulators coming apart), but there will be insufficient air pressure in the cavity between the lips and coronal closure to produce a plosive release. The release is then made into alveolar plosion. The whole sequence can be transcribed as [tak ˥ t ap ˥ t].

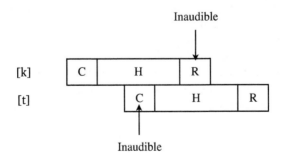

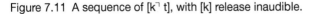

Figure 7.11 A sequence of [k˥ t], with [k] release inaudible.

The third possibility is a common way to end utterances where the speaker has no more to say: most notably, word forms like 'yep', [jɛpʼ], and 'nope', [nəʊpʼ], for 'yes' and 'no' are not produced with audible release. One likely explanation for these kinds of forms is that they end with labial closure, which is visible: a mouth that is closed is a mouth that is not talking. By making a bilabial closure, the 'completed' nature of the utterances that end this way is highly visible.

7.8 Taps

Taps are stop articulations, but unlike plosives, the closure for a tap is non-maintainable. For taps, the closure is made by two articulators when one articulator – usually the front of the tongue – strikes another in passing. The closure lasts for about 30–40 ms. Because the active articulator is in motion, the closure cannot be maintained.

Taps occur very commonly all over the English-speaking world as forms of [t] and [d] between vowels. The cluster [nt] is sometimes produced with a nasalised tap [ɾ̃], so that e.g. 'winter' can be pronounced [wɪ̃ɾ̃ɚ]. Taps are especially common in many varieties of American English, but are by no means limited to those varieties.

Figure 7.12 shows a production of the word 'city', ['sɪɾi], by a speaker from southern Michigan. The portion labelled 'C' corresponds to the short closure period characteristic of taps. Notice how short it is (about 25 ms). It is voiced all the way through. Immediately after the labelled portion there is a transient which corresponds to the release of the tongue.

There are many pairs of words distinguished by [t] and [d] which sound very alike or even identical when pronounced with taps: 'writer' and 'rider' ([raɪɾɚ]) are well-known cases. Sometimes, however, the distinction is still made through e.g. vowel duration (longer duration in [t / ɾ] words) and vowel quality (e.g. Canadian speakers use [aɪ] in 'rider', but [ʌɪ] in 'writer'). This loss of distinction between originally different words has given rise to some interesting 'eggcorns' – words which are misheard and then given peculiar spellings. ('Eggcorn' is an eggcorn from 'acorn'.) Examples arising from confusion over whether to interpret [ɾ] as /t/ or /d/ include: 'Catillac', 'radify', 'color-coated', and 'don't know X from atom'. (See eggcorns.lascribe.net for more.)

Here are some taps as produced by Anglo-English speakers in unscripted conversation in places where [t] might also be expected:

(4) VT 020104

a little bi[ɾ] of acid
I've go[ɾ]a go by my husband's opinion

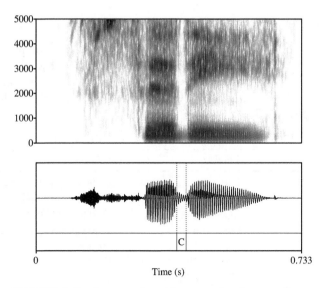

Figure 7.12 'City', ['sɪɾi], as produced by a speaker from southern Michigan. 'C' marks the closure portion for the tap [ɾ] (IPA).

le[ɾ] it cool
I think I know wha[ɾ] i[ɾ] is
i[ɾ] is del:icious

Taps occur in conservative varieties of Anglo-English as one form of rhotic. They are commonly heard in old British black-and-white films where the actors speak RP. Taps also occur dialectally in England as tokens of rhotics, e.g. in many parts of Yorkshire and Liverpool. Many speakers who do not normally produce <r> as a tap use a voiceless tap in the cluster [ɾ̥], as in 'three'.

Here are some narrow transcriptions of words with taps in Liverpool English (Scouse) (Watson 2007). Scouse is known for its open articulations, of which there are many here, including aspiration for [d] in 'around'.

(5)   Liverpool English

        free   fɾiː
        around   ʌˈɾ̃ãnˠd̪ʰ
        stronger ˈs̪ˌt̪ˌɾ̃õŋɡə̞
        agreed   əˈɡɾiːd̪ʰ
        probably on aggregate   ˈpɾɒβəβli ɒn ˈaɡɾiˠəh
        stronger of the two   ˈst̠ɹɒŋɡəɾə̞ vð̪ɪ ˈtsɪʉ

Summary

We have seen in this chapter that the phonetic details of plosives depend very much on the context and variety of English. One of the most complex aspects of plosives is the way that the voicing contrast is produced. These differences are summarised (for Standard Southern British English) in Table 7.3.

Table 7.3 Phonetic characteristics of voicing with English plosives.

	Voiceless	*Voiced*
Vocal fold vibration	None during closure	In the early part of the closure; occasionally throughout closure
	Except after [s], voicing starts late after release; aspiration	
		Voicing starts early after release
Voice quality	Glottalisation possible in preceding vowel, nasal or lateral	Possible whispery voice quality
Durational aspects	Short preceding vowel, nasal or lateral	Long preceding vowel, nasal or lateral
	Long hold phase	Short hold phase

Exercises

1. Give a phonetic description of the plosives in your production of the words below, paying particular attention to how you get into and out of them:

> lock – log – locking – logging
> ramp – ramping – rant – ranting – rank – ranking
> hump – Humber – hunt – hunter – under – hunk – hunger

Are there any pairs where the voice quality is different?

2. The spectrograms and waveforms at 1–5 in Figure 7.13 correspond to the underlined portions of five of the phrases at (a)–(g) below. By looking at the friction, voicing and transients in the acoustic data, try to match 1–5 with the appropriate data. Can you use the acoustic data to provide a narrower transcription?

a. churches
b. cocktail
c. jukebox

d. robin
e. pecking
f. tapestries
g. and trust

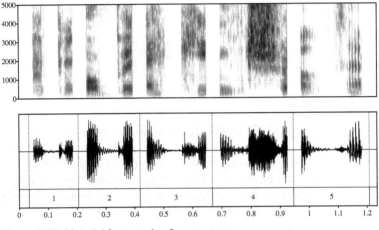

Figure 7.13 Material for exercise 2.

Further reading

For more on the general phonetics of plosives, see especially Jones (1975), Cruttenden (2001) and Laver (1994). For an acoustic description of plosives, see Johnson (2002). Crystal and House (1988) give a good overview of instrumental findings on plosives. For a comprehensive description of the phonetics of glottal stops in English, see Dilley et al. (1996).

The voicing of English plosives is highly variable by dialect, so general references such as Wells (1982), Foulkes and Docherty (1999) and Wolfram and Fasold (1974) are very useful. For a study of two ways of implementing voicing, take a look at Jacewicz et al. (2009), who examine voicing in Wisconsin and North Carolina.

8 Fricatives

8.1 Introduction

At the systematic level, English has nine fricatives (Table 8.1). This makes them the largest class of consonants in English by manner of articulation. One determining factor in the auditory quality of fricatives is the shape of the tongue; the shape of the surface where friction is generated (such as the teeth or the roof of the mouth) is also important. Although they are not explicitly represented on the IPA chart, these factors explain why it contains so many fricatives.

Table 8.1 Fricatives in English.

	Labiodental	*Dental*	*Alveolar*	*Postalveolar*	*Glottal*
Voiceless	f	θ	s	ʃ	h
Voiced	v	ð	z	ʒ	

8.2 The production of fricatives

Friction can be generated in two ways in the vocal tract. One way is to produce a constriction of close approximation. To achieve this, two articulators are far enough apart so that air can pass between them, but close enough together so that when it does, it becomes turbulent and produces friction noise just forward of the maximal constriction. This is how friction is produced for labiodental fricatives [f v] and dental fricatives [θ ð] (as in 'think' and 'then'). The other way is to direct a channel of air at another surface, such as the back of the teeth or the alveolar ridge, and when the moving air hits this surface, it becomes turbulent. This is how friction is produced for alveolar fricatives [s z] and postalveolar fricatives [ʃ ʒ] (as in 'ship' and 'pleasure').

How much friction is generated depends on a number of variables. First, the width of the channel between articulators affects the pressure of air through the constriction. With a narrower channel (e.g. for [s] and [ʃ]), the pressure increases, and so the turbulence increases too. With a wider channel (e.g. for [f] and [θ]), there is less pressure and therefore also less friction.

Secondly, the volume of air affects the volume of friction generated. The more air forced through the constriction, the greater the pressure, and therefore the greater the turbulence and the amount of friction noise. This will depend on the amount of air being expelled from the lungs.

If this seems a bit abstract, imagine watering a garden with a hosepipe. If the pipe is not blocked and the water pressure is not too high, water flows through the hose and comes out in a steady stream. If you narrow the end of the pipe by putting your finger over it, the pressure within the pipe increases, generating turbulence in the flow of water, and producing a spray. You can also increase pressure in the hose by opening the tap, which increases the flow of water through the pipe and therefore also the pressure behind the stoppage. To get a really good spray (in other words, a lot of turbulent water), you can increase the pressure by both opening up the tap and making the constriction narrower. Air moving through the vocal tract is a little similar: the constriction in the vocal tract corresponds to your finger at the end of the hosepipe, and the water moving through the pipe corresponds to the air being pushed out of the vocal tract.

Fricatives are often classed as **strident** or non-strident. Strident fricatives, [s z ʃ ʒ], have a lot of friction noise, especially at higher frequencies, caused by a comparatively narrow constriction. Non-strident fricatives are [f v θ ð]. If you compare the sounds [θ] and [s] in particular, you will hear that one of the main differences between them auditorily is that [θ] has a much 'flatter', quieter sound than [s], which sounds 'sharper' or 'brighter' and louder.

Fricatives in English all have airflow down the mid-line of the vocal tract. You can tell this by producing a fricative, holding the articulators in place and then sucking air in. The part of the mouth that goes cold and dry as you do this should be symmetrical around the middle of the vocal tract.

Some speakers use fricatives with lateral airflow: the voiceless lateral fricative [ɬ] is a Welsh sound (spelt <ll>) that occurs in many place-names, such as 'Llandudno', 'Llangollen' and 'Llanfair'. Many English speakers replace this sound with a sequence like [tl kl θl]; but it is not difficult to produce [ɬ]. First, make a [l] sound, and hold it; secondly, remove the voicing (as in the [l̥] of 'p[l̥]ay'); thirdly, raise and tense the sides of the tongue a little. This should produce a good [ɬ].

English fricatives all have oral airflow: the velum is raised and forms a tight seal preventing air from flowing through the nose. This can be demonstrated by pinching the nose while producing a sustained fricative such as [s:::]. It makes no difference to the sound that comes out because [s] requires a good seal, preventing leakage of air through the nasal cavities and therefore weakening the friction.

Affricates have no place on the IPA chart, because they are sounds composed of two elements, plosive + fricative. In English, there are two such sounds at the systematic level, [tʃ dʒ], usually represented by <ch -tch> and <j ge- gi- -dg-> respectively in the spelling. Affricates are also discussed in Chapter 7, but their fricative components [ʃ ʒ] are described in this chapter.

There are fricatives at five places of articulation in most standard varieties of English: labiodental, dental, alveolar, postalveolar and glottal; and two degrees of voicing: voiced and voiceless.

Other fricatives also occur in English, for a range of reasons. These are discussed towards the end of this chapter.

8.3 Details of English fricatives

We start with a consideration of generic properties of fricatives, before looking at the specific details of individuals.

8.3.1 Voicing

English has four pairs of fricatives which are traditionally said to be distinguished by voicing: [f – v; θ – ð; s – z; ʃ – ʒ]. Say the sounds continuously, alternating between the voiced and voiceless sound: e.g. [s::z::s::z::]. If you do this while covering your ears, you will hear the vocal fold vibration for the voiced sound conducted through your bones, but otherwise, the articulators remain in the same configuration.

The phonetic detail of voicing is more complex for many speakers. We will see that the contrast actually involves a cluster of phonetic features, only one of which is vocal fold vibration.

If you compare a voiced and a voiceless pair of fricatives, such as [s z] or [f v], you will notice that there is less friction noise for a voiced fricative than for a voiceless one. The best way to hear this is to compare pairs, or near-pairs like 'loser' – 'looser'; 'ever' – 'heifer'. The reason for this difference is that when there is vocal fold vibration, the vocal folds are closed for about half of the time, and so there is less air flowing through the vocal tract. With voicing, the flow of air is reduced, and consequently the amount of friction noise is reduced.

Figures 8.1 and 8.2 show waveforms of a stretch of about 300 ms from the words 'sip' and 'zip' as produced by a speaker of RP in isolation. In these figures, friction and voicing are marked. As can be seen, for 'sip', the initial friction and voicing do not overlap at all: the waveform has no periodicity until after the aperiodic friction has ended. By contrast,

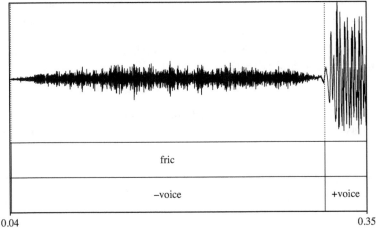

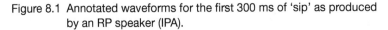

Figure 8.1 Annotated waveforms for the first 300 ms of 'sip' as produced by an RP speaker (IPA).

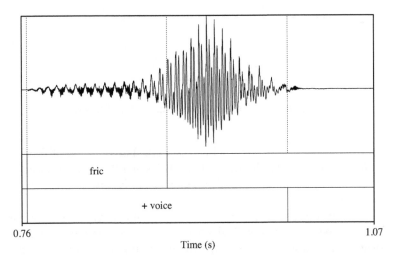

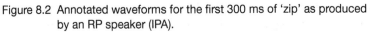

Figure 8.2 Annotated waveforms for the first 300 ms of 'zip' as produced by an RP speaker (IPA).

in the case of 'zip', friction and voicing overlap throughout the period of friction. The waveform contains signs of aperiodic and turbulent airflow; and superimposed on it can be seen a low-amplitude, regular, periodic waveform, which indicates vibration of the vocal folds.

Other differences are visible too. The friction in 'sip' lasts about twice as long as the friction in 'zip'. (The graphs are shown on the same scale, with marks on the x-axis every 100 ms.) The friction for 'sip' is also louder, which can be seen in the vertical displacement in the waveforms. These differences in duration and amplitude are consistently found in the pairs [s – z; f – v; θ – ð; ʃ – ʒ], even though the alignment of voicing and friction is highly variable.

Figure 8.3 shows a spectrogram of 'sip' and 'zip' as produced in Figures 8.1 and 8.2.

The differences that have already been mentioned can be seen here too. [s] and [z] have turbulence centred at 4000 Hz and above. For

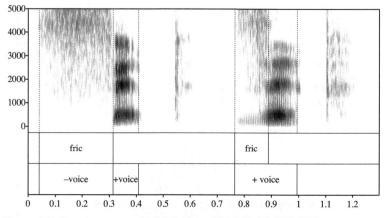

Figure 8.3 Spectrograms of 'sip' (left) and 'zip' (right) (RP) (IPA).

[z], voicing can also be seen below 1000 Hz. The duration of friction is much longer in 'sip' (between about 0.05 s and 0.3 s on the spectrogram) than in 'zip'; and it is louder, which means it appears as darker on the spectrogram.

Now by way of contrast let us look at a similar pair, also citation forms, as spoken by a New Zealander. This speaker often produces the fricatives transcribed as [v ð z ʒ] without vocal fold vibration, but the other differences are still found – the amount of friction noise produced is lower for [v ð z ʒ], and the duration of the frication is shorter.

Figures 8.4 and 8.5 show productions of 'fie' and 'vie' by a New
Zealander. For 'fie', as expected, friction is produced without voicing.
But the same is true for 'vie', where voicing and friction do not coin-
cide. This is unexpected, and we might assume that 'fie' and 'vie' are
homophones for this speaker. But they are not: as can be seen from the
vertical displacement in the waveforms, [f] is produced louder – with

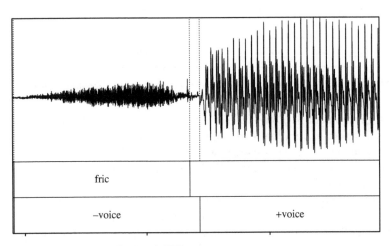

Figure 8.4 'Fie' (New Zealand) (IPA).

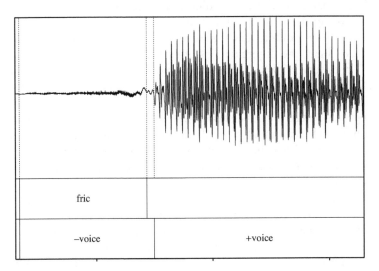

Figure 8.5 'Vie' (New Zealand) (IPA).

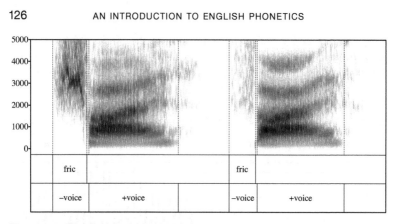

Figure 8.6 'Fie' (left) and 'vie' (right) as spoken by a New Zealander (IPA).

more turbulent friction – than [v]; and at about 145 ms the friction for [f] is longer in duration than that for [v], which is about 110 ms. These productions of voiced fricatives, where there is little or no voicing along with friction, are very common in English, so we will look at them in a bit more detail.

Figure 8.6 shows a spectrogram of the utterances in Figures 8.4 and 8.5: note the lower-amplitude friction for [v] than for [f]: between about 0.1 and 0.2 s the fricative portion corresponding to [f] on the spectrogram is darker than the corresponding portion between about 0.8 and 0.9 s, which corresponds to [v].

These patterns of partial voicing are recurrent in English. On first noticing them, it is common to worry about how to name and transcribe these differences. There are a number of solutions to this problem. First, the difference has often been referred to as 'tense' [f θ s ʃ] and 'lax' [v ð z ʒ] (rather than 'voiced' and 'voiceless'), to avoid the implication that [v ð z ʒ] are necessarily accompanied by regular vocal fold vibration. This is not a solution that has been universally accepted, because it can be seen as just a difference in the way names are used, and is not much more descriptive or factually accurate than the term 'voiced'. Secondly, conventions should be stated for transcription symbols so that they can be interpreted accurately. The details are set out in Table 8.2.

We may want to represent the overlap of friction and voicing more accurately in our transcriptions: for instance, there may be variability within a speaker's productions so that some instances of [v ð z ʒ] are fully voiced while others are not. In this case, we might transcribe [v ð z ʒ], but use the diacritic for 'voiceless', [̥], along with the symbol for 'voiced' fricatives: [v̥ ð̥ z̥ ʒ̊]. These symbols might seem to be equivalent

Table 8.2 Voiced and voiceless fricatives.

Symbols	Conventions
[f θ s ʃ]	Voicing and friction do not overlap Friction is loud and turbulent as compared with [v ð z ʒ] Friction is long in duration as compared with [v ð z ʒ]
[v ð z ʒ]	Voicing and friction may (but do not necessarily) overlap Friction is quiet (low amplitude) as compared with [f θ s ʃ] Friction is short in duration as compared with [f θ s ʃ]

to [f θ s ʃ], but conventionally they are thought of as implying lower-amplitude friction and shorter duration of friction, so that they do not refer to the same sounds as [f θ s ʃ].

By using this diacritic, we can transcribe three kinds of fricative, such as [s z̥ z]. This does not represent the phonological facts of English, because there is no evidence that three kinds of fricatives contrast in any variety of English, but it may be that the distribution of [z̥] and [z] is regular and patterned (e.g. related to location in syllable structure), and therefore the differences between them could be linguistically informative details.

These differences are not true of medial fricatives. Typically, in a vowel + voiced fricative + vowel sequence, there is a short period of voicing and friction at the beginning and the end of the fricative portion, and the middle part of the fricative is often either voiceless or has only low-amplitude (quiet) voicing. Usually, there is a little more overlap of friction and voicing going into a fricative from a vowel than there is coming out of a fricative portion into a vowel. In either case, the period of overlapping friction and voicelessness is usually just a few cycles of voicing as the vocal folds stop (or start) vibrating. This can be seen in Figures 8.7 and 8.8: compare the duration of friction for the voiced and voiceless fricatives; the amplitude; and the point at which the voicing goes off (V off) and on (V on).

If you compare words with voiceless and voiced fricatives finally, such as 'race' and 'raise', or 'leaf and 'leave', you will hear that although there is little or no voicing towards the end of the words with [z] and [v], the friction is quieter than in the words with [s] or [f]: [reɪs·, re·ɪz̥, liˑf, liːv̥]. For many speakers of English, this reduction of friction noise compared with their voiceless counterparts is one of the properties of the sounds [v ð z ʒ]. This reduction in friction noise happens even when the sounds are produced without voicing throughout, as when they are word final.

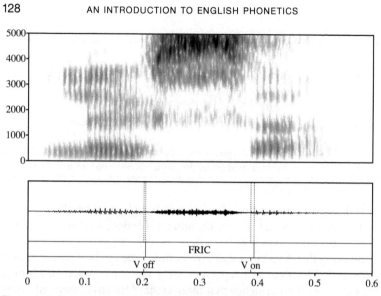

Figure 8.7 Spectrogram of 'looser', with friction ('FRIC') and the offset and onset of voicing ('V off', 'V on') marked.

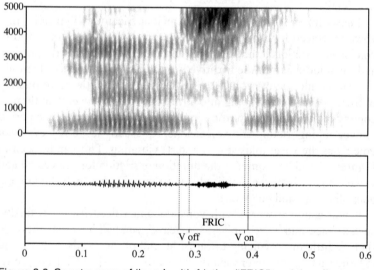

Figure 8.8 Spectrogram of 'loser', with friction ('FRIC') and the offset and onset of voicing ('V off', 'V on') marked.

8.3.2 Place of articulation

We will now look at the main English fricatives by place of articulation: labiodental, dental, alveolar, postalveolar and glottal. Having done that, we will look at a few other fricatives in English which occur but which are not treated as lexically important in most standard varieties.

Labiodental

For labiodental fricatives [f v], air passes between the upper teeth and lower lip. Labiodental articulations are made with the upper teeth on either the outside or the inside of the lower lip. The two do not sound very different from each other and, as far as is known, no variety of English exploits the difference.

Because they are made without involvement of the tongue, labiodental fricatives are highly susceptible to secondary articulations made by different tongue postures: for example, compare the sounds at the beginning of 'feast' and 'fool', and you will probably hear an [i]-like secondary articulation in 'feast' – with the tongue close and front in the mouth, [fʲ] – but an [u]-like one in 'fool', with the tongue body raised towards the velum, and perhaps with some lip-rounding [fˠʷ]. Retroflexion can also co-occur with labiodental articulation, and is common in productions of the word 'from', where there is often a period of friction and rhoticity simultaneously: [fʴəm, f͡ɹ̥əm].

Dental

The fricatives [θ ð] can be made at a couple of places of articulation. For many speakers, the articulation is interdental, i.e. made with the tongue blade between ('inter-') the upper and lower teeth. In this case, it may protrude, or be barely visible between the teeth. Such articulations are frequently reported for varieties of American English. The IPA has no symbol for interdental sounds, but we could combine the symbol [θ] with [̟], which marks an advanced articulation: [θ̟]; or we could use the symbol [θ̪͆], which is found on the **Extensions to the IPA** (for the transcription of clinical and disordered speech). (The diacritic [̪] marks 'dental'; the dental diacritics above and below [θ] iconically represent the upper and lower teeth.)

In other varieties, the friction is generated against the back of the teeth and the tongue is held relatively flat so that the air escapes through quite a wide channel. This wide channel is what makes the fricatives [θ ð] so quiet in comparison with [s z]. If you make a [θ] sound and then suck air in, you should be able to feel the place where friction is generated: it is the part of the mouth which goes cold and dry.

In the case of dental fricatives, this is a wide area at the front of the tongue.

Some speakers do not use dental fricatives, replacing them with labiodental ones instead, giving [fɪŋ] for 'thing', [faŋks] for 'thanks', [və] for 'the', and [fɑːvə] for 'father'. This phenomenon has gained a lot of attention in sociolinguistic literature and is commonly known as th-fronting.

The sounds [θ ð] are not always produced as fricatives. In some varieties of English, notably some Irish varieties and the East Coast of the USA, they are produced as dental plosives instead, [t̪ d̪], in all situations. Another possible pronunciation is as an affricate, i.e. a plosive with a fricative release: [t̪θ d̪ð]. See Chapter 7.

For many speakers, [ð] in particular is highly variable in its manner of articulation, ranging through plosive, nasal, fricative, lateral approximant, and approximant articulations:

(1)   Variability in voiced dentals:

plosive (utterance initial)	that's good	d̪ᵟ ats gʊd
nasal	in the (park)	ɪn̪ːə pɑːk
lateral	all those (people)	ɔːlˠəʊz piːpəl
approximant (intervocalic)	weather	wɛð̞ə

Alveolar

The alveolar fricatives [s z] are made with a groove in the centre of the tongue. This groove directs air towards the alveolar ridge, and the main source of turbulence for these fricatives is the air striking the alveolar ridge, which is an obstacle in its path. (It is hard for people without front teeth to produce good [s z] sounds.) The jaw is fairly close, so that the upper and lower teeth are close together: to hear the effect of jaw height, say a [s] sound and slowly open the jaw, and you will notice that the friction decreases in loudness. The second feature of these fricatives with respect to tongue shape is that there is a hollow behind the groove, so the tongue has a concave shape, with the tongue sides raised and pressed against the upper teeth to produce a good seal. Without this, air would leak out, and the sibilance of the fricatives would be much diminished.

[s] and [z] can be made with the tongue tip either up or down; in fact, the precise articulation of these sounds is very variable between individuals. The huge variety in individuals' dentition and the shape of the inside of the mouth leads to a great variety in articulation, but the resulting acoustics are similar.

[s] and [z] are made with the front part of the tongue, leaving the lips and tongue back free. These sounds can take on a range of secondary

articulations, especially before a vowel: compare the [s] sounds of 'see', 'saga' and 'soar', and you will hear something like [sʲ, s, sᵞʷ].

Postalveolar

The fricatives [ʃ ʒ] are made with a constriction that is further back than [s z]. Their place of articulation is variously described as palatoalveolar or postalveolar. The tongue has a wider channel than for [s z], and it is convex behind the groove, rather than concave as for [s z]. Like [s z], [ʃ ʒ] can be produced with the tongue tip either up or down.

[ʃ] is usually accompanied in English by a secondary articulation of labialisation (lip-rounding). If you compare the words 'lease' – 'leash', and 'said' – 'shed', you will probably notice quite different lip postures. For the alveolar sounds, the lips have the same shape as for the vowel; but for the postalveolars, the lips are rounded, even though the vowels are not. So a narrower transcription would be [liːʃw]. One possible reason for this secondary articulation is that the postalveolars have friction at a lower frequency than the alveolars. If the lips are rounded, then the friction sounds as though it has a lower pitch. Try this for yourself: isolate the [ʃw] sound of 'shed' and then unround and round the lips so you can hear the acoustic effect. The reason this happens is that by rounding the lips, you effectively lengthen the vocal tract, and longer tubes resonate at lower frequencies than shorter tubes.

Figure 8.9 shows a spectrogram of an Australian male speaker saying the words 'sigh' and 'shy'. Note that the centre of the energy in the fricative portion is lower for [ʃ] than for [s], having significant energy at

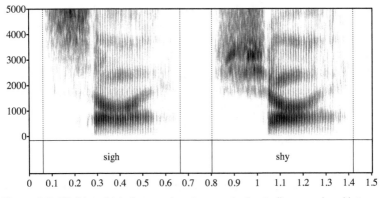

Figure 8.9 'Sigh' and 'shy' as spoken by a male Australian speaker. Note the lower-frequency energy for [ʃ] than for [s] (IPA).

2000 Hz and above. Lip-rounding for [ʃ] can be thought of as enhancing one of the acoustic differences between [s] and [ʃ].

Not all [ʃ] sounds in English are rounded. This reflects one source of the sound [ʃ] historically, which is a combination of [s] + [i] or [j]. Many words across varieties of English can vary between the alveolar + palatal sequence and the postalveolar sound: 'tissue', [tɪsju: tɪʃu:], illustrates this. In some words one or the other possibility has become lexicalised, that is, it has become the normative pronunciation of the word: examples include 'sugar', where modern English has [ʃ], but the spelling indicates that it was originally [sj-], and 'suit', which is usually [su:t], can be [sju:t] but cannot be [ʃu:t].

In the words with the alveolar + palatal sequence, the rounding does not start till the frication ends. In words like 'tissue', the rounding can start later during the fricative, so that the last syllable of 'tissue' is not homophonous with the word 'shoe'. For some speakers, there are the odd pairs like 'fisher', [fɪʃʷø], and 'fissure', [fɪʃʲə], where in the first case there is rounding throughout the friction and in the second syllable ([ø] stands for a rounded version of [ə]), while in 'fissure' the friction is slightly longer than in 'fisher' and has a palatal off-glide and lip-rounding with a later onset. These are small, subtle details which not all speakers of English have in their speech.

Another place where there is some subtlety about the lip-rounding is across words, in phrases where in between [s] and [j] there is a word boundary, as in 'I miss you'. Here, a wide range of possibilities occurs, from [s j] through to articulations that are more like [ʃ] throughout.

The fricative [ʒ] in many instances derives historically from [z] + [i], which makes it somewhat parallel to [ʃ] (which has other sources as well). It has a much more restricted distribution than [ʃ], however: the main difference is that [ʒ] cannot be word initial or word final in native English words. [ʒ] often alternates with [ʃ] and/or [zi]: 'Parisian', [pəˈrɪziən, pəˈriːʒən], or 'nausea', 'anaesthesia', [-ziə -ʒə -ʃə]; also with [dʒ] in some loanwords like 'garage', whose last syllable can be [-ɑʒ -ɪdʒ]. The other main source of [ʒ] is indeed loanwords, such as 'negligee', 'beige', 'rouge'. It does not occur, however, at the boundary of morphemes where the rightmost morpheme is <-er>: words like 'rosy', 'cosy', 'cheesy' have comparative forms with [-zi-], and not [-ʒ-] (so e.g. [ˈrəʊziə], not [ˈrəʊʒə]).

Glottal

Finally, we come to the glottal fricative, [h], which does not occur at all in some varieties of English. This is usually classed as a fricative on the grounds that its friction noise is generated at the glottis. Because of this, its quality is very different depending on what follows. If you say the words 'heat', 'heart' and 'hoot', and isolate the initial fricative, you will hear very different qualities, which are determined by the quality of the vowel that follows. This is because although there is friction being generated at the glottis, the rest of the vocal tract above the glottis (the supralaryngeal tract) excites and amplifies some parts of the friction more than others. One commonly suggested analysis of [h] is that it is a period of voicelessness superimposed on a vowel, so that it might also be transcribed as e.g. [i̥ ɑ̥ u̥]: [i̥i̥t ɑ̥ɑːt u̥uːt]. Usually this transcription is not used because it requires a different symbol for each voiceless vowel, and in broad transcription, we avoid diacritics; [h] on the other hand captures the initial voicelessness consistently, but in some ways is less precise phonetically.

Between vowels, voiced glottal friction is common. Examples of this are to be found in the words 'ahead', 'ahoy' and 'behold'. One analysis of this sound is to treat it as a period of voicing with glottal friction, or breathy voice. So we might transcribe 'ahead' as [əˈɦɛd] (with a voiced glottal fricative) or [əˈɛ̤d] (with breathy voicing and a vowel).

[h] is usually counted as a fricative of English, though phonologically it patterns more closely with /w/ and /j/, which are also limited in distribution to syllable-initial position. /h/ also has phonological similarities with /w/ and /ð/: for instance, it occurs at the start of many function words (including some related ones: 'where', 'there', 'here'), and can be dropped from the start of words (e.g. will/'ll, them/'em, her/'er). Connected to this, the distribution of [h] is related to stress: it appears in stressed syllables, but not in unstressed ones – compare 'he likes it', [\hi ˈlaiks ɪt], with 'does he like it?', [dʌz i /laik ɪt]. 'Dropping one's h's' in unstressed syllables is normal for even conservative speakers. This discussion shows that phonetic classification is not always straightforward; and while it may make sense to classify [h] as a fricative in phonetic terms, in phonological terms, the classification is a bit less straightforward.

8.4 Non-lexical fricatives

Having discussed the nine fricatives of English that are likely to be represented in a dictionary, we will now discuss other fricatives which are found more sporadically. They fall into three main sets: those fricatives which arise from sequences of other sounds and which have a set of alternatives which can be analysed as a sequence (Section 8.4.1); those which are regularly used in certain varieties of English in place of other sounds (8.4.2); and those which are the result of incomplete closure for plosives (8.4.3).

8.4.1 Fricatives which arise out of a sequence of sounds

Postalveolar fricatives

A common combination of sounds across morphemes in English is [-s + j-], as in phrases like 'this year', 'I miss you'.

These sequences can be produced as [-s j-]. The two sounds can also merge to produce a postalveolar fricative with a palatal off-glide [-ʃj-]. A phrase like 'this year' can be produced as [ðɪs jiə(r)] or [ðɪʃjiə(r)], where the last syllable is not homophonous with 'shear', [ʃiə(r)]. These two possibilities are extremes of a spectrum of possibilities, including portions during which the friction changes from [s] to [ʃ].

Palatoalveolar fricatives

The sequence [t + j] sometimes gives rise to palatoalveolar fricatives, as in words like 'Tuesday' and 'question', which can be pronounced with [tɕ] or with the sequence [tj]. For some speakers, the first syllable of 'Tuesday' may be homophonous with 'chews'; but for others, there is a distinction between the two kinds of word. 'Chews' has lip-rounding throughout and an overall dark resonance; on the other hand 'Tues-' has increasing lip-rounding throughout the consonantal portion until the [u] vowel is reached, when lip-rounding is at a maximum. The friction is also not in the same place as for [ʃ]: it is further forward and is made with the blade of the tongue. It is alveolopalatal and transcribed as [ɕ].

Similar observations could be made for 'question'. Phonemicising this word as /kwɛstʃən/ predicts that the consonant cluster /stʃ/ in the middle of the word should sound the same as in the sequence 'nice church'. However, this does not seem quite accurate for all speakers, because the lip-rounding and tongue body posture in the two are different. In 'question', the friction is front and clear, and close to palatoalveolar, [ɕ].

Palatal fricatives

In discussing the approximant [j], we noted that there is the possibility of voicelessness + palatality as in words like 'pew'. Voiceless palatal fricatives are also common in English as realisations of the sequence /hj/, as in 'hue', 'huge', 'human', etc. This is not surprising: as we have seen, [h] has no associated tongue shape and represents voicelessness. It must be accompanied by some supralaryngeal articulation, and in the case of the sequence [ju] (represented in English orthography as 'long <u>'), this means that the accompanying supralaryngeal articulation will be that for a palatal approximant. If this is produced without voicing, there will be greater airflow through the vocal tract, and in turn this will generate friction, resulting in voicelessness, palatality and friction, which is represented as [ç]. Notice that (as with [pj-], etc.) other transcriptions suggest themselves on phonological grounds, such as [hj] or [j̊]. It may not be a coincidence that there are varieties of English where these words have initial voicing, not voicelessness: [juːdʒ, juːmən].

8.4.2 Fricatives in place of other sounds

Some varieties of English, notably Liverpool and Irish English, regularly use fricatives for sounds that are produced as plosives in other varieties. These fricatives correspond to the places of articulation of plosives, so there are bilabial fricatives, alveolars and velars corresponding to the plosives [p b; t d; k g]. How these fricative sounds should be transcribed is a matter of debate. In some varieties of English, especially Liverpool and Irish, such sounds are normal productions, not just common productions, of the sound [p t k b d g], but especially [t], in many contexts. In all varieties of English, fricatives like these arise in speech that is often described as 'fast' or 'casual', though perhaps a more accurate description would be 'ordinary'. What is special about Irish and Liverpool English is that these are normal productions of 'plosives'.

Alveolar 'slit-t'

Irish English has a form of [t] which is sometimes described as 'slit-t'. It is made with an incomplete closure. The tongue shape is flatter than for [s], and the onset of the friction is rather sudden: this gives a very different impression from a 'real' [s], which has a more gradual build-up of friction. The period of friction is shorter in duration than for [s]. There is no agreed way to transcribe this sound. Possibilities include modifications of [s], but [s] implies a grooved tongue shape, which is not accurate; variations of [t], which captures the fact that the sound does the work of [t] in other varieties; and [θ], which implies a sound with the tongue shape of [θ], but an alveolar place of articulation, marked with the diacritic [=], taken from the Extensions to the IPA (for the transcription of clinical and disordered speech). This sound occurs between vowels and word finally, but not if another consonant occurs either before or after. A similar sound can also be heard in some varieties of Australian English.

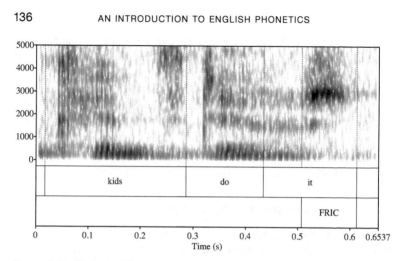

Figure 8.10 'Kids do i[θ]'. Speaker: 18-year-old male, Dublin (IViE file f1mdo).

Velar

Velar fricatives are regularly found in at least two varieties of British English: Scottish English and Liverpool English. In Scottish English, the velar fricative occurs in a few peculiarly Scottish lexical items such as 'dreich', [drix], a term to describe dark, grey, cloudy weather, and 'loch', [lɔx], a kind of lake or inlet from the sea.

Liverpool also has fricatives where other varieties have [k] after vowels. The friction is made with the tongue body or back, from palatal

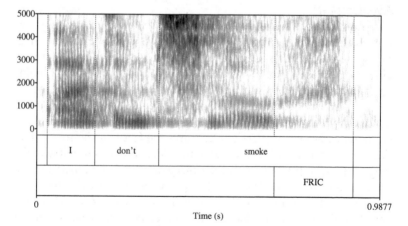

Figure 8.11 'I don't smo[x]e'. Speaker: 18-year-old male, Liverpool (IViE file f1sgw).

through to uvular articulations, depending on the preceding vowel: a more forward place of articulation with front vowels, a backer place of articulation with back vowels, as in 'week', [wiːç], 'back', [bax], 'dock', [dɒχ]. Figure 8.11 shows a spectrogram of a Liverpool speaker saying 'I don't smoke', [sməʉx]. Notice the last portion, labelled 'FRIC', which has no voicing, but has prolonged friction all the way through.

8.4.3 Fricatives from undershoot

The third group of fricatives we will consider in this section can be thought of as plosives that do not have the complete closure needed to create plosion. These are fricatives that arise from **undershoot**: that is, where articulators fail to make the complete closure needed to produce a plosive. These are rather common in ordinary speech in all varieties of English.

In normal speech, these sounds are barely audible as fricatives; often, it is only through close inspection of a recording that they are clearly hearable as fricative rather than plosive articulations. The entry into these fricatives is rather tight and fast; and they are short in duration in comparison with the fricatives we looked at in the early part of this chapter.

Table 8.3 Fricatives from undershoot.

	Labial	Coronal	Dorsal
Complete closure	p, b	t, d	k, g
Incomplete closure	ɸ, β	ʂ, ʈ, ʐ, ɖ	x, ɣ

Here is an example of two such fricatives. The speaker speaks a variety of London English.

(2) London:

what are you going to cook for us today?
['wɒʂjəɣər̃ə 'kʊk fəɹəs təˈdeɪ]

The utterance is produced with a pitch high in the speaker's range. It is quiet and fast, until it gets to the word 'cook'. On the word 'cook', there is a fall in pitch, and then the pitch remains low to the end of the question. In the fast talk that precedes the stressed word 'cook', there are a number of unusual sounds. The first one is [ʂ]. The diacritic [̺] marks that the articulation is closer than close approximation: that is to say, the tongue tip is raised quickly, so that friction starts abruptly. This articulation is similar to that of the Irish 'slit-t' we looked at earlier, but has a sharper, more [s]-like quality; you could think of it as a 'fast [t]', which in some sense it is.

The sound transcribed [ɣ] at the start of the word 'gonna' is made with voicing + friction + velarity. It is achieved in the same way that [ş] is: that is, the tongue body is raised towards the velum, as if to make a velar closure, [g], but it fails to make a complete closure and instead generates a short period of friction, [ɣ]. As with [ş], the speed with which the articulation is made and its short duration both contribute to the perception of these sounds as [t] and [g] respectively.

Here is another example from English spoken in the north west of England (around Manchester), although this pattern is common in other varieties of English too (Kelly 1967). In clusters of the shape [-sPs], where P stands for a voiceless plosive [p t k], complete closure is not made; what happens is that two articulators approximate each other, producing a short period of friction. In the case of labials and dorsals, the friction is concurrent with alveolar friction. In the case of coronals, there is a slight change in the quality of the friction as the tongue is raised:

(3)   Northern English
      the wasp's here   [-s ɸ͡s s-]
      the mast's here   [-s ş s-]
      the desk's here   [-s x͡s s-]

Summary

As with plosives and approximants, we have seen that fricatives form a phonetically rich set of sounds in English. This richness stems in part from the fact that tongue shape, the volume of air flowing through the vocal tract and place of articulation all affect the quality of friction. The way that fricatives are entered and exited is also a linguistically signifi-cant feature, distinguishing 'real' fricatives from those which arise from the failure to achieve a complete closure to form a plosive. Although the number of fricatives in the words of English (nine) is larger than that of plosives (six), we have also seen that some of these fricatives cannot occur everywhere in words, and sometimes alternate with other frica-tives. Fricatives, then, are also a phonologically complex set of sounds.

Exercises

1. Transcribe, broadly and then more narrowly, your productions of the words and phrases below. Pay particular attention to the secondary articulations. The first one is done for you.

future	ˈfjuːtjə	ɸjy̯ːʔtɕə
shop		
this shop		
disgusting		
sneezing		
all the horses		
from the summer		
a thin veil		
for his father		
to hush up		
thank you		

Further reading

For a more complete description of Liverpool English see Watson (2007) and references therein. Pandeli et al. (1997) discuss the production of Irish English 'slit-t'.

Zsiga (1994) and Nolan et al. (1996) are instrumental studies of variations in word-final /s/. Overviews of plosives changing to fricatives in speech can be found in Brown (1977) and Shockey (2002).

9 Nasals

9.1 The production of nasals

At the systematic level, English has three nasal sounds, which are all voiced (Table 9.1). In conversational speech, we can observe nasals at other places of articulation as well, in ways that are contextually etermined. It is also reasonably easy to find stretches of talk which have **oro-nasal airflow**, i.e. airflow through both the nose and the mouth.

Table 9.1 English nasals.

Bilabial	Alveolar	Velar
m	n	ŋ

The nasals have different distributions: [m n] occur both syllable initially and z finally, but [ŋ] occurs only syllable finally.

Nasal sounds are so called because when they are produced, air flows through the nasal cavity. The nasal cavity is a space above the palate and behind the nostrils. It has a large surface area because it is filled with 'conchae', long, curled bone structures that resemble seashells (the name is related to the word 'conch'). The primary function of the large surface area is to warm and humidify air as it passes from the outside into the body. The complex structures of the nasal cavity mean that they absorb sounds at some frequencies (much as soft furnishings do) so that the acoustic structure ovf nasals is also complex. The effect of airflow through the nasal cavity in speech is to dampen the sound that comes out: nasal sounds are relatively quiet and low in volume compared with non-nasal sounds. Compared with oral sounds, they sound 'dull'. It is harder to distinguish fine details of nasals auditorily than it is for e.g. plosives or fricatives.

Nasal consonants require three main articulations in English. First, they require the velum to be lowered. This lowering of the velum is what allows air to flow out of the vocal tract via the nasal cavity. Learning to control the raising and lowering of the velum is not very easy, since most people are not aware of the velum. One way to become more awarve is to open the jaw (as if to make an [ɑ] sound), and then breathe in through the nose, but breathe out through the mouth, and then repeat this. At the transition between breathing in through the nose and out through the mouth, you might hear a quiet popping sound as the velum is lowered. This can make you more aware of the velum's position.

Secondly, nasal consonants require a complete closure to be made somewhere in the vocal tract: the oral gestures for [m n ŋ] are the same as those for [b d g] except that the velum is raised for [b d g] and lowered for [m n ŋ]. For this reason, nasals are often classed as 'stops', alongside plosives: in this case, the term 'stop' refers to a sound with a complete constriction in the oral tract, rather than a complete constriction in the vocal tract as a whole.

Thirdly, nasals in English are voiced.

Most of these properties of nasals can be tested simply. Make a long nasal sound such as [mːːː] or [nːːː], and then pinch your nose. You should find that the sound cannot be sustained for very much longer once the nose is pinched: this is because the closure in the vocal tract seals off airflow through the mouth, so there is no oral airflow; and by pinching the nose, airflow through the nose is also blocked.

Next, make a [sːːː] sound. You may be able to make a nasalised [s] sound, [s̃], by lowering the velum. If you achieve this, the amount of friction will diminish rapidly as you move from [s] to [s̃], and the fricative will sound weak and 'thin' compared with [s]. However, you can restore some of the volume to [s̃] by pinching the nose again, blocking nasal airflow.

Finally, try a simple experiment with a friend. Make nasals at a few places of articulation, including labial, labiodental, dental, alveolar and postalveolar; but do this out of sight, e.g. with your back turned or with your hands in front of your mouth, so that they cannot see the articulation. Ask them to guess the place of articulation. Most likely, they will not be very successful. The reason is that that nasals are not, by themselves, very distinctive, because the nasal cavity absorbs a lot of acoustic energy. Most information about place of articulation for nasals is located in the transitions into and out of the nasal occlusion which correspond to the closing phase of plosives.

9.2 Details of English nasals

In looking at the details of nasals in English, we will first consider how speakers come out of a nasal sound, normally into a vowel. Secondly, we will consider how speakers get into a nasal sound – the process of going into a nasal is not a mirror image of the process of coming out of a nasal. This is because two articulations have to be co-ordinated in time: the velum has to be lowered (to produce nasal airflow) or raised (to stop nasal airflow); and remember also that there must be an oral closure as well. The timing of these two events relative to one another can be varied.

9.2.1 Releasing nasals into vowels

In coming out of a nasal into a vowel, the oral closure must be released, and the velum must be raised to block airflow through the nasal cavity. These two articulations are generally simultaneous, so that when the oral closure is released, the airflow becomes oral. This produces a discontinuity in volume, which can be seen in waveforms and spectrograms as a rapid change in amplitude. Sometimes, movements of the velum can be seen in a spectrogram.

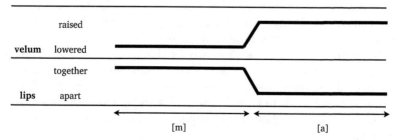

Figure 9.1 Co-ordination of articulations in nasal + vowel sequences.

Figure 9.1 gives a schematic representation of a nasal followed by a vowel. The upper line represents the action of the velum, and the lower line represents the action of the lips; the two articulations are temporally aligned so that they co-occur. The transition in time from [m] to [a] is quite fast (a few tens of milliseconds).

Figure 9.2 gives a spectrogram and a waveform of the start of the word 'map', as produced by a male speaker of RP. The nasal and vowel portions are labelled 'm' and 'æ' respectively: notice the rather abrupt

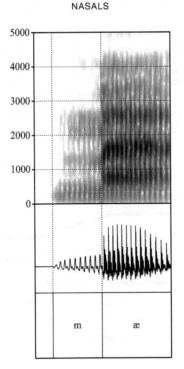

Figure 9.2. Initial part of 'map', [mæ-] (RP) (IPA).

change in amplitude as the nasality ends. What can also be seen is that during the spectrogram of the portion labelled 'm', there are some areas of low amplitude, such as around 1600 Hz. This is because the nasal cavities absorb some of the acoustic energy, and gaps like this (called zeroes) are often evident on spectrograms. Although there are formants visible during the nasal portion, they are less distinct than in the vocalic portion; this is because the formant peaks are wider, which makes them also quieter and less visually prominent. This is particularly noticeable for Fl.

9.2.2 Vowel + nasal sequences

In vowel + nasal sequences, nasality starts early and is slow compared with the onset of the closure in the vocal tract, meaning that there is a period of oro-nasal airflow. A common sequence is: oral airflow only (i.e. velum raised, allowing air to flow out of the mouth only); oro-nasal airflow (i.e. velum lowered, vocal tract open, allowing air to flow out of the mouth and nose); nasal. This description slightly misleadingly suggests that there are three discrete segments. In the middle part, the nasal airflow gradually increases, so that the transition from oral to nasal is generally quite smooth. Individuals' (and dialectal) co-ordination of the velum lowering and the formation of the oral closure is variable: some speakers lower the velum rather quickly and the vowel + nasal sequence is more like a reflection of the nasal + vowel sequence.

Figure 9.3 represents vowel + nasal sequences schematically. The lowering of the velum is represented as starting early, and happening slowly.

Figure 9.4 shows the vowel + nasal portion for a male Australian English speaker saying the word 'hang'.

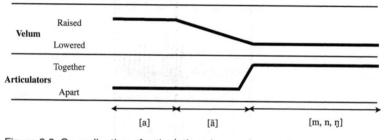

Figure 9.3 Co-ordination of articulations in vowel + nasal sequences.

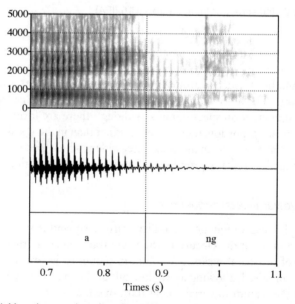

Figure 9.4 Vowel + nasal portion from the word 'hang', [(h)æŋ]. Speaker: Australian male (IPA).

The vowel + nasal portions are much less distinct than in the case of nasal + vowel sequences. Fl, around 1000 Hz, gently falls, but its amplitude fades away too (that is, it gets lighter in colour on the spectrogram). The waveform has a smooth diminuendo, and the amplitude falls off gradually. F2 and F3 come together into a pattern distinctive for velars at around 0.87 s, where the boundary between [a] and [ŋ] is marked, and then they fade away in amplitude and are no longer visible.

The nasalisation of vowels before nasal consonants is an example of anticipatory co-articulation (cf. Section 7.6.3): a vowel anticipates a later sound (in this case a nasal) by adopting some aspect of the production of the later sound.

9.2.3 Nasals between vowels

As we saw, the transition into syllable-final nasals is not a mirror image of the transition out of nasals into vowels. When between vowels, the entry into the nasal portion tends to be quicker than syllable final, which means that there is shorter (and less) nasalisation than we saw in the earlier section.

Figure 9.5 is a spectrogram of a female RP speaker saying 'the more (he blew)', [ð̞ðə mɔː hi bluː].

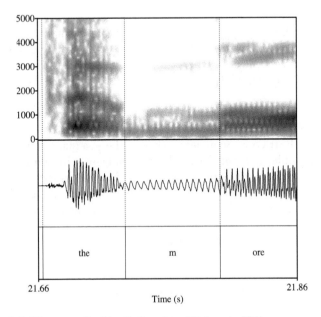

Figure 9.5 'The more (he blew)'. Speaker: RP female (IPA).

As can be seen from the diminution in amplitude in the latter portion of 'the', nasality increases slowly, but then the amplitude drops abruptly once the bilabial closure is made, and the transition out of the vocal portion into the nasal one is more abrupt and obvious than in the case of 'hang' earlier. As the nasal is released, there is a spike corresponding to the opening of the lips, which can be seen at the boundary between the segments labelled 'm' and 'ore'.

9.2.4 Places of articulation with nasals

There are three main places of articulation for English nasals: bilabial, alveolar and velar, as illustrated by e.g. 'simmer', 'sinner' and 'singer'. However, other places of articulation also occur, and are in many ways parallel with plosives.

Bilabial
Bilabial nasals occur both syllable finally and syllable initially.

Labiodental
Labiodental nasals are sometimes found before labiodental fricatives, in words like 'emphasis', [ˈɛɱfəsɪs], and 'invariant', [ɪɱˈvɛəriənt].

Dental
Dental nasals are rather common in English but are limited to word-final clusters within words and morpheme boundaries between words.

Within words, they occur before the dental fricative [θ] in words like 'plinth', [plɪ̪n̪θ], 'tenth', [tɛ̃n̪θ] – which contains two morphemes, 'ten' and '-th'.

The fricative [ð] occurs initially only in function words, such as 'this', 'that', 'the', 'those', 'they'. When nasals occur in this context, there may or may not be friction. So in phrases like 'in the –', a range of pronunciations is possible, including [-n̪ dð -], [-n̪ð-] and [-n̪ː-]. In addition to this, dental nasals in English typically have a 'dark' secondary resonance, with some degree of velarisation. The entry and exit into dental nasals is also slower and less crisp than for alveolar consonants. These details make quite a strong contrast between the definite form 'in the –', [ɪn̪ːˠə], and the indefinite form 'in a –', [ɪnə].

Alveolar
Alveolar consonants occur syllable initially and syllable finally in English.

Postalveolar
Postalveolar nasals (transcribed [n̠]) occur before the postalveolar sounds [ʃ tʃ dʒ], in words such as 'French', 'lunch', 'grunge' (narrowly: [frɛn̠tʃ, lʌn̠tʃ, grʌn̠dʒ]).

They are also reported as variants of alveolar nasals in Indian English; and as variants of [r] + nasal in some rhotic dialects.

Velar
Velar nasals in English, like velar plosives, have a range of places of articulation, from rather front ([ŋ̟]) through to rather retracted or back ([ŋ̠]). Velar nasals, however, must follow a vowel (i.e. they are not syllable initial or word initial), and the range of vowels that can precede them is limited: they must be short, and are the vowels of kit, trap, lot and strut. Compare the place of articulation for 'sing', 'sang', 'song', 'sung', and they should feel different: probably frontest for 'sing', backest for 'song', and roughly the same for 'sang', 'sung', depending on the quality you have for these vowels.

The place of articulation of velar plosives is more dependent on the vowel that comes after than before them; and when they occur between vowels, the place of articulation is somewhere between the places of articulation expected for the vowel sounds. The same is roughly true for velar nasals. Compare the place of articulation for 'singer' and 'singing': you should notice that it is slightly advanced for 'singing' compared with 'singer'. However well these differences can be felt in production, in perception they are less easy to notice, especially compared with the various [k] sounds.

9.2.5 Clusters with nasals

The case where things do not quite work this way is where a nasal comes before a plosive consonant which shares the same place of articulation, in the clusters [mp nt nd ŋk ŋg], as in 'lamp', 'rant', 'land', 'lank' and 'finger'. In these clusters, the oral closure is held and the velum is raised in order to produce oral airflow

The three clusters with voiceless plosives deserve some comment. Recall that vowels are longer before voiced plosives, and before voiceless plosives, many speakers produce creaky voice during the vowel. The same is also true for nasal + plosive clusters: compare 'lend' and 'lent'. For 'lend', you will probably produce something like [lɛn·d], but for 'lent', it will probably be something more like [lɛ̆n̆t]. (The diacritic [˘] here is used to mark 'shorter than expected'.)

When it comes to nasal + voiced plosive clusters, the situation is more complex. There is a gap in English, in that there is no word-final [-mb] cluster, [-nd], on the other hand, is very common. The velar cluster [-ŋg] is more problematic. There are varieties of English where there is no final [ŋ], since it is always pronounced as [ŋg]. This means there are varieties of English where 'singer' and 'finger' rhyme, and have the same rhythm: [sĩŋgə, fĩŋgə]; and others where they do not: [sĩŋgə(r), fĩŋgə(r)]. The difference is occasioned by the different morphological structure of the words: 'finger' has one morpheme; but 'singer' has two: 'sing' ([sĩŋ(g)]) + <-er> ([-ə(r)]).

There is also a phonetic explanation for the origin of the [ŋ/ŋg] variation. To exit a nasal, the velum must be lowered, but the oral closure must also be released. This velar can be seen in Figure 9.4 above at around time 0.98 s. In this case, the velar release is produced simply as a percussive, that is, it is a transient noise that arises from the separation of the two articulators. We will transcribe this as [ᵍ], using superscript to represent its shortness and low amplitude. But if it is preceded by more airflow, and there is more pressure behind the closure, it is a short step from [-ŋᵍ] to [-ŋg].

9.3 Nasalised vowels

9.3.1 The production and transcription of nasalised vowels

As we have seen, in cases where a nasal is syllable final, nasality starts before oral closure, giving rise to a period of oro-nasal airflow. The result of this is typically a nasalised vowel, which can be transcribed as a vowel symbol + the diacritic [˜], resulting in transcriptions like [hãŋ], 'hang', [sũːn], 'soon', and [mɛ̃n], 'men'.

The same kinds of symbols are used for vowels in languages which use the distinction between oral and nasalised vowels lexically, such as French and Portuguese. It is often said in fact that English does not 'have' nasalised vowels, because the vowels that we can find with oro-nasal airflow are different from languages which 'do have' nasalised vowels in two respects. The first is that in English, the occurrence of nasalisation in vowels is predictable from context and therefore is not seen, especially in phonemic accounts of English, as being significant for meaning. The second difference is that in French and Portuguese (and indeed other languages) nasalised vowels are more heavily nasalised than in English: that is to say, the velum is lower than in English, allowing more airflow through the nasal cavity.

9.3.2 Nasalised vowels in conversational speech

Vowels are commonly nasalised in conversational speech. This happens in the context of a nasal consonant, and may be quite extensive. Here are some examples of naturally occurring talk which illustrate nasalisation. In this first example, from a Liverpool speaker, nasality is found both before and after a nasal consonant: in 'don't' and in 'anything', nasality extends from the vowel portions to the subsequent consonant, and in the case of 'anything', the vowel after the alveolar nasal [n] is also nasalised.

(1)   Liverpool nasalisation:
      'We don't grow anything after that'
      [wɪ dɔ̃ʊ̃ŋ ɡɹɔʊ ɛ̃nĩθĩŋk ʔaftə ðat]

The next example comes from the United States. This speaker produces, in the word 'one', a nasal consonant where the nasal airflow starts at the same time as the closure is achieved, meaning that she does not have nasality in the vowel before nasal consonants. On the other hand, vowels in the words 'only', 'on', 'and', 'means' and 'committee' are nasalised. The reason for this difference may lie in the fact that 'one' carries the main accent in this utterance, and it bears a falling intonation contour which starts high in her range.

(2)   USA (Santa Barbara) nasalisation:
      'There's only one on the ways and means committee'
      [ðɚz õːnli ↑ \ wʌn ʔãn̩ːə weːz ə̃n mĩːnz kə̃mɪɾi]

9.3.3 Nasalised vowels in the place of nasal consonants

In some varieties of English, syllable-final nasal consonants do not always occur, but are manifest only through the nasalisation of vowels. This phenomenon is reported for English in the Southern USA (Wells 1982: 541), where a sequence of vowel + nasal + voiceless plosive can be produced as a nasalised vowel + voiceless plosive. All the same 'ingredients' are present, but they are reordered in time so that nasal airflow occurs concurrently with the open resonant articulation needed for the vowel, and there is no discrete portion which has nasality + closure. (This variety, in common with many others in the USA, has vocalic on-glides into some consonants.)

(3)   Southern USA (Wells 1982):
      lump   [lʌ̃əp]
      pint   [pã̃ɪt]

drink   [drĩk]
tint/tent [tĩə̃t]
glance   [glæ̃ĩs]
can't   [kæ̃ə̃t, kẽĩt]

This can be seen as a 'natural' process, in that it has a simple phonetic explanation: the velum lowers early, producing nasality + vocalicity followed by nasality + a stop articulation.

Here are some examples taken from Cockney English (the traditional dialect of London, especially the eastern part of the city), recorded in the early 1950s from the speech of people born in the 1890s (Sivertsen 1960). What is recorded here, then, is 'conservative' or 'traditional', from a modern perspective. The distribution of nasalisation in Cockney is under-researched: it occurs in the context of nasal consonants, and is commonly found on open vowels; it is also a property of the voice quality used by Cockney speakers. The transcriptions have been simplified a little.

(4) Cockney (Sivertsen 1960):

ə'peərɔ̃?ləi   apparently
ɑ 'wẽ?   I went
'nʌθĩk   nothing
ə 'pã·? ṇə 'ɑ·f   a pint and a half
ɪts nã·s   it's nice
'fʌ̃nĩ 'ĩnĩ?   funny isn't it
ði 'ɔod 'ɛ̃əs   the old house
əz ðɛɪ 'lãɪ?   as they like

It can be seen from these transcriptions that some vowels are nasal-ised in words which in the spelling contain nasals: 'apparently', 'went', 'pint' are all examples of this. Then there are words where there is nasalisation also after a nasal consonant, as in 'funny', 'isn't it', 'nice'. But there are also words with nasalised vowels where there is no nasal in the spelling: 'house' and 'like' are examples of this. These details are very characteristic of this dialect, and they show that sometimes phonetic parameters do not behave in the same way in all varieties.

9.4 Syllabic nasals

Nasals can be syllabic in English. This means that they occur in syllables without vowels in unstressed syllables. The patterns of distribution for syllabic nasals are not well understood, and there is some disagreement in the literature and among dictionaries over which words have syllabic nasals (which could be a matter of personal or social preference), and over what the definition of a syllabic nasal is.

The most straightforward cases of syllabic nasals are ones where there is a homorganic plosive + nasal sequence. Some examples of words like this are:

(5) Syllabic nasals:
     open, happen [-pⁿm̩]
     button, sudden [-tⁿn̩, -dⁿn̩]
     bacon, wagon [-kⁿŋ̩, -gⁿŋ̩]

Syllabic nasals can be thought of as a product of the join between the plosive and the nasal portions of the words. We will start with the simplest case, 'button'. This word has an alveolar plosive [t] with nasal release into an alveolar nasal [n]. (See Chapter 7 on nasal plosive release.)

Between the [t] and the [n], then, there is no intervening vocalic portion. This is because by definition vowels have unimpeded airflow through the vocal tract, but all through the sequence [tnn], the tongue makes a complete closure against the alveolar ridge. For this reason, the nasal in a sequence like [tnn] in words like 'button' is considered to be syllabic. This is more precisely transcribed as [tⁿn̩].

Similar sequences can be made at other places of articulation: so words like 'happen' can be pronounced as [hapⁿm̩], and words like 'bacon' can be pronounced as [beɪkⁿŋ̩], with syllabic bilabial and velar nasal portions respectively.

Figure 9.6 shows spectrograms for the words 'bottom', [bɑɾəm], and 'button', [bʌʔtnn̩], as spoken by an Australian male speaker.

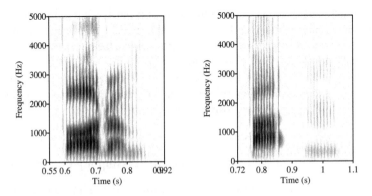

Figure 9.6 'Bottom', [bɑɾəm], and 'button', [bʌʔtⁿn̩]. Speaker: Australian male (IPA).

The spectrograms show very clear differences between the non-syllabic and syllabic nasals. The non-syllabic nasal is on the left: at about time 0.74 s, there is a short vocalic portion followed by a portion starting around 0.8 s which has the low amplitude associated with nasals. In the case of 'button', there is a glottal stop at around 0.85 s, followed by a silent portion, during which airflow through the vocal tract ceases and an alveolar closure is made; and then at about 0.95 s, voicing starts again. Notice the low amplitude of this portion of the spectrogram: this is consistent with a nasal release.

These cases are straightforwardly syllabic nasals, because the plosive and nasal portions are homorganic: they share the same place of articulation. Slightly more difficult is the case of e.g. fricative + nasal, as in 'prison', 'reason', 'often', 'rhythm', 'oven'. In these cases, the two consonants do not necessarily share a place of articulation. For them to be syllabic, the join between the fricative portion and the nasal portion requires the oral closure for the nasal consonant to be made without a more open gesture intervening between the gesture of close approximation for the fricative and the oral closure needed for the nasal. This is easy to achieve in words like 'prison', where the tongue needs merely to be raised so as to make a complete closure against the alveolar ridge, giving [-zn̩]. But such words can easily be produced with a lowering of the tongue tip first, so that the transition between [z] and [n] does allow for a vocalic portion, [-zən]. This is likely also to be nasalised, [-zə̃n]. Auditorily, there might not be much difference between the syllabic and non-syllabic versions, especially if the vocalic portion is short.

The word 'and' is regularly pronounced as a syllabic nasal (with varying places of articulation), even when it comes at the start of an utterance.

Syllabic nasals can also be found in nasal + plosive + nasal sequences, which are more common than one might expect. The distribution here is more difficult to explain: e.g. the name 'Clinton' (the former US president) is [klɪntən], [klɪntⁿn̩] or [klɪnʔn̩].

Here is an example of a syllabic nasal by an American speaker, where the word 'something' has two different forms in the same turn. The second one has a nasal + plosive + nasal cluster:

(6)   NB II 4R 7-9 ESRC-O34

   N   I mean can I get you [sʌmθɪŋ]? or [sʌmpⁿm̩]? or [sʌmpⁿm̩]?

Syllabic nasals are often used as response tokens in conversation. Both mono- and di-syllabic versions are found. Monosyllabic tokens are mostly bilabial in English. In the disyllabic tokens, there is usually a glottal stop or a portion of voicelessness or breathiness in the middle. The place of articulation is usually bilabial, but alveolar tokens are also found. These are one of the few places in English where voiceless nasals are found. The transcriptions in (7) below are all taken from conversational data. For the sake of completeness, intonation is marked on the syllabic nasal portions: \/ means the intonation falls then rises; ↑ means the syllable has a relatively high, level pitch; / means the intonation rises. Neither the forms nor the functions of tokens like these are very well understood.

(7) NJC 02:20
     1   Wen: I'm looking forward to going to the library
     2   (.)
     3   Mar: →   [\/mːː]
     4   (.)
     5   Mar: [you sad individual ((laugh)) .hhh]hh
     6   Wen: [(((laugh————————)))]

(8) JDC 1077
     1   W   cos we did like communal food
     2   G   →   \m[ːː
     3   W   [there was like eleven of us

(9) SBL:2:1:6R:4-7 ESRC-O40
     52   Bea: A̲h̲-haːh .hh because pa̲r̲t̲ of them were
                         going to drink coffee you see
     53   Tess: →   [↑-m / m̥m]

(10) SBL:3:1R:1-3, 8-9 ESRC-O42
     187 Claire: that's one reason I didn't take the thin[g
     188 Mary: [yeːah
     189   →   [m / m̥m]

So far the syllabic nasals we have looked at have all been word final, but they can also occur word medially too, especially when there is a morpheme after the nasal. For example, the word 'instances', which has a plural morpheme [-ɪz], can have a syllabic nasal: [ɪstⁿn̩sɪz].

One good place to observe this is in verbs formed from adjectives with the suffix '-en'. For instance, the adjective 'bright' has a related verb 'brighten', which can be produced as [braɪtn̩n̩]. This verb can be inflected, producing the form 'brightening' (as in: 'the weather's brightening up now'), which can be pronounced as [braɪtn̩n̩ɪŋ]. The past tense form is correspondingly [braɪtⁿn̩d]. Words like this can also be produced without the syllabic nasal, in which case the release of the alveolar closure is different: compare [braɪtⁿn̩d and [braɪtənd].

Syllabic consonants are not obligatory in these contexts, and in cases where the morphological form is less transparent, syllabic nasals are less likely. A well-known pair is 'lightening' ('light' + '-en' + 'ing'), [laɪtⁿn̩ɪŋ] (with three syllables), and 'lightning', [laɪtⁿnɪŋ] (with two syllables). Another example is 'frightening' – although this is derived from 'fright' + '-en' + '-ing', it behaves more like a monomorphemic word, and is more likely to be [fraɪtⁿnɪŋ] (parallel with 'lightning') than [fraɪtⁿn̩ɪŋ] (parallel with 'lightening').

Summary

Although there are only three nasal phonemes in English, we have seen that nasal airflow is common in a range of sounds in English, and syllabic nasals are an important feature of everyday speech.

Exercises

1. Transcribe the words below, paying particular attention to the place of articulation for the nasal consonants.

emphasis; hangar; unreal; unbalanced; in bad shape; in good shape; in dubious taste; ungrateful; hymn; mind; anthropology; in that manner; I'm going to (or: gonna) mime it

2. Do you produce syllabic nasals in the following words? Try to put them in different but comparable contexts; e.g. bacon – bacon and eggs – I like bacon; I like baking.

bacon; baking; ribbon; ribbing; London; fatten; redden; darken; organ; even

3 In some varieties of English, sequences of fricative + nasal in words like 'seven', 'isn't', 'eleven' are produced as plosive + nasal, as in [sɛbⁿm̩]. Do you do this? How might this phenomenon be explained?

4 There are modern loanwords in English from French which (in French) contain nasalised vowels. How do you produce them? They are underlined in the examples below:

restaurant, croissant, bon vivant, bon mot, entrepreneur, rapprochement, liaison, gratin, timbre, seance, crouton

Is there variability in your pronunciation? How do you explain their treatment in English?

Further reading

As ever, Cruttenden (2001) and Jones (1975) cover the main details and discuss assimilation in some detail. Sivertsen (1960) is a study of Cockney English. For discussion of response particles like 'mhm', see Jefferson (1985). For a phonological account of assimilation, see e.g. Giegerich (1992).

10 Glottalic and velaric airstreams

10.1 Airstream mechanisms

Airstream mechanism is the term we use to describe the means by which air is moved out of or into the vocal tract. So far, in almost all the sounds we have looked at, the airstream is pulmonic and egressive (see Section 2.2 for a recap of those terms). Every spoken language uses this mechanism. There are two other important airstream mechanisms in the world's languages, and it is possible to illustrate them from spoken English. They are:

- **velaric airstream**, where there is a complete closure of the back of the tongue against the velum (sometimes uvula), with another closure somewhere forward of that, making a cavity between the two closures
- **glottalic airstream**, where the glottis is closed and the larynx is raised to compress, or lowered to rarefy, air trapped between the glottal closure and a constriction higher up in the vocal tract

In this chapter, we explore and illustrate these two airstreams with material from English.

While sounds that are made with the velaric and glottalic airstream mechanisms can be observed in English, very little is known about the uses to which these sounds are put, what their distribution in speech is, and who is likely to use them. This is an area for much further work. It is a challenging area, because velarically and glottalically initiated sounds are not easy to elicit from speakers (e.g. in eliciting word lists), but in many varieties of spoken English they are common in spontaneous, conversational speech.

10.2 The velaric airstream mechanism

Velarically initiated sounds have two closures in the vocal tract. One of these is the back of the tongue against the velum (hence the name 'velaric') and the other closure is further forward: usually the front of the tongue, but it is also possible to make a bilabial closure. In between these two closures there is a cavity filled with air; and this cavity can be expanded, so that when the forward closure is released air flows into the vocal tract. It is also possible to compress the air in the cavity and force it out, but such sounds are not known to occur in any of the world's languages. The IPA treats all velarically initiated sounds as ingressive. To make a velarically initiated sound, start off by making a [k] sound silently. Do not release the velar closure; leave the back of the tongue in contact with the velum. Now make another closure: while keeping the [k] closure, make a dental closure as well, [t̪], with the tongue against the back of the upper teeth. Make sure that the sides of the tongue are pressed firmly against the upper teeth. (We could transcribe this gesture as [k͡t̪˺].) What you will have now is a cavity between the roof of your mouth and the upper surface of the tongue: the tongue should have a concave shape (that is, the midpoint of the tongue will be lower than the sides of the tongue). There should be a pocket of air trapped between the upper surface of the tongue and the roof of the mouth, with the sides of the tongue making a seal around the edges. While holding these closures, you should be able to breathe in and out normally: this shows that the velum is lowered, and that the velaric airstream is independent of the pulmonic airstream.

Now, while holding the two closures, tense your tongue and pull it downwards without releasing either of the closures. At this point, the cavity will expand, and so the pressure of the air within the cavity between the two closures will decrease. You will probably be able to feel the pressure on your tongue, as if it is being sucked. Release the front closure but retain the velar closure. What happens now is that air rushes into the cavity, and a noise is made: this will probably be a very familiar sound, because it is the **click** [|]. This sound is typically produced English by speakers many times in a conversation: you have probably seen it in written form as 'tut-tut' or 'tsk'.

Sounds like this are often called 'clicks' – shorthand for the longer more technical description: velarically initiated **ingressive** plosives, or suction stops. No words of English contain them so they are not phonemes of English. But, as is well known, they do occur in English speech.

They are ingressive because when the forward closure is released, the pressure between the forward closure and the velar closure is lower than the air pressure outside; so once the closure is released, air moves into the vocal tract. It is possible to produce velarically initiated sounds with egressive airflow, by pushing the tongue upwards to the hard palate and squeezing air out of the cavity, or letting it out by withdrawing the tongue's contact from the upper surfaces of the mouth. These sounds are not known to occur in the world's languages, although a velarically initiated, bilabial egressive plosive or trill can be used in English to mean something like 'nothing', or 'I have no idea' ('and I don't care').

In learning to produce clicks in phonetics classes, students commonly allow the tongue to plop down on to the floor of the mouth. This produces a secondary sound known as a **percussive**. Percussives are sounds made when two articulators strike each other, but there is no airstream necessarily involved in producing the noise. When English-speaking children mimic the sound of a horse walking on a road, they often make a sequence of click + percussive, which mimics the 'clip clop' of the horse's feet. In producing clicks, it is important to try to eliminate any percussive element.

Clicks can be produced at a range of places of articulation. In English, the commonest ones are probably dental [|], bilabial [ʘ] and alveolar lateral [ǁ]; other possibilities include palatoalveolar [ǂ] and alveolar [!]. We will look at dental clicks in Section 10.2.1 below.

Clicks are complex articulations, but in their simplest form, we can think of them as a velar plosive accompanied by another complete closure which is released before the velar closure. It is quite possible to produce more complex click articulations by changing the 'accompaniments' that go with them. For instance, it is possible to produce a click with voicing, by combining velar closure and voicing: so instead of voicelessness at the same time as velar closure, [k], as the accompaniment, we have voicing and velar closure, [g]. Voicing and nasality are also combinable with clicks. These are easier to produce than might be thought. Start off by making a protracted [ŋ] sound, and simultaneously start to make a clicking sound: this should be easy to do, because the airstream needed for clicks is located forward of the velum, so air can flow through the nasal cavities while a click is being made. The resulting sound can be transcribed [ŋ͡|].

It has become usual to think of clicks as 'click + accompaniment' (a point of view that originated in the work of Ladefoged and Traill 1994), and it is common to transcribe clicks in two parts: the first part describing the velar (or uvular) articulation (as e.g. [k g ŋ]), the second part describing the click type. The two parts are joined with a 'tie bar', [͡]. So a fuller transcription of the click [|] (the 'tut' of English) would be [k͡|].

Figure 10.1 shows a spectrogram of a click (from extract (5) below). Point 1 marks the release of the forward closure, in this case a dental closure. This closely resembles the burst of the release of [t]: it has most energy higher up in the frequency range. Notice that there is a transient burst followed by a longer period of noise. Very soon after that comes

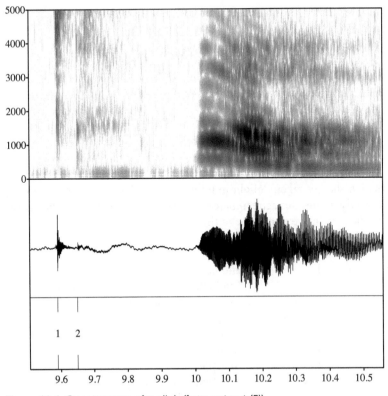

Figure 10.1 Spectrogram of a click (from extract (5)).

the second release, that of the velar closure. This is marked 2. Notice the centre of energy is very different: around 1500 Hz. This is consistent with the kind of burst we find for velars. After the release of the velar closure there is a lot of ingressive aspiration noise, which is the sound of air entering the vocal tract; and then the particle 'ah'. This spectrogram, then, shows clearly the two releases associated with the velaric airstream mechanism.

10.2.1 Clicks in English

Clicks can be produced at a range of places of articulation. In English, the commonest ones are probably bilabial, alveolar lateral and dental.

Bilabial clicks, when produced with pursed lips, resemble a peck on the cheek. These clicks are used to mimic kissing (or even done instead of kissing, as in the stereotyped 'mwah!' of insincerely warm greetings).

Lateral clicks are sometimes used to 'gee up' horses (and usually come in pairs).

The dental click is so ubiquitous in English that we even have a verb to describe making it: 'tutting'. Stereotypically, we associate this with an expression of disapproval (accompanied in our mind's eye by rolling one's eyes heavenwards). In the next few paragraphs, we look at some instances of [|] taken from naturally occurring English conversation.

We start with an example of a click used as part of a response to a story. Lesley has been telling Joyce about a visit to a church fair. At this fair, an acquaintance of theirs said something Lesley finds offensive, and which she has taken delight in telling Joyce about. At lines 2–3, Lesley directly quotes this acquaintance and brings his objectionable behaviour to the fore in the punchline of the story.

(1)   Holt C38 4

1	L		and he came up to me and he said
2			"oh hello Lesley, still trying to buy
3			something for nothing"
4	J	→	[	ɑ↓ː]
5			[ooh
6	L		[ooh
7	J		isn't [he
8	L		[what do you say
9	J		oh isn't he dreadful

Joyce's immediate reaction to the punchline at line 4 is a dental click followed by an open vocalic gesture accompanied by ingressive airflow. This is a display of understanding of Lesley's story: a complaint about the behaviour of their acquaintance. The click is only the beginning of the sequence of talk in which Joyce and Lesley complain about him, and Joyce's turn continues with an assessment of this acquaintance as 'dreadful'.

Perhaps it is significant that both the click and the vowel sound that come after it are ingressive: having air in the lungs is a prerequisite for talking, and in-breaths are often used to mark: 'I have more to say'. Sharp in-breaths are also a reflex reaction to unexpected physical events: perhaps the in-breath here is an iconic device to express 'shock' – although it is unlikely to be a spontaneous shock, since the story has been constructed to achieve precisely this response.

Clicks can also be used to initiate turns at talk in less emotionally charged contexts, as in the following cases:

(2) ell sum 04 cheese

   1   P   what's on offer at the market then today
   2   I   →   [| h ↓] well we've got lots of different cheeses

(3) klm sum04 housing

   1   I   ((complains about new houses to be built in M——))
   2   M   and you're unhappy about that
   3   I   yes and so's a lot of people in M——
   4   M   thank you
   5   Councillor P——?
   6   P   →   [| h ↓] oh hello Imogen
   7   the issue is, as you know, is the Government...

In (2), the click in line 2 prefaces the answer to a question; in (3), the click in line 6 starts Councillor P's response to I's point, having been selected as the next speaker in line 5 by M.

Again the clicks are followed by ingressive airflow, this time an in-breath (marked in the transcriptions as [h ↓]). In these cases, the clicks do not seem to 'express disapproval'. Rather, they seem to be used to project more talk by the speaker, i.e. to mark 'I have more to say'.

Clicks can be used as part of turns that display other kinds of stance. For example, they can occur at the start of turns that mark some display of sympathy. In the example below, Agnes complains about the weekend she has had. In response to this telling, Billie produces a click followed by a long and creaky [ɑ::]. The click is produced on beat with a rhythm established by Agnes: the stars above lines 2 and 3 mark the beats, which are evenly spaced in time.

(4) CK/SW #63

   1   A   it's just kinda dull

                       *   *   *   *

   2   A   God what a miserable miserable   [weekend
   3   B   [|]   [[ɑ::::::]
   4   B   that's a shame

Billie comes in at line 3 before the completion of Agnes's turn 'what a miserable miserable weekend' with a click. Agnes and Billie both continue their talk on beat (i.e. they talk in overlap), Agnes producing the completion of her turn, 'weekend', Billie producing a long, creaky open vowel. Since the rhythm was established by Agnes, we could interpret Billie's use of it to time her talk as a display of attention to the details of

Agnes's talk, and in doing that, going along with the complaint made by Agnes. This is consistent with her display of sympathy in her next turn: 'that's a shame'. So here we have a click which seems to be produced as the first part of a display of sympathy with another's situation, and which seems to be temporally placed to display attentiveness to that other person's telling of the situation.

Clicks can also be used to mark receipt of positive news. In the next extract, Jade tells Kate how two people they know became a couple. Once she has completed her story, Kate offers an appreciation of the story (line 6), which starts with a click followed by a long, breathy open vowel with falling pitch. If clicks marked 'disapproval', then Kate would be treating this story as bad news; but in fact she makes a positive assessment of the story: 'that's lovely'. Indeed, we might even say that the stretch [ʔɑ̤::] marks a positive receipt of the news.

(5) nrb reluctant lover
     1   J   he wouldn't stop asking her out
     2   he used to ring her like three times a day
     3   and she'd go "no no"
     4   or she'd say yes and not turn up
     5   and then she just completely fell for him
     6   K   →   [| ʰ (.) ʔɑ̤::] that's lovely

So, here we have a few instances where clicks initiate turns that provide assessments or appreciations of a telling; in these turns, the recipient of a story demonstrates their understanding of the kind of story it was, which can include 'disapproval', but also 'a story deserving of sympathy' and 'good news'.

Another common use for clicks is to signal the transition from one activity to another (Wright 2007). A good place to observe this is at the end of phone calls, where there is a sequence that English speakers commonly use to manage how they will both get to the point of putting the phone down. (This may seem trivial, but putting the phone down before it is due is a big *faux pas* in English-speaking societies.) The extract in (6) below displays this well. The current topic is closed down in lines 8–9 ('oh splendid'/'yahp'); then there follows a click in line 9; then there is a short sequence in lines 9–10 where a proposal is made to close the call ('Okay then'), which is accepted ('right'), and then greetings are exchanged, and the speakers hang up the phone. Clicks are common in this sequence in between the closing down of the topic and the 'OK':

(6) Holt.C.1985.6/splendid (Wright 2007)

```
1    Bod:          It might be mo:re I don't [know.]
2    Les:   →                                [Yes:  ] I was going
3                  to bring Missiz La:amp (0.2) from North
                   Cadbury
4                  (.)
5    Les:          but she can't come because her husband's
6                  unexpectedly .hhh had to go away so she's
                   coming
7                  to the first one after Christmas.
8    Bod:          Oh: splendid
9    Les:   →      Yahp. [ | ] Okay the [n
10   Bod:                             [Righ[t, well I shall ] see you
11   Les:                                  [See you later]
12                 (.)
13   Les:          B[ye bye:
14   Bod:           [Bye
     – end of call –
```

The click occurs in a single turn which has two parts. The first part, 'yahp', closes down the earlier sequence about Mrs Lamp's attendance at a meeting. The second part of the sequence, 'Okay then', marks the beginning of the closing of the call ('Okay then/right', after which the speakers start to exchange greetings). The click marks the transition between two activities.

While we commonly find velarically initiated clicks in turns like this, we also find other kinds of ingressive sounds and percussives: the most usual are audible lip smacks or releases of other closures, where the articulators are separated from one another, which may produce a sound loud enough to be heard. If the speaker breathes in loudly enough to be heard, this can sound like e.g. an ingressive voiceless bilabial plosive, [p↓]. It is perhaps an important feature of clicks in these particular sequences that they stand in free variation with other (related) sounds; whereas the clicks that express some kind of stance are not, and cannot be, produced in this way, but must be velarically initiated.

The clicks we have looked at so far are all accompanied by [k] and then sometimes followed by a vocalic articulation which is either ingressive or egressive. The next, and final, example of a click is accompanied by voicing and nasality, [ŋ͡ǁ]. In this example, the click occurs at the start of the receipt of a compliment.

(7)   nrb/01.red hair.aiff
    1   J   's very red but it's very ni[ce
    2   K   [it is very red
    3   [isn't it
    4   J   [looks in really good conditi[on   ]
    5   K →   [[ŋ͡ɑː]]
         [thank   you]
    6   J   [(*) lovely and] shiny

(In line 6, (*) marks an indistinct syllable.) Kate has dyed her hair red, and Jade has been complimenting her on it. In line 5, Kate produces a nasalised click with a breathy-voiced and long open vowel, with a pitch contour that falls from high to low in her range. It is immediately followed by 'thank you'. The commonest lay interpretation of clicks, 'disapproval', is once again unlikely to be what Kate does in line 5.

In summary then, we can find a range of clicks in naturally occurring spoken English. Their distribution and functions are not well researched; but they seem to occur at the start of turns, or to mark the transition from one kind of activity to another within a turn. They commonly seem to be involved in assessing stories or situations, but (contrary to English speakers' general intuitions) they do not necessarily imply 'disapproval', or even anything negative at all.

10.3 The glottalic airstream mechanism

The glottalic airstream mechanism relies on air being moved into or out of the vocal tract by raising the larynx while the glottis is closed (in the case of egressive sounds) or by lowering the larynx while there is a glottal constriction (in the case of ingressive sounds). Some varieties of English use an egressive glottalic airstream, so we will concentrate on that.

To make an *ejective*, start off by making a glottal stop, [ʔ]. You should be able to feel that you can breathe neither in nor out while the glottal stop is held. If you flick your index finger against the larynx while the glottis is closed and the mouth is open there will be a hollow ringing sound, rather like tapping a wooden tube. (If the glottis is open, the sound will be altogether more dull and less resonant.)

Now try to get a sense of raising and lowering the larynx. One way to do this is to sing a very high note, and then a very low note. On reaching the high note, it is likely that you will raise your larynx; and conversely, on reaching the low note, the larynx is likely to be low. If you do this silently, you should be able to feel the larynx raised for the 'high' note, and lowered for the 'low' note. If you can do these two things in quick succession, you will feel the larynx bobbing up and down. To make good ejectives, you need to be able to control the upward movement of the larynx.

Now make a glottal stop again, and this time combine it with another complete closure, for instance at the velum, as for [k]. (We could transcribe this as [ʔ͡k̚].) Having two complete closures – the glottis at the lower end and the velum at the upper end – means that the air between them is trapped. If the larynx is now raised, the air pressure between the closures will increase, because there is the same amount of air, but in a smaller space. In the case of a pulmonically initiated plosive, the increase in air pressure behind a closure comes from the lungs; but in the case of a glottalically initiated egressive plosive, the increase in air pressure comes from the raising of the larynx. If the velar closure is now released, there will be a sound rather like a [k] sound, but it has a much harsher, louder character than a pulmonically initiated plosive.

Egressive, glottalically initiated plosives like this are called 'ejectives'. (The Latin origin of this term is quite descriptive: 'e-', 'out'; '-ject-', 'thrown'.) The IPA uses the convention of an apostrophe after the symbol for the corresponding pulmonic sound: in the case of a velar ejective, then, the symbol is [k'].

Since ejectives require a closure at the glottis, they are necessarily voiceless sounds.

10.3.1 Ejectives in English

Ejectives occur in a good number of British English varieties, though remarkably little is known about which ones. Nor is anything much known about the distribution of ejectives. The material on which the observations in this section are based is collected from a range of sources in Britain, and the following observations seem to be true, but are only indicative. Ejectives occur:

- word finally (and not e.g. before vowels)
- in stressed syllables
- after vowels, nasals and laterals (which are all voiced), and after the voiceless fricative [s]
- within utterances (before pauses), as well as at the end of utterances

Ejectives may be a development of glottal reinforcement (Chapter 7). In glottal reinforcement, a glottal constriction is made before an oral one; once the oral constriction is made, the glottis is opened, and air is forced from the lungs across the open glottis. In the case of ejectives, a glottal constriction is also made simultaneously with an oral constriction; but is released after the release of the oral constriction. So ejectives involve a rearrangement in time of the constrictions needed to produce glottally reinforced voiceless plosives.

Another explanation for ejectives in English lies in the fact that the plosive release of ejectives is typically loud (or at least louder than the release of the corresponding pulmonic sound): this enhances the audibility of the burst, and makes it easier to perceive the place of articulation of the plosive.

Here are some examples of ejectives taken from a narrative by a woman from Aberdeen in her early twenties. She is telling about applying for a job. (Timings between brackets within transcriptions mark pauses in the speaker's talk; e.g. (0.5 s) means the speaker is not talking for 0.5 seconds.)

(8)   Ab KU23F CS

    (a) so that was quite lengthy to fill all that ou[t'] (0.7 s) [tʰ↓] and I
        was really nervous
    (b) so they told me about th[a:ʔt' a̰:n:ɖʰ] (0.8 s) they didn't really . . .
    (c) they didn't ask for specific examples which was gr[ḛ:t' h↓ a̰:n:ɖʰ]
        (0.5 s) [p͡t↓] after that I had to . . .

The ejectives here all come in the context of a pause in her talk, either immediately or shortly after the ejective. In (a), the ejective comes before a pause, which is exited with an audible percussive alveolar release, followed immediately by an in-breath (marked here with [tʰ↓]). In (c) too, there is an in-breath just after the ejective. In (b) and (c), the ejective is followed by a long production of 'and' which starts with creaky voice: we might expect creak after a glottal closure, as the vocal folds start to vibrate modally again. In all these cases, the speaker continues speaking after the stretch which contains the ejective.

In the extract in (9) below, a conversation between two students from the north of England, there are two ejectives: one turn-finally, the other in the middle of a turn.

The turn-final ejective is in line 2, a reformulation of a question (line 1) which makes it more specific what kind of answer is required (a reference to which week in term, rather than e.g. a calendar date like '15 June'). This one is at a place in the conversation where the other person can be expected to talk next.

The turn-medial one comes in line 15 between the words 'week' and 'three', which is part of a list (week one, week two, week three). Although the word 'three' is highly predictable from the context, there is a hitch in the speaker's production, and the ejective occurs before a 0.2-s pause.

(9) gw lab 0701 weeks
    1   H   when are your finals then
    2   →   what wee [k']
    3   E   (0.6 s)
    4   H   [ʔ]uhm (.) wee [kʰ] (0.5 s) [b] one (1.2 s)
    5   I've got my exams from this term
    6   E   [pt↓] yeah
    7   H   wee[kʰ ʔ⌐] (1.1 s) two [ʔ] and three is then [ʔ]
    8   write my open paper
    9   (0.3 s)
   10   E   yeah
   11   H   ooh I wonder when that's gotta be in
   12   cos that might be quite good
   13   (0.5 s)
   14   [h↓] cos David's brother's: (0.3 s) wedding's
   15   →   at– [[ʔ] on the week] end of wee [k' (0.3 s) ʔ] three
   16   E   [ohh yeah   ]
   17   H   (0.3 s) [h:↓] (.) [ʔ]and the:n (0.8 s)
   18   is that right weekend

In line 15, in between the release of the plosive of 'week' and the start of the friction of 'three' is a pause of about 0.3 s. The fricative [f] at the start of 'three' starts with a glottal stop. So the glottal closure made earlier at the same time as the velar closure in 'week' is held until the speaker starts to speak again with 'three'. Articulations which are held across gaps in speaking within a speaker's turn like this have been shown for English to mark: 'I may not be speaking now but I have more to say and I am keeping the turn' (Local and Kelly 1986). So perhaps the ejective in this environment is a side-effect of some other work that is being done by a glottal stop.

We can compare Helen's production of 'week' here with her other productions of 'week' in lines 4 and 7. In line 4, the plosive is produced with aspiration, followed by a long pause. There is evidently labial closure too: the word 'one' is preceded by a bilabial plosive with approximately 0.07 s of voicing during the closure. In line 7, the plosive at the end of 'week' is produced with lengthy aspiration (0.45 s), which is abruptly cut off by a glottal stop before a pause of 1.1 s. The pause is released into an alveolar plosive.

For comparison, spectrograms of the tokens of 'week' from lines 4 ([k]) and 15 ([k']) are shown in Figure 10.2.

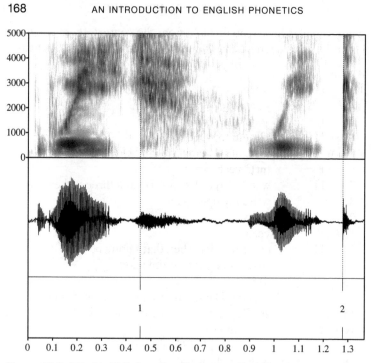

Figure 10.2 'Week'. (1) Pulmonic; (2) ejective. Speaker: female.

The first production (on the left) shows voicelessness and closure co-occurring: notice the high-frequency friction around 3000–4000 Hz between 0.3 and 0.4 s on the spectrogram. The plosive is released with a considerable amount of aspiration: the release is marked at 1 on the spectrogram. The second production is an ejective production, marked at 2 on the spectrogram. Notice the glottal closure at around 1.15 s, and the very abrupt way that the energy for the vowel dies away. The plosive release marked at 2 is sharp and loud (darker than at 1), and although there is some friction noise, it is much shorter in duration than in the pulmonic production. This is because the amount of air available between the glottal and velar closures is rather small, which makes it difficult for friction to be sustained for very long; whereas for pulmonically initiated productions, there is far more air in the lungs which can be forced out to produce aspiration noise.

So while not all the tokens of 'week' contain ejectives in this extract, they do all have some kind of closure which is held in the pause after the word 'week', and two of these, in lines 7 and 15, involve also glottal closure. In making sense of the distribution of ejectives, then, we probably need to look at the wider context. This way, we can see the ejectives as part of a longer stretch of phonetic events, which includes a plosive, a pause, and an exit from the pause.

10.3.2 Implosives

Ingressive glottalically initiated plosives (**implosives**) can also be made. These sounds are made by lowering the larynx while there is a forward closure. As the larynx is lowered, the air pressure between the glottal constriction and supralaryngeal closure drops, and when the supralaryngeal closure is released, air flows into the vocal tract. It is possible to produce voiceless glottalically initiated ingressive plosives, but these are thought not to occur in the world's languages. Much more commonly for these sounds, the vocal folds vibrate as the larynx is lowered. This is also the case for Jamaican Creole (see below).

Auditorily, these sounds are rather distinctive. As the larynx is lowered and the vocal folds vibrate, a peculiar 'swallowing' sound can be heard. As might be guessed, voiced implosives are fully voiced. The IPA represents implosives with modified plosive symbols which contain a rightward hook on the upper part of the letter: [ɓ ɗ ʄ].

In many languages, implosives seem to have derived historically from fully voiced plosives. Remember that the vocal folds can only vibrate when there is a pressure difference above and below the glottis; and when there is a complete closure in the vocal tract, the pressure above and below the glottis will eventually equalise. One way to enable the vocal folds to continue vibrating while there is a supralaryngeal closure is to expand the size of the vocal tract. If this is done, then there is more volume, which means that the pressure in the supralaryngeal tract will fall. Expanding the vocal tract can be achieved by puffing out the cheeks, or expanding the pharynx by lowering the larynx: this may account for how some languages develop fully voiced glottalically initiated ingressive plosives.

Implosives have not been formally reported for any varieties of English, though there are hints in the literature that they may occur in Appalachian English (e.g. Jacewicz et al. 2009). One reason for this absence is probably that most varieties of English do not have fully voiced plosives. One prediction that we might make is that implosives – perhaps even weak ones, with a short hold period and a short portion of voicing along with larynx lowering – might be found as an innovation or a development in varieties which do have fully voiced plosives.

Implosives do, however, occur in at least one English-derived Creole, Jamaican Creole (Harry 2006), where they occur as realisations of voiced plosives when they are initial in syllables that are auditorily prominent, especially word initially.

A spectrogram of an implosive [ɠ] in the word 'good' in Jamaican Creole is shown in Figure 10.3. At the point marked 1, a short transient noise burst can be seen. This corresponds to the tongue back making a complete closure against the velum. In between points 1 and 2, there is a rather lengthy voiced portion, about 135 ms in duration, during which there is complete closure. Notice how the amplitude of the voicing dies away shortly before the release of the closure at point 2. This is what we would expect as the pressure difference above and below the vocal folds becomes smaller, and the pressure equalises. Point 2 is where the velar closure is released. The [d] at the end of the word is also fully voiced, but not implosive.

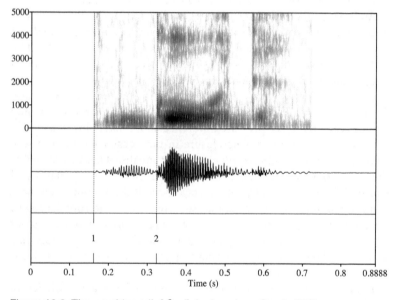

Figure 10.3 The word 'good', [ɠuːd], in Jamaican Creole (IPA).

Summary

In this chapter, we have looked at a group of sounds produced using the velaric and glottalic airstream mechanisms that are not typically thought of as 'sounds of English'. However, it is relatively easy to find examples of both clicks and ejectives in English. These sounds are not part of the phonemic inventory of English. Nevertheless, both kinds of sound do seem to pattern in an orderly way, but currently we have only a poor grasp of this orderliness.

The study of 'non-lexical sounds' in English may prove to be a rich and rewarding aspect of study.

Exercises

1. Make a collection of stretches of talk with clicks. Good places to start might be radio phone-in shows, or panel discussions, where the activities of the show move on rapidly. Word searches are another place where clicks seem common. Compare what you find with the descriptions in this chapter.

2. Ejectives are very understudied in English. One place to search for them might be where speakers need to give a quick answer, as in a game show or a quiz; and in the examples in this chapter, they were often found before pauses in word searches. See whether you can find ejectives in a variety familiar to you; try to reproduce them.

Further reading

See Ladefoged and Maddieson (1996) for an overview of clicks, ejectives and implosives in languages other than English; and Ogden (2013) and Wright (2007, 2011) on clicks in spoken English.

McCarthy and Stuart-Smith (2013) is a rare systematic study of ejectives in English; they explore the production and distribution of ejectives in the speech of female teenagers from Glasgow.

11 Sounds and structures

11.1 Introduction

We have now worked our way through the consonants and vowels of English. In this chapter, we focus on a sample of conversational speech, and study the speakers' phonetic systems in more detail. In doing this, we will see something of what it means to provide a phonetic description of running speech, and we will notice many phonetic details, including some that relate to how words are put together into bigger phrases, and where the speakers come from.

The data comes from Salford, a city next to Manchester in north west England. It was collected as part of a sociolinguistic project on varieties of northern English. The speaker we will focus on is a middle-aged woman who grew up in Salford, and she is with her friend, who grew up in the same neighbourhood. We will call our speaker Diane, and her friend Marie. They are pretty representative for their age and location; so while we are describing the speech of particular individuals, and can make very specific observations of their production, it is reasonable to treat this speech sample as representative of a wider community.

The data is conversational, like much of the material in this book. Talking in time with another person places very particular demands on us, and conversational speech is very variable: it varies in tempo, loudness, voice quality, articulatory precision, and along many other dimensions. Conversation is the most natural and most basic use of speech; many of its phonetic details are meaningful, and we have the resources from earlier chapters in the book to make sense of these details. So the focus of this chapter is to show how some phonetic details relate to simple structures of spoken conversation.

11.2 Data

Our data is part of a conversation between Marie and Diane. The top line shows in regular English orthography what the speakers are saying. This was determined by a field worker who knows the variety well. The line below contains a systematic phonetic transcription with some extra details included, so it is relatively narrow.

As in previous examples in the book, '[' marks the start of overlapping talk, and ']' the end. '#' is used to mark places where the speaker has reached a place of syntactic completion and stops talking. Where '=' is used at the end of one line and the start of another, it means that the utterance is immediately connected to the next phrase at the start of the next line. '-' at the end or in the middle of a word means that it is abandoned suddenly, usually with a glottal stop. Durations of pauses are given in seconds between brackets. (.) means a pause of 0.1 s or less. Underlining in the orthography marks accented syllables; the more underlining, the stronger the accent. The intonation contour is marked in the phonetic transcription, using the symbols from Chapter 4. This is not a complete transcription of intonation, which is out of the scope of this book; but it will give you a reasonable idea of how it sounds.

11.2.1 Conventions for consonants

Here are some brief notes on the phonetic values of the symbols given:

- The voiceless plosives [p t k] are aspirated when syllable initial, but not in clusters [sp st sk].
- The plosive [t] is usually quite heavily affricated, [tˢ]. On release, the tongue shape is similar to that for [s], so that as the tongue comes away from the alveolar ridge, a short period of friction is heard, rather like a [s] sound. The same is not true for [d].
- The plosives [b d g] are generally voiceless during most of the closure portion, and have a short VOT after release. They are sometimes fully voiced in the closure if the syllable is accented.
- The lateral [l] is regularly velarised ('dark', [lˠ]), even when it is syllable initial.
- There are two kinds of sound used for /r/: an approximant, [ɹ], and a tap [ɾ]. The tap is regularly used after [θ]; otherwise the two seem to be in free variation. The transcription shows both the approximant and the tap.

11.2.2 Conventions for vowels

The vowels are presented here in IPA quadrilaterals to show their approximate qualities. For diphthongs, the arrows show the start and end points. The transcription of vowels is systematic rather than impressionistic. In principle it would be possible to provide impressionistic transcriptions, and indeed we will do that later for some details. [aɪ] is especially variable, so that before a voiced consonant or in an open syllable, it is barely diphthongal [a̰ːe̥], but before a voiceless consonant and in [aɪə], the first component is shorter, and the second component longer, closer to [ɪ]. [ʉː] is also variable, and sometimes starts unrounded, closer to [ɪʉ].

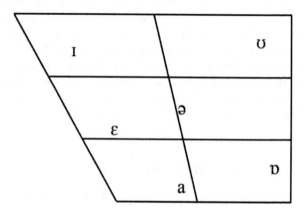

Figure 11.1 Short vowels in Salford.

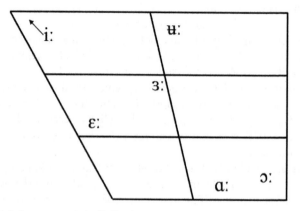

Figure 11.2 Long vowels in Salford.

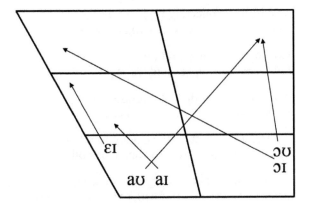

Figure 11.3 Diphthongs in Salford.

11.2.3 Transcription

01 D   one of my favourite things was bonfire night=
        wɒn ə 'maɪ \feɪvɹɪ? 'θɪŋz wəz \bɒnfaɪə naɪ?

02   =I us[ed to love bonfire night]#
        aɪ jʉːstə \lʊv bɒnfaɪə naɪ?

03 M   [oh I loved that as well] <laugh>
            ɔʊ \aɪ lʊvd̪ 'ða? əz \wɛl

04   [<laugh>]

05 D   [and that's-] that's (0.3) that's all changed=
        ən̩ `na?s \d̪a?s ɔːl /tʃɛɪnd ʒd̪

06   =I'm [sure the]se displays are lovely but (0.5)
        am \ʃʊ ði:z dɪ'splɛɪz ə \lʊvlɪ bʊ?

07 M   [mm   ]

08 D   you know you'd have your own bonfire-=
        jə ∨nɔʊ jəd av jəɹ `ɔʊm \bɒnfa̠?

09   =we used to build it in the entry=
        wɪ \jʉvst̪ə 'bɪld ɪ? ɪn̩ːi /ɛnt̠ɹ̥ɪ

10   =you'd have the houses on fire <<laugh>but- [you know>
        (0.5)
        jəd av ðə̠ ∧a̠ᵃ ʊzɪz ɒn 'faɪə bʊ? jə \nɔʊ

11 M   [<laugh>

12   D   we'd be (0.3) coll<u>e</u>cting w<u>oo</u>d for <u>weeks</u> (.) #
         wɪd bɪk⌐   kə\le͡ʔktɪn \wʊd fə \wiːks

13   and we had um an <u>air</u> raid shelter (0.5) #
         ʔə̃w̃ wi ad-ɜm | ən \ɛː ɹeɪd 'ʃɛltə̥

14   D   at the back of our (0.3) our <u>house</u>=
         ə̥ʔ ð̥ə 'bak əv ɑːʔˋ   ʔɑː \haʊs

15   =so <u>we</u>('d) got to store the <u>bonfire</u> wood #
         sɔʊ \wiːd⌐ gɒt tə 'stɔː ðə \bɒnfaɪə 'wʊ̥d

16   my m<u>o</u>ther'd be chasing off r<u>i</u>val <u>gangs</u>=
         hiːↆ mɪ \mʊðər əd⌐ bɪ 'tʃeɪsɪn ɒf \'ɹaɪvəl \gaŋgz

17   =cause they'd [be coming   pi[nching your <u>woo</u>]d
         kəz ðɪd bɪ \kʊmɪn   \pɪntʃɪn jə \wʊd

18   M   [they'd come and [<u>pin</u>ching   it]
                      ðɪd kʊm ən \pɪntʃɪn iʔ

19   M   (you/that's) <u>right</u>
         ðjaʔʃ ˋɹaɪʔ

20   D   and I'd be s<u>a</u>ving up for (0.2) for <u>fireworks</u> and g<u>oi</u>ng (0.5)
         ʔən ab⌐ bɪ \sɛɪvɪn 'ʊ͡ʔp⌐ fəːʔˋ ʔfə \faɪəwɜːʔs əŋ ˋgɔʊɪn

21   s- g<u>ett</u>ing me <u>spends</u> and (.) and g<u>ett</u>ing it tog<u>ether</u> #
         ᵗs ˋgeṭɪm mɪ \spɛnz ən   ʔəŋ ˋgetɪn ɪt⌐ tə\geð̥ə̥

22   (0.8)

23   D   and <u>I'd</u> be getting (0.4) sp<u>ar</u>klers and uh
         ən \aɪd⌐ bɪ 'getɪnː   \ᵗspɑːkləz ə̥n̥d̥ə̥

24   sn<u>ow</u>storms and <u>cat</u>herine wheels=
         \snɔʊstɔːmz ə̥ŋ \kaθɾ̥ɪm wi<u>ː</u>l̥z

25   =and me br<u>o</u>ther'd be getting b<u>a</u>ngers and those <u>ae</u>roplane
         thing[s that]
         əm mi \bɹʊðəb bɪ 'gɛʔɪm /baŋgəz ən hↆ ðɔʊz \ɛːɹəpleɪn̥'
         θɪ̥ŋgz ðə?

26   M   [oh <u>ye</u>]ah
         ˋɔʊ \jeː

27   <u>whizzed</u> #
         \wɪzd

SOUNDS AND STRUCTURES   177

28   D   <u>yeah</u> (.) I mean you <u>wou</u>ldn't be able to <u>sell</u> things like that
         <u>now</u> (0.8) #
         \jɛː   m̩ʲ jə \wʊm? bi ɛɪbəl tə \sɛl̪ θɪŋgz laː? 'ð̥a? ∨naʊ

29   but <u>oh</u> I used to <u>love</u> bonfire night (.)
     bʊ?˙ \?ɔʊ a juːstə \lʊv 'bɒɱfaɪə naɪ?

30   me 'd<u>a</u>d'd come home <u>ea</u>rly from <u>work</u>=
     mɪ ˋdad əd kʊm 'hɔʊm ˋɜːlɪ fɹəm /wɜːk˙

31   =me m<u>o</u>ther'd put her <u>bon</u>fire boots <u>on</u>=
     mɪ ˋmʊðər əbˊ pʊ? ə \bɒɱfaɪə bʉː?s /ɒn

32   =these f<u>u</u>nny little <u>boots</u>=
     n̪iːz ˋfʊnɪ 'lɪtʲl̩ \bʉː?s

33   =d'you rem<u>e</u>mber those <u>boots</u> that had a zip up (.) [up there] #
     ɹ̩ˋɹɛmbə ðɔʊz \bʉ ːʔs ð̥ə? ad ə 'zɪp ʊpˋ   h↓ʊp \ðɛː

34   M   [I   <u>do</u>] #
                                                    a /dʉː

35   D   I think they only had an <u>ou</u>ting once a y<u>ear</u> at
         <u>bon</u>fire night (0.4) #
         ?a θɪŋ? ðɪ 'ɔʊnlɪ ad ən \aʊtɪn wɒns ə /jiər ə?
         /bɒɱfaɪə 'naɪ?

36   and o- (0.2) <u>off</u> we'd <u>go</u> and (0.2)
     ən ɒh   ˋ?ɒf wɪd /gɔʊ ən

37   oh I love-
     ɔʊ a 'lʊf-

38   I <u>liked</u> that more than Christmas <u>rea</u>[lly (0.5) #
     ?a \laɪkˋtˋ ða? mɔː ðən /kɹɪsməs /ɹɪːlɛ

39   M   [\mm

40   D   used to think it was <u>great</u> #
         ʷs θɪŋk ɪ? wəz /gɹɛɪ?

A careful reading of the transcription shows a lot of variability or
unexpected detail. The focus of this chapter is to explain some of these
details, and to show how context shapes phonetics. Some phenomena
occur at very particular places in the structures of speech, whether
between words, sentences or turns at talk. We can only look at a few of

these things; there are some more ways for you to explore the data here (or data you collect yourself) in the Exercises section.

11.3 Assimilation: place of articulation across word boundaries

We begin by looking at structures where one word ends in a consonant, and the next one starts with a consonant. We can see that in some of these joins, the end of the first word and the start of the next share the same place of articulation. For example: in citation form (that is, the form we would find in a dictionary, or the form produced if the word is said in isolation), the word 'own' ends with an alveolar, [n]. But in the phrase 'your own bonfire' (line 08), the nasal at the end of 'own' is bilabial, [m], which is the same place of articulation as the [b] at the start of 'bonfire'. Likewise, various forms of 'and' have forms like [əm] and [əŋ] alongside [ən]: the place of articulation of the final consonant can vary according to what follows. In the examples below, look at how the consonants corresponding to the underlined parts are pronounced. The numbers on the left are the line numbers in the transcription.

Bilabial
08   your ow<u>n b</u>onfire-
       jər 'ɔʊm 'bɒnfa̰?-

25   and my brother'<u>d be</u> getti<u>ng b</u>angers
       əm mi 'brʊðəb bɪ 'gɛ?ɪm 'baŋgəz

31   me mother'<u>d p</u>ut
       mɪ mʊðər əbˈ pʊ?

31   bo<u>nf</u>ire boots
       bɒm̩faɪə bʉː?s

Dental
05   a<u>nd th</u>at's-
       ə̪n̪ 'n̪a?s

28   to se<u>ll th</u>ings
       tə 'sɛl̪ θɪŋgz

Postalveolar
19   (you/that's) <u>right</u>
       ðja?ʃ ˋɹaɪ?

(Labio)velar

13 and we had
    ʔə̃w wi ad

21 and getting it together
    ʔəŋ 'gɛtɪn ɪtˀ tə'gɛðg̟

24 and catherine wheels
    əŋ 'kaθrɪm wiːlz

These are examples of assimilation, which we first saw in Section 7.6. More specifically, this is assimilation of place of articulation. The stretches [-m b-, -ṇ ð/ṇ -, -b b-, -l̟ θ-, -ŋ g-] etc. have the same place of articulation across the word boundary. The voicing and manner of articulation of the word-final consonant remain constant, but place of articulation can vary.

In English, assimilation affects mostly consonants which in citation form are produced as alveolar, but when they are followed by a consonant that has a different place of articulation, the 'alveolar' one may match it. You can see that this generalisation is also true of our Salford data, except that words ending in '-ing' in the spelling are included. (In citation form, or when followed by a vowel, these most often end in alveolars in Salford, as in line 21: 'getting it together', ['gɛtɪn ɪtˀ tə'gɛðg̟].)

Shared place of articulation across the word boundary, then, is a way to stick two adjacent sounds together. This makes the sounds across the word boundary more alike. Assimilation is one of the main ways that we get the percept of 'words being run together'.

Assimilation is not compulsory: there are places where Diane produces word-final consonants with alveolar place of articulation even though the next word starts with a consonant with a different place of articulation:

12 we'd be collecting wood
    wɪd bɪkˀ (0.3) kə'lɛʔktɪn 'wʊd

15 we'd got to store
    'wiːdˀ gɒt tə 'stɔː

16 my mother'd be chasing
    mɪ 'mʊðər ədˀ bɪ 'tʃɛɪsɪn

30 me dad'd come home
    mɪ 'dad əd kʊm 'hɔʊm

We can explain assimilation in terms of articulatory gestures, as in Figure 11.4. Imagine two gestures for place of articulation, one alveo-

time →

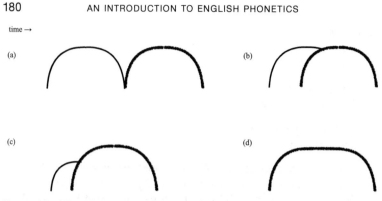

Figure 11.4 Explaining assimilation with articulatory gestures. (a) Two
adjacent gestures; (b) one gesture overlapped by another; (c)
one gesture weaker and overlapped by another; (d) two
gestures merged.

lar, the other bilabial, as in 'own bonfire'. Figure 11.4(a) shows very
schematically how we might represent this. (It is also possible to make
actual measurements of the movements of articulators; that is outside
the scope of this book, but the principles are the same.) The curves show
the articulations through time. The curve on the left, with the clean line,
represents the raising of the tongue tip to the alveolar ridge till it makes
a closure, at the point where the gesture reaches its maximum. It is held
there, released, then followed by a bilabial gesture, which has the same
kind of articulation in time; this is represented in the crayon-like line.

Figure 11.4(a) represents two distinct gestures, one after the other;
but this is not very natural, even in careful speech. Figure 11.4(b) shows
a more likely arrangement of the gestures: first, the alveolar gesture is
made, and while it is at its peak, or in the later part of the gesture, the
bilabial articulation is made. When the lips are closed for the bilabial gesture, the alveolar gesture is released, but this is not audible
or visible. This is the sort of arrangement we find when there is no
assimilation: the first articulation is made but inaudibly released. In fact,
we saw something like this in Figure 7.11 when we discussed plosives.

Figure 11.4(c) shows another possibility. Here, the first gesture is
considerably weaker, represented by the lesser height of the line. For
example, for a weaker alveolar articulation, the tongue tip might move
towards the alveolar ridge but not make complete closure, as we saw
in Section 8.4.3, when we discussed undershoot. Figure 11.4(c) shows
a case of partial assimilation: these are usually heard as a kind of blend
of two articulations, where the first one is usually much less prominent
than the second.

Figure 11.4(d) shows one last possibility: complete assimilation. Here, there is no perceptible gesture for the first consonant, and the second one dominates. The only sign that there is assimilation and that there are 'really' two consonants is that the second articulation can be held for longer than a single one might be.

These figures show some things that it is very hard to capture using the IPA. First, they highlight the reality that articulations unfold in time. IPA symbols focus on the points at which the articulations reach their maxima, but articulations are in fact almost constantly in flux. Secondly, they show that articulations can be changed along two dimensions: time and magnitude, that is, the 'size' of the articulation. The symbol [n] represents simultaneous voicing, nasal airflow and alveolar closure; [ɳ] (a voiced nasal alveolar approximant rather than stop) would be one way to capture the same gesture with reduced magnitude for the alveolar gesture. Thirdly, these representations capture better the co-ordination of gestures relative to each other: it is much easier to see, this way, how assimilation comes about, and it is also easier to understand that it is not straightforwardly present or absent, but in fact a more complex phenomenon. Complexity in speech is a frequent source of sound change.

11.4 Glottal stops

We saw in Chapter 7 that at the systematic or phonemic level, English is considered to have six plosives, based around a contrast for voicing (voiced vs. voiceless) and place of articulation (bilabial, alveolar, velar): [p t k b d g]. Although the basic system contains six items, at the phonetic level there is a lot of scope for variability.

In Salford English, as in many other varieties of English, glottal stops are frequent. They appear in four main contexts, all of which we can see in this transcription:

1. A realisation of /t/ (occasionally of /k/ or /p/) syllable finally or between vowels (replacement).
2. Part of a simultaneous articulation with [p t k] when syllable final (reinforcement).
3. Phrase-initially when the phrase starts with a vowel.
4. Before and after pauses.

Glottal stop simultaneous with another voiceless closure (glottal reinforcement; Section 7.4) is found in line 12 ('collecting', [kə'lɛʔk̂tɪn]), and line 20 ('saving up for', [sɛɪvɪn 'ʊʔp̂ fə]). As we have already seen, this is found in other varieties of English too.

Replacement is common in this variety. In the words below, Diane uses [ʔ] where on the basis of spelling or etymology we might have expected a voiceless alveolar plosive. These are all words with final /t/ in citation form and <t> in the spelling:

night	naɪʔ
but	bʊʔ
put	pʊʔ
great	grɛɪʔ
went	wɛnʔ
favourite	fɛɪvrɪʔ

In 'that's', [ḏaʔs] (line 05) and 'boots', [bʉːʔs] (lines 32 and 33), there is a consonant cluster which contains a morpheme boundary: the verb 'is' is cliticised to 'that', and the noun 'boots' has the plural marker -s. In 'getting', ['gɛʔɪm] (line 25), the glottal stop coincides with a syllable boundary. So [ʔ] for /t/ is not limited to postvocalic, word-final positions. Diane does not always use [ʔ] for /t/. She also has 'getting', ['gɛtɪn] (line 21); 'little', ['lɪtˡl] (line 32); and 'outing', ['aʊtɪn] (line 35).

Figure 11.5 shows 'getting' from line 21, 'getting it together'. Around 0.2 s friction is visible which corresponds to the release of the alveolar,

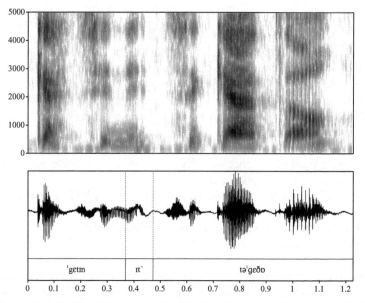

Figure 11.5 'Getting it together', line 21. Note the incomplete closure for [t], seen as frication at around 0.2 s.

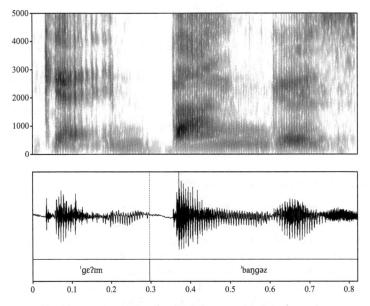

Figure 11.6 'Getting bangers', line 25. Note the glottalisation between 0.1 and 0.2 s, corresponding to /t/.

though from the spectrogram it looks like the closure is very short and probably incomplete, and the plosive is released with a lot of friction; this could be transcribed more narrowly as [ʈˢ]. (By way of contrast, the initial [t] of 'together' just after 0.7 s is clearly plosive and much less fricated.) Figure 11.6 shows 'getting', ['gɛʔɪm], from line 25. The spectrogram shows no closure, but between about 0.1 and 0.2 s, creaky voice is visible in the waveform and spectrogram as irregular, aperiodic vocal fold vibration, which is followed by low-volume, non-creaky nasal airflow between about 0.2 and 0.3 s. This is a realisation of /t/ without any sign of alveolar closure: this is partly why we need to distinguish phonological units like /t/ from phonetic ones. It has been transcribed as [ʔ], partly because it sounds like a glottal stop rather than creak, and partly because it functions like a glottal stop.

This variability shows that for Diane, the choice of [t] or [ʔ] is not lexically distinctive; but that is not to say that they cannot carry other kinds of meaning, such as indexical meaning marking her out as a speaker of this variety, or of a particular generation or gender.

Diane uses [ʔ] occasionally when we might expect a voiceless velar, [k], in the same position: 'fireworks', ['faɪəwɜʔs] (line 20; see the period of glottalisation at around 1.6 s in the spectrogram in Figure 11.8), and 'like that', [laː? 'ð̩a?] (line 28). Elsewhere in the conversation she says [laɪ? skuːl] for '(didn't) like school'; and also [pɹ̩'a?s] for 'perhaps'. There are far fewer of these cases than of the alveolars, and they seem to be common before fricatives.

Elsewhere we find [a 'θɪŋ?], 'I think'. Velarity is present in the nasal, [ŋ]; [?] is voiceless and plosive, and the nasal is not long, so the phonetic piece [ŋ?] has several features in common with the more standard [ŋk]. Words and phrases that are common often have special weak forms like this (see 'like that' and 'I mean' in line 28).

11.5 Silent pauses within an utterance

Normal conversation contains moments when one or neither party speaks. Some silences are in the middle of something that is meant to continue; other silences are meant to indicate 'I've finished talking, now it's your turn'. Both kinds of silence sound alike; but the way a speaker gets into (and out of) silence says something about how that silence should be understood by others. The next sections look at the phonetics of getting into pauses. This lays the foundations for how we might start to understand a basic fact of conversation: turn-taking.

We will start by looking at the phonetics of pausing within an utterance: what happens when Marie stops talking momentarily in the middle of something that is incomplete? Here are pauses which occur in places where the sentence she is producing is incomplete:

05   [and that's-] (.) that's all changed
       ən'na?sː (.) 'ða?s aːl 'tʃeɪndʒd̩

12   we'd be (0.3) collecting
       wɪd bɪk˺ (0.3) kə'lɛktɪn

14   of our (0.3) our house
       əv aː?˺ (0.3) ʔaː 'haʊs

20   saving up for (0.2) for fireworks and going (0.5)
       'seɪvɪn 'ʊ͡ʔp˺ fəː?˺ (0.2) ʔfə \faɪəwɜː?s əŋ ˋgəʊɪn (0.5)

21   s- getting me spends
       ˈs ˋgɛʈɪm mɪ \spɛnz

23   I'd be getting (0.4) sparklers
       'aɪd˺ bi 'gɛtɪnː (.) ˈ˺spɑːkləz

Before these pauses, a closure is made and held, but not released until the end of the pause. Line 12 shows this well: 'be' is produced with a velar closure which is held for 0.3 s. Because making a closure is audible (Section 7.2.4), the place of articulation of the next consonant is already hearable in the vowel of 'be'. Figure 11.7 shows a spectrogram of this. In the portion labelled [bɪkˀ], F2 and F3 can be seen at around 0.3 s to be coming together in a 'velar pinch'. (The same phenomenon can be observed in Figures 7.4 and 7.9.) This is a sign that velar closure is made. The release comes at about 0.66 s, at the start of the word 'collecting'.

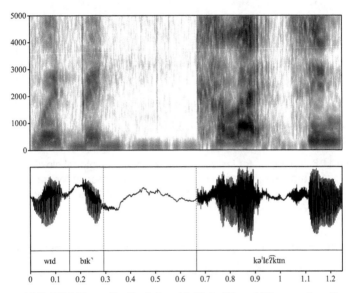

Figure 11.7 'We'd be collecting', line 12. Note F2 and F3 come together as the closure is made between 0.2 and 0.3 s, reflecting the velar closure.

In line 20, 'for' ends in a vowel which is lengthened ('stretched'). This is shown in Figure 11.8. A glottal closure is made, visible on the spectrogram at around 0.55 s, and released at the end of the pause before friction: notice the transient in the spectrogram and on the waveform just after 0.7 s.

Figure 11.9 shows a spectrogram of line 23, 'getting (0.4) sparklers'. At the start of [s] in 'sparklers', a transient is visible in the spectrogram. This corresponds to the release of the tongue against the alveolar ridge, as the alveolar closure for [n] is held across the silence and is released at the start of [s]. This transient is represented as [ᵗ] in the transcription. (A similar thing is found at the start of lines 20–1, 'going (0.5) s-', where [s] is the beginning of something that is abandoned.)

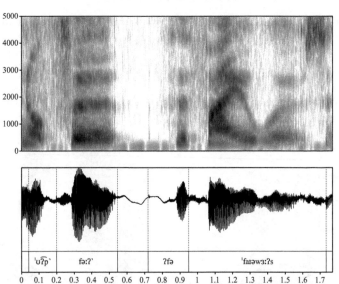

Figure 11.8 'up for . . . for fireworks', line 20. Note the glottal closure around 0.55 s, and its release, which is seen in the transient just after 0.7 s. Note the glottalisation at 1.6 s corresponding to /k/.

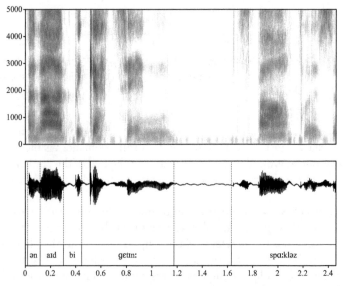

Figure 11.9 'I'd be getting sparklers', line 23. Note the transient just after 1.6 s.

We won't look at the function of these pauses, just notice that they occur; and consider that when another speaker hears a current speaker cease talking, it might offer the other speaker an opportunity to come in and talk. As you can see from the transcription, this does not happen in these cases. Partly this is because these pauses fall at places where the current sentence is not finished.

11.6 Silent pauses after syntactic completion

In the previous section, we looked at pauses that occur where the syntax is incomplete. Now we will look at some of the phonetic features we commonly find when the syntax is complete, and the speaker stops speaking: in other words, possible utterance-finality before a silence that is meant to be filled by someone else.

As well as syntactic completion, sentences can have intonational completion. This usually falls after the main accented item in the intonation phrase, which is itself marked by the occurrence of an intonation contour, greater loudness and a slower tempo than what comes before. In line 02, this item is the word 'love'. A falling intonation contour starts on 'love', and the initial lateral is long. The fall continues to the end of the sentence.

I used to love bonfire night   <<fast> aɪ juːstə>   \lːʊv bɒnfaɪə naɪ?

After the accented item, features of production may change to mark finality. Finality is marked phonetically in a number of ways in English, including: slowing down; possibly a drop in loudness; a change of voice quality (usually to creaky, whispery or breathy); a final pitch level that is not mid. (The precise details have been shown to be different in different varieties; see the suggestions in Further Reading, p. 194.) These features do not necessarily all co-occur, but we find them in this extract. Before these features, there is usually a stressed syllable that bears an intonation contour, and this syllable is the most prominent one of the sentence: typically, it has a higher or lower pitch than, and is louder and longer than, the surrounding talk.

11.6.1 Examples of places with syntactic completion + pause

Places in the transcription where Diane or Marie stop speaking at a place of syntactic completion are marked with '#'. These are places where the turn so far is possibly complete, and they exhibit features of finality, which we explore here.

A canonical way to show finality is slowing down: the syllables after a final tone-bearing syllable are usually longer in duration. We can see this by comparing the version of 'bonfire night' in line 01, which goes straight into the next phrase, with the one in line 35, which is followed by a pause. A labelled spectrogram and waveform are shown in Figure 11.10. The production on the left is the one that is from line 01 and the word 'night' lasts about 210 ms; the one on the right is from line 35 and 'night' lasts about 360 ms, so is much longer and slower than in the first one.

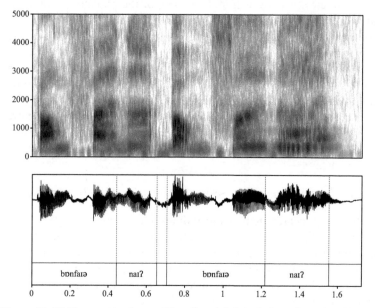

Figure 11.10 Two productions of 'bonfire night'. Left: from line 01, which is final but immediately joined to the next phrase; right: from line 35, which is also final but before a pause.

A change of voice quality may also occur finally. This is not consistent in this data, but lines 13, '... air raid shelter', and 15, '... the bonfire wood', end with creaky voice. Figures 11.11 and 11.12 show this. It can be seen on the spectrogram as greater distance between the vertical striations (cf. Figure 4.5). Notice that the three-part list in lines 23–4 also has creaky voice at the end, in 'wheels'; one hypothesis might be that creak can serve as a more general marker of finality or completion.

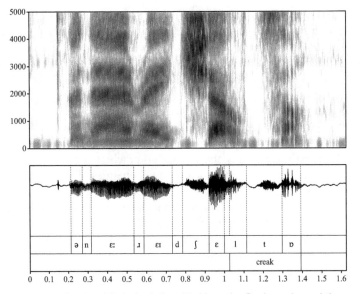

Figure 11.11 'An air raid shelter', line 13. Note the final creak, and the open back vowel (high F1, low F2).

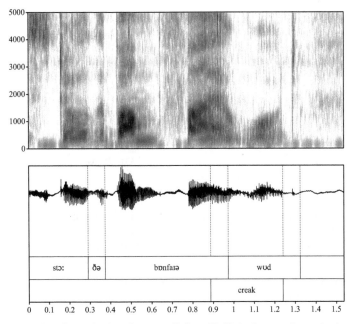

Figure 11.12 'Store the bonfire wood', line 15. Note the creak, and release of [d].

It is also often the case that final plosives are released when utterance final (in contrast with those before pauses in the middle of an utterance that we saw previously). There are only two clear examples of that in this transcription, 'wood' in line 15, and 'whizzed' in line 27, where the word-final [d] is audibly released. This can be seen also in Figure 11.12 with the transient at 1.3 s. In line 27, Marie finishes Diane's turn for her, but she designs 'whizzed' as a continuation of Diane's turn, not as e.g. a suggestion for the word Diane is looking for. The other final plosives in this extract are glottal stops, whose release is not very audible.

Aside from these features, there is one other which is especially interesting in this data, and a bit unusual: vowel qualities. The final vowels of the COMMA/LETTER and HAPPY sets seem to be variable, with the qualities [ə ɪ] respectively when not before a pause (e.g. line 06, 'lovely'; line 23, 'sparklers'; line 31, 'mother'; line 32, 'funny') but the qualities [ɒ ɛ] when syntactically complete and pre-pausal (e.g. line 13, 'shelter'; line 21, 'together'; line 38, 'really'). Here are some more examples from elsewhere in the conversation:

End of a syntactically complete sentence followed by silence from the speaker:

nativit̲y̲	nə'tʰɪvɪtɛ
big and beef̲y̲	'bɪg əm 'biːfɛ
lovel̲y̲	'lʊvlɛ
wealthy famil̲y̲	'wɛlθɪ 'famlɛ
frightened m̲e̲	'fɹaɪʔn̩ mɛ
is h̲e̲?	'ɪzɛ
had i̲t̲?	'hadɛ?
do th̲e̲y̲?	'dʉː ðɛ
came to talk to h̲e̲r	tɔːkˈ tɪʉ ɒ
. . . had been a weav̲e̲r	'wiːvɒ
one anoth̲e̲r	'wɒn ə'nʊðɒ

Followed by more talk from the same speaker:

wealth̲y̲ family	'wɛlθi 'famlɛ
Mar̲y̲'s chair	mɛːɹɪz̟ tʃɛː
beef̲y̲ woman	'biːfɪ 'wʊmən
bon̲y̲ fingers	'bɔʊnɪ 'fɪŋgəz
we get on so well togeth̲e̲r don't we	tə'g3ðə
a weav̲e̲r of-	'wiːvər əv

Now we have seen two different ways for speakers to cease talking. One way is to hold articulations across silence, as a way to mark 'I have more to say'; the other is a set of practices that involve longer preparations to stop talking, as a way to mark 'I'm going to stop talking, someone else can come in'. It turns out that these are different kinds of activity phonetically; and this is useful, because it tells us something about how speakers manage the transition from one speaker to another.

11.7 Syntactically complete phrases followed immediately by more talk

Our next and final structure is the kind of join between one possibly complete phrase followed immediately by another one. These are marked with '=' in the transcription. In these cases, the speaker continues speaking and starts to produce a new phrase immediately, without even a pause for breath. Phonetically, these joins are marked by features which are quite unlike those we saw in the other two cases, but resemble those of word joins: the speech does not slow down, and may even speed up; there can be assimilation of voicing or place of articulation across the join (line 32, 'these funny little boots'; line 33, 'do you remember . . .'); lack of audible release (e.g. line 30, 'from work'); lack of e.g. glottal stops or other features to separate similar sounds as in lines 09–10, '. . . entry = you'd . . .'. All of these features make the boundaries between phrases more alike, rather than keeping them separate.

Figure 11.13 shows the end of line 09 and the start of line 10. Notice how between the end of 'entry' and the start of 'you'd', voicing continues (if you look at the waveform closely you will see the striations getting closer together as f0 rises); the voiced portion at the end of 'entry' is very short; and other features such as silence, closures, or glottal stops are missing.

Figure 11.14 shows the end of line 31 and the start of line 32, '. . . boots on, these funny'. Notice that voicing continues all the way across the join. The dental nasal shows assimilation between the end of the first phrase and the start of the next; as we saw, assimilation is a kind of 'glue' between words. This nasal is about 80 ms long, which for a combination of final + initial nasal is quite a short duration.

Summary

In this chapter, we have looked at a longer stretch of talk between two people, focusing on the speech of one of them. As well as assimilation between words, we have seen some examples of phenomena that are specific to spontaneous speech or conversation, such as pausing in the

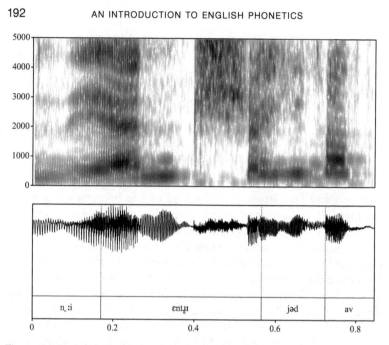

Figure 11.13 '. . . in the entry, you'd have . . .'. Note the lack of pause or lengthening at the end of 'entry', and the continuity of voicing across the join between the two phrases.

middle of ongoing talk, and producing talk which is designed to be heard as complete or designed to be heard as projecting more to come. There is, despite a great deal of variability, an orderliness to these practices. We have only touched the surface of a very rich and complex field, using a small amount of data. What we have seen though is that there is structure at many levels, from words upwards to whole turns at talk; and much of this structure is made available through aspects of phonetics.

Note on the data

Thanks to Bill Haddican for access to the data used in this chapter. It was collected under ESRC Project RES-061-25-0033. The audio file is available online from edinburghuniversitypress.com/englishphonetics.

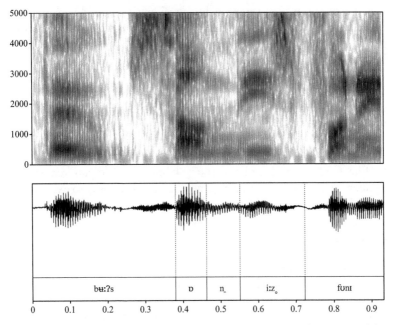

Figure 11.14 '. . . boots on, these funny . . .'. Note the lack of pause, and the continuity of voicing and nasality across the join between the two phrases.

Exercises

1. Read aloud the transcription as best you can.

2. If you work through the list of keywords in Chapter 5, how do the vowels of Salford pattern, and how do they compare with other varieties of English we have seen or that you know?

3. Is Salford a rhotic or a non-rhotic variety (Section 5.5)? What evidence can you find from the transcription?

4. The spectrograms and accompanying waveforms in this chapter are more difficult to read than many others in the book: they are of richer, more complex stretches of speech. See if you can identify the following things in them and match them to the transcriptions provided (Section 3.3):

a. periodic sounds
b. continuous aperiodic sounds
c. transient sounds

If you can do this, you can probably also identify individual sounds by manner of articulation and voicing. Try this out for some of the spectrograms, and cross-check your findings with what is described elsewhere in the book.

5. In line 28, 'wouldn't' is pronounced [wʊmʔ]. This is an extreme form of reduction: the shortening of longer forms (in this case ['wʊdənt]). Can you explain how this form might come about using what we have learnt about assimilation, glottalisation and syllabic nasals (in Chapter 9)?

6. The fieldworker heard the start of line 33 as 'd'you remember'. Phonetically, it is transcribed as [ɹ̥ˈɹɛmbə]. Is there a way to explain this reduction using what we have seen about the joins between utterances?

Further reading

The original work done on pausing in conversation is Local and Kelly (1986). For more on the phonetics of turn-taking, see e.g. Local et al. (1986), and Local and Walker (2012). For more on the phonetics of conversation, Shockey (2002) is a good introduction. For a more fully worked out model of phonetics in terms of articulatory gestures, see Gick et al. (2013).

12 Conclusion

This book has, I hope, shown some of the richness and complexity of the sounds of English. We have seen a great deal of phonetic diversity for sounds which intuitively we think of as 'the same'. In many cases, what started off looking like a simple system turned out to be more complex. For example, /l/ is not always produced as a lateral in English, a fact that we explained with secondary articulations. Syllable-initial and syllable-final /l/ have different secondary articulations, with the syllable-final lateral being (labio)velarised, [lˠ], and we saw that in some cases, the alveolar closure is lost, leaving only the secondary articulation, giving fairly close, back, vocalic articulations like [ɣ ö] or [ʊ]. We also noted that the kind and degree of secondary articulation vary according to the variety of English. The linguistic interpretation of this kind of complexity is a problem for phonology, which is largely beyond the scope of this book.

If we consider critically what we have learnt, we can draw a number of conclusions.

First, we have seen that sometimes the phonetic details are more complex than we might first imagine. This is especially obvious for voiced and voiceless fricatives and plosives (as in 'race' vs. 'raise' or 'hit' vs. 'hid'). For these sounds, we have seen that the phonetics of the voicing contrast in English is more complex than just vocal fold vibration. The timing of the start and end of voicing with, for example, the onset and offset of friction, or closure and release, is complex in English. There are also differences in the volume of air passing through the vocal tract, possible differences in voice quality, and differences in the duration of resonant articulations that precede such sounds. We have seen also that in many cases, the location of a sound in a syllable or a word is an important determinant of how it is pronounced: for example, syllable-initial nasality and syllable-final nasality are co-ordinated with oral gestures (such as complete closure) in different ways. Likewise, syllable-initial [k] matches closely the articulation of an adjacent resonant (as in 'keep', 'car', 'corn', 'creep'), while syllable-final [k] is a lot less variable in its place of articulation. Phonetic details like these provide listeners with a lot of information about linguistic structure: and this is information that they can use to make sense out of the sounds of speech.

Secondly, we have seen that there are many things we can observe phonetically that relate to 'meaning', but not to word meaning. For example, the use of voice quality to convey a stance towards the thing being talked about; the use of in-breaths, clicks and closures that are held across silence to project 'I have more to say'; the phonetic details around pauses of particular types to accomplish different tasks in interaction: all these things are used by speakers to mark something that goes beyond word meaning. Another kind of non-lexical meaning involves the use of one sound in place of another that is found in more standard varieties. Examples of this include the use of glottal stops or taps in the place of [t] or [d], or the more open articulations found in Liverpool, or the particular voice quality found in Glasgow. These details index another kind of meaning: 'I am from (where I am from)', or 'I belong to such-and-such a social group'.

Phonetic details at all levels are not 'extras', but are often an indispensable part of speakers' phonetic repertoires. Some of the most exciting work in phonetics at the moment comes from the systematic exploration of how such details work in everyday talk, taking into account speakers' sociolinguistic background, marking 'stance', 'attitude' and 'affect', and looking at how talk is organised in conversation. There is still a great deal that we do not know, for example, about the way speakers use intonation, voice quality, sounds made with non-pulmonic airstreams, and other phonetic parameters to generate meaning.

In our studies, we have used our eyes (through the use of symbols, spectrograms, waveforms and other diagrams), our ears (listening and reflecting on our own productions), and our awareness of our own vocal tracts (reflecting how it feels to make a sound), as well as data from carefully controlled recordings and everyday conversation. Phonetics is, by its very nature, a multisensory discipline. Human communication is also a multisensory phenomenon: whether our language is spoken or signed, language is ultimately produced, sensed and mediated through our bodies. One growing area for research in phonetics is how our speech is co-ordinated with other physical activities like body posture, pointing gestures, eye gaze and eyebrow movements; another is how the brain handles speech and language.

What comes next for you, the reader? This will depend on your own interests, but a better understanding of acoustics will make it easier for you to appreciate how speech perception works. There is much more to say about the way that phonetics and phonology relate to one another. We have not even scratched the surface of the phonetics of the intonational and rhythmical systems of English. The small details of today's English sometimes become the lexically contrastive of tomorrow's, just as the details of today's English have developed from earlier pronunciations. Historical change and sociolinguistic variability are closely related, and often have phonetic explanations. There are many varieties of English (let alone other languages) whose phonetic details have not been recorded: it's a healthy stance to approach each variety as a foreign language, noticing as many details as possible, because in many cases we still do not know what details are important to speakers and hearers. To develop as a phonetician, constant practice and observation are needed. We are lucky that the stuff of our trade surrounds us.

Glossary

accent-bearing syllables – Stressed syllables which carry an intonation contour.

acoustic phonetics – The aspect of phonetics which looks at the physical properties of sounds, such as their frequency, amplitude, duration, etc.

active articulator – When two articulators are involved in making a sound, the active articulator is the one that moves. E.g. in [t] the active articulator is the tongue tip. Cf. passive articulator.

advanced – Advanced articulations are further forward than might be expected. Diacritic [₊] e.g. 'key', [k̟]. (Cf. 'cart' or 'court'.) Cf. retracted.

airstream mechanism – The way in which air is made to flow into or out of the vocal tract in order to make a speech sound. There are three major airstream mechanisms: pulmonic, velaric, glottalic.

allophone – A contextually determined variant of a phoneme. For example, /p/ is realised as a voiceless aspirated plosive [pʰ] when initial in a stressed syllable, as in 'pit', unless there is a /s/ before it in the same syllable, when it is realised as voiceless but unaspirated, [p], as in 'spit'.

alphabetic principle – The principle of writing one symbol per sound.

aperiodic – Aperiodic signals have no regularly repeating part, as in e.g. voiceless friction.

approximant – A frictionless consonantal sound with a stricture of open approximation; in English the sounds [j w l r] are approximants.

articulatory phonetics – The aspect of phonetics which looks at how the sounds of speech are made with the organs of the vocal tract such as the vocal folds, tongue, lips, velum, etc.

arytenoid cartilage – The vocal folds are attached at their rear to the arytenoid cartilages, which are at the back of the larynx. The arytenoids can swivel and rotate, changing the tension and thickness of the vocal folds, which affects pitch and voice quality.

aspiration – A period of glottal friction after the release of a plosive. Diacritic [ʰ], e.g. [pʰ].

assimilation – The process of one sound becoming more like another in some respect, e.g. place of articulation.

Bernoulli effect – An aerodynamic effect which causes two articulators to come together and move apart, as in the production of voicing and trills.

breathy voice – A voice quality generated by incomplete closure of the vocal folds during vibration because the vocal folds are slack, not tense. Diacritic [..], e.g. [a̤]

cardinal vowels (CVs) – A set of reference vowels used in the description of the vowels of languages. There are eight primary cardinal vowels, [i e ɛ a ɑ ɔ o u].

central airflow – Airflow along the centre of the vocal tract. Cf. lateral airflow; nasal airflow.

citation form – The phonetic form of a word when spoken carefully; the usual form found in a dictionary.

click – A type of ingressive plosive made on a velaric airstream. In English speech, clicks do not form parts of words but are common in everyday talk; often represented as 'tut' or 'tsk'.

close approximation – An articulation which generates turbulent airflow between two articulators, resulting in friction.

co-articulation – The articulation of aspects of two or more sounds at the same time. E.g. the velar closure in [k̟] in 'keep' is front (advanced); it is co-articulated with the following front [i] sound.

complete closure – An articulation which blocks the passage of air through the vocal tract because a seal is made between two articulators.

consonant – One of two kinds of segment recognised by the IPA, the other being vowels. Consonants are produced with a stricture of at least open approximation in the vocal tract. Consonants are described in terms of voicing, place and manner of articulation.

coronal (adj.) – A term used widely in phonology, referring to sounds made with the tongue tip and blade, i.e. the active articulator, without specifying what the passive articulator is. Alveolar consonants, e.g. [t z n l], as well as dental consonants, [θ ð d̪ l̪], are coronal.

creaky voice – A voice quality generated by slow, tense, sometimes random vibration of the vocal folds. Diacritic [̰], e.g. [a̰].

cricoid cartilage – A ring of cartilage at the base of the larynx.

diacritic – A character which modifies the basic value of a phonetic symbol and is placed around simple letter shapes. E.g. [̥] is the diacritic for voicelessness. Since there is no special symbol for a voiceless alveolar nasal, this diacritic can be combined with the symbol for the voiced sound [n], giving [n̥].

diphthong – A sequence of two vowels within the same syllable. The vowels of CHOICE, MOUTH and PRICE in most varieties of English are diphthongs, as in RP [ɔɪ, aʊ, aɪ].

distribution – A statement of where something occurs in a language, e.g. syllable initially, word medially, utterance finally.

dorsal (adj.), dorsum (n.) – A term referring to sounds made with the tongue back, i.e. the active articulator, without specifying what the passive articulator is. Velar consonants, [k g ŋ], are dorsal.

double articulation (doubly articulated) – A sound with two articulations with the same degree of stricture. [w] has open approximation at the lips and the velum, and is a double articulation.

egressive – A sound made with air flowing out of the vocal tract.

ejective – A type of egressive plosive made on a glottalic airstream. Ejectives occur in some varieties of British English. Diacritic ['], e.g. [k'].

Extensions to the IPA (ExtIPA) – Extensions to the IPA system for the description of disordered speech, but often useful in the notation of details from everyday talk.

falsetto – A voice quality generated by making the vocal folds long, thin and tense, causing them to vibrate at a much faster rate than usual. May be marked using ExtIPA conventions, e.g. {falsetto [wɑt də jə seɪ] falsetto}.

formant – A broad, dark band on a spectrogram. It indicates an area of the acoustic signal which is boosted by the natural resonances of the vocal tract. Formants are counted upwards, from the first formant, F1 (the lowest). In speech, F1–F3 are the most important formants.

frequency – Frequency is a measure of the rate of how many cycles occur per second. It is measured in Hertz.

fricative – When there is turbulent airflow through the vocal tract, generally as the result of close approximation, fricatives are generated. English fricatives include [f v θ ð s z ʃ ʒ h].

fundamental frequency (f0) – In speech, the lowest component frequency of the speech signal, generated by the vibration of the vocal folds.

glottalic (airstream) – Airflow caused by the raising or lowering of the larynx. When egressive, the glottis is closed. When ingressive, there is usually vocal fold vibration.

glottalisation – The accompaniment of creaky voice and/or glottal stop while a sound is made. Common for syllable-final voiceless plosives, e.g. 'hat', [hæ̰ʔt], when it is often known as glottal reinforcement.

glottis – The space between the vocal folds.

Hertz (Hz) – A measure of frequency. 1 Hz = one complete cycle per second. If there is voicing at a frequency of 150 Hz, it means the vocal folds open and close 150 times in a second.

homophone – Two words which are different but sound alike are homophones, e.g. 'whole' (adj.) and 'hole' (n.).

homorganic – Two sounds are homorganic when they share the same place of articulation, as in the clusters [mp lt ŋk].

implosive – A type of voiced ingressive plosive made on a glottalic airstream. They are said to occur in parts of the Southern states of the USA, and occur in some English-derived Creoles. The IPA represents implosives with modified plosive symbols which contain a rightward hook on the upper part of the letter: [ɓ ɗ ʄ].

ingressive – A sound made with air flowing into the vocal tract. Symbol (ExtIPA) [↓].

intonation – A linguistic use of pitch, spread out over whole utterances.

intrusive-r – In non-rhotic varieties: a [r] sound (produced as e.g. [ɹ ɹ r]) used to join two words where the second starts with a vowel but there is no historical warrant for the presence of [r]. E.g. 'China [-r-] and Japan'.

IPA – International Phonetic Association; International Phonetic Alphabet.

labialisation – A secondary articulation where the lips are rounded in a gesture of open approximation. Diacritic [ʷ], e.g. [ʃʷ].

labiovelarisation – A secondary articulation which combines velarisation and labialisation. Diacritic [ˠʷ], e.g. [ɹˠʷ].

larynx – Voice box; Adam's apple. A structure made of cartilage, located in the neck. Houses the vocal folds.

lateral airflow – Air passes down one side of the vocal tract; in English only for the sound [l].

linking-r – In non-rhotic varieties: a [r] sound (produced as e.g. [ɹ ɹ r]) used to join two words where the second starts with a vowel. E.g. 'far and wide', [fɑːr ən waɪd] (but cf. 'far sighted', [fɑː saɪtɪd], without [r]).

modal voicing – Vibration of the vocal folds along their full length with regular vibration.

morpheme – The smallest meaningful unit in words. For example, 'misunderstanding' has the morphemes 'mis+under+stand+ing'.

nasal – A consonant sound made with a complete closure in the oral tract and the velum lowered. English nasals include [m n ŋ].

nasal airflow – Air passes through the nose, but not the mouth.

nasalised – Sounds made with oro-nasal airflow are said to be nasalised. Diacritic [˜], e.g. [ã], a nasalised, front open vowel.

non-rhotic – Varieties of English which do not allow [r] sounds before consonants are known as non-rhotic. E.g. in non-rhotic varieties, the word 'start' is pronounced as [staːt] or]staːt]. Cf. rhotic.

off-glide – Off-glide describes the way speakers get out of a sound; aspiration is a kind of voiceless off-glide out of a plosive.

on-glide – On-glide describes the way speakers get into a sound; preaspiration is a kind of voiceless on-glide into a plosive.

open approximation – An articulation where two articulators are brought towards each other, but not close enough to generate turbulent airflow. Used in the production of approximants [jwɹ].

oral airflow – Air passes through the mouth.

oro-nasal airflow – Air passes through the nose and the mouth, resulting in nasalisation.

palatalisation – A secondary, [i]-like articulation where the tongue body is raised towards the hard palate in a gesture of open approximation. Diacritic [ʲ], e.g. [lʲ].

passive articulator – When two articulators are involved in making a sound, the passive articulator is the one that does not move. E.g. in [t] the passive articulator is the alveolar ridge. Cf. active articulator.

perception – That part of phonetics, speech sciences and psychology more generally that investigates how the sounds of speech are recognised, organised and classified.

percussive – A sound made when two articulators strike each other, but there is no airstream necessarily involved in producing the noise, e.g. the sound of the lips coming apart in preparation for speaking.

periodic – Periodic sounds are those which repeat themselves. In speech, periodicity is normally the result of the vibration of the vocal folds. Other sources of sounds are aperiodic. Voiced fricatives contain both periodic and aperiodic components (voicing and friction respectively).

phoneme – A unit of phonology: sounds which can differentiate one word from another, e.g. the sounds [t] and [d] in 'hit' and 'hid'. Transcribed between slash brackets, e.g. /t d/.

pitch – A percept generated by f0. High pitch is caused by high f0, low pitch by low f0.

plosive – An oral consonant made with complete closure in the vocal tract. Plosives have three possible stages: closing, hold and release.

preaspiration – A period of voiceless friction as a closure into a plosive is made. Transcribed with [ʰ] e.g. 'loop', [luːʰp], or with a homorganic fricative symbol, e.g. [luːᵠp].

primary articulation – In complex articulations, the primary articulation is the closest of two or more articulations. In English, syllable-final laterals are velarised: compare 'leaf', [l-], and 'feel', [-lˠ]. The primary articulation is [l], the secondary articulation is velarisation.

pulmonic (airstream) – Airflow originating from the lungs; pulmonic airstream; cf. glottalic; velaric.

Received Pronunciation (RP) – The traditionally prestigious variety of British English. This is the variety of British English which has most commonly been described, and is taught to learners of English.

reduced vowel – The use of one of a limited set of vowels (such as [ə ɪ]) in unstressed syllables.

release, central – The most usual way to release plosives, by letting air flow down the middle of the vocal tract.

release, fricative – The release of a plosive into a period of friction. Affricates, such as [tʃ dʒ], are plosives with fricative release.

release, inaudible – A form of release without audible plosion. Diacritic [̚] e.g. [-k̚ t-].

release, lateral – A way to release alveolar plosives, by lowering one side of the tongue and allowing air to flow down the side(s) of the vocal tract. Diacritic [ˡ], e.g. [dˡ].

release, nasal – A way to release plosives, by lowering the velum while retaining the oral closure and allowing air to escape through the nose. Diacritic [ⁿ], e.g. [bⁿ].

resonance – As a physical space, the vocal tract boosts the amplitude (loudness) of some parts of the speech signal (frequencies) more than others. These amplified parts are known as resonances. The values of the resonances of the vocal tract depend on the shape of the vocal tract, which is why different sounds sound different from one another.

resonant articulation – Sounds made without friction.

retracted – Retracted articulations are further back than might be expected. Diacritic [-], e.g. 'court', [k̠]. (Cf. 'cart' or 'key'.) Cf. advanced.

retroflexion – Curling back of the tongue tip. Diacritic for vowels [˞], e.g. 'mother', [mʌðɚ], in rhotic varieties. Symbols for retroflex consonants all have a right-facing downward hook, e.g. [ʈ ɖ ʂ ɳ].

rhotic (adj.) – Varieties of English which allow [r] sounds before consonants are known as rhotic. E.g. in rhotic varieties, the word 'start' is pronounced as [start] or [stɑrt]. Cf. non-rhotic.

rhotic (n.) – A cover term used to refer to a [r] sound; one of a family of sounds, such as [ɹ ɾ ɻ], which is a realisation of <r>.

secondary articulation – The more open of two or more articulations in the same sound. In English, syllable-final laterals have a secondary articulation of velarisation: compare 'leaf', [l-], and 'feel', [-lˠ].

segment – Speech is conventionally thought of as being composed of segments: consonants and vowels. In acoustic phonetics, 'segment' may refer to any stretch of the sound wave which can be identified consistently, such as the hold portion of plosives.

spectrogram – A graphical representation with time on the horizontal axis and frequency on the vertical axis. Amplitude (loudness) is represented by darkness.

stop articulation – An articulation made with complete closure in the oral tract. Plosives and taps are stop articulations.

striation – A vertical line on a spectrogram corresponding to one opening of the vocal folds: a good indication of voicing.

strident – Strident fricatives are those which have a lot of friction noise, caused by a narrow constriction. Strident fricatives in English are [s z ʃ ʒ].

suprasegmental – Properties of speech which extend over segments. Suprasegmental features of speech include intonation, loudness, rhythm, voice quality and tempo.

syllabic lateral/nasal – A nasal or lateral which forms a syllable by itself, usually after a lateral or nasal release. Diacritic [ˌ], as in 'bottle', [bɑtˡl̩], 'button', [bʌtⁿn̩].

tap – A sound made by a short complete closure in the vocal tract as one articulator strikes another.

thyroid cartilage – One of three cartilages that make up the larynx. The thyroid has two prominent plates which form a notch at the front of the larynx.

transcription – The practice of representing speech in writing.

transcription, allophonic – A transcription which uses the phoneme symbols of a language and includes some allophonic detail. Allophonic transcriptions are narrower than phonemic transcriptions.

transcription, broad – A transcription which contains a limited amount of phonetic detail. Cf. transcription, narrow.

transcription, comparative – A transcription whose purpose is to compare sounds within or between varieties.

transcription, impressionistic – A transcription which uses the full potential of the IPA to record much observable detail. Impressionistic transcriptions (or 'impressionistic records') are necessarily narrow.

transcription, narrow – A transcription which contains some phonetic detail. There is a gradual scale from broad to narrow transcription. Cf. transcription, broad.

transcription, phonemic – A transcription which uses only the phoneme symbols of a language. Phonemic transcriptions are necessarily systematic and broad.

transcription, simple – A transcription which uses familiar Roman letter shapes in preference to non-Roman letter shapes. E.g. the sound [r] in English can be transcribed [r] in a simple transcription unambiguously; in a non-simple transcription, the symbol [ɹ] (or variants with diacritics) might be used.

transcription, systematic – A transcription which uses a limited set of symbols. Phonemic transcriptions are necessarily systematic.

transient – Short-lived sounds which appear as spikes in waveforms and spectrograms. The release portions of plosives are transients.

trill – A sound made by the repeated striking of one articulator against another using aerodynamics. Sounds called 'rolled <r>' are often trills.

triphthong – A series of three vowels within the same syllable. The vowel of hire can be a triphthong in RP, [aɪə]. Triphthongs are also found in Southern varieties in the USA.

undershoot – When articulators do not reach their target, they are often said to 'undershoot'. This is common in ordinary speech. For example, in making a [b] sound, the lips might not make a complete closure, producing a fricative-like sound instead, [β].

velaric (airstream) – Airflow originating from an enclosed space between a closure at the velum and another closure further forward. Cf. click.

velarisation – A secondary articulation where the dorsum is raised towards the velum in a gesture of open approximation. Diacritic [ˠ], as in 'feel', [lˠ].

velum – Also known as the soft palate; tissue at the back of the roof of the mouth. The velum can be lowered to allow airflow through the nose, or raised to seal off the nasal cavities.

vocal folds (cords) – Two fleshy folds which are stretched across the larynx. They can be held wide open, as in breathing; completely closed, as in a glottal stop or cough; or made to vibrate to produce voicing. Different kinds of vibration produce different voice qualities.

voice onset time (VOT) – The time between the release of a plosive and the start of voicing, measured in milliseconds. Positive VOT means the voicing starts after the release of the plosive; negative VOT means the voicing starts before the release of the plosive.

voice quality – Different modes of vibration of the vocal folds generate different voice qualities. Cf. breathy voice; creaky voice; falsetto; whisper.

voiced – Sounds made with vibration of the vocal folds. Voiced sounds are made with vibrating vocal folds. Voiced sounds in English include [b d g v ð z ʒ m n ŋ l r w j] and all vowels.

voiceless – Sounds made without vibration of the vocal folds. Voiceless phonemes in English include [p t k f θ s ʃ]. Other sounds can be voiceless in English in the appropriate context. Diacritic [̥], e.g. [m̥].

voicing – Use of vocal fold vibration in speech.

vowel – One of two kinds of segment recognised by the IPA, the other being consonants. Vowels are voiced oral resonant sounds made with central airflow. Vowels may occasionally be voiceless or nasalised. Vowels are described in terms of height, frontness/backness and lip posture.

vowel frontness/backness – One of three dimensions for describing vowels. The IPA recognises three arbitrary points along a continuum: front, central and back.

vowel height – One of three dimensions for describing vowels. The IPA recognises four arbitrary points along a continuum: close, close-mid, open-mid and open. 'High' and 'low' are sometimes used instead of 'close' and 'open' respectively.

vowel – lip posture – One of three dimensions for describing vowels. The lips can be held in a number of postures, such as spread and close (as for CV1, [i]), compressed and protruded (as for CV8, [u]) or open and rounded (as for [ɒ]). The IPA represents lip postures implicitly in symbols.

vowel quadrilateral – The four-cornered chart which is used to represent the vowel space.

vowel space – An abstract space which represents the possible configurations of the vocal tract that produce vowels. Articulations outside the vowel space generate friction and are consonantal.

waveform – A graphical representation with time on the horizontal axis and sound pressure level on the vertical axis.

whisper – A type of voice quality where the vocal folds are narrowed, so as to produce turbulent airflow across the glottis. The vocal folds do not vibrate in whisper.

yod-dropping – A term applied to some varieties of English which have no [j] sound after alveolars before [u] in words such as 'dew', 'new', [d(j)uː, n(j)uː].

Discussion of the exercises

Chapter 2

1a. velar plosive; alveolar lateral; bilabial plosive

b. glottal fricative; labiodental fricative

c. alveolar plosive; labiodental fricative

d. velar plosive; alveolar fricative

e. alveolar approximant; alveolar fricative; alveolar plosive

f. alveolar plosive; postalveolar affricate

g. velar plosive; alveolar nasal; alveolar plosive; velar plosive; alveolar plosive

h. velar plosive; bilabial nasal; alveolar nasal; alveolar plosive (or tap)

i. alveolar nasal; alveolar plosive; alveolar fricative; alveolar plosive

j. alveolar nasal; alveolar plosive. (NB <g> and <h> are not pronounced.)

k. alveolar fricative; velar plosive; alveolar lateral approximant; post-alveolar affricate

l. glottal fricative; alveolar approximant; velar nasal

m. bilabial plosive; (alveolar approximant); labiodental fricative; (alveolar approximant); bilabial nasal. Not all speakers will pronounce this word with [r] sounds.

n. alveolar plosive; alveolar approximant; alveolar nasal; alveolar fricative; alveolar lateral approximant; alveolar plosive

2.

	Symbols	Set 1	Set 2
a.	p m t n k ŋ	p t k (oral plosives)	m n ŋ (nasals)
b.	s l p m v ʃ	p m v (labial)	s l ʃ (made with tongue tip)
c.	f j w l z θ	f z θ (fricatives)	j w l (approximants)
d.	s v h ð ʒ θ	v ð ʒ (voiced fricatives)	s h θ (voiceless fricatives)
e.	r k n l w g	k w g (velar)	r n l (alveolar)
f.	t w s m b g	t w s m b g	
g.	ʃ ʒ ʈ θ ð ɗ	ʃ ʒ ʈ (postalveolar)	t̪ θ ð (dental)
h.	h z fi l ʔ s	h fi ʔ (glottal)	z l s (alveolar)
i.	n a p k j w	a j w (made with open approximation)	n p k (made with complete closure; stops)
j.	j w b d ɗ ɹ	j w r (approximants)	b d ɗ (plosives)

Chapter 3

2. (a) is a phonemic transcription, based on citation forms. It is a broad, systematic transcription. (b) is a more allophonic, narrower transcription which contains some predictable details such as aspiration and the unstressed vowels in 'was' and 'because'. (c) is much the same, but it is simpler; it uses the familiar letter shapes [e] and [r]. (d) is a narrow transcription, and is more impressionistic. It uses a full range of diacritics to mark e.g. voicelessness and lip-rounding; it also shows many details of the consonants that are not evident in (a)–(c).

3.

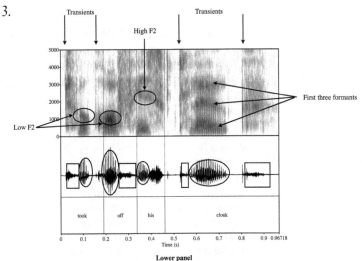

Lower panel
Periods of voicing in ellipses; aperiodic noise in rectangles. Both have corresponding portions of spectrogram immediately above.

Chapter 4

1. Finding contrasting pairs for [s – z], [f – v] and [θ – ð] should be straightforward where these are word final. Word initially, it is harder, because the distributions of [z ð ʒ] are limited in this position. This kind of test is useful for working out the distribution of sounds.

2. You should find that some kind of phrase boundary must be marked with punctuation at major syntactic breaks, but not generally between words that are closely related syntactically. In the sentence below, < | > marks a possible phrase boundary, <*> where a boundary could not occur.

> you're * a * caterer | with * a * big * firm | small * firm | your * own * firm |
> e.g. You're a caterer. With a big firm? Small firm? Your own firm?

In spoken language, names used to identify the next speaker are generally phrases: 'As I understand it, Marguerite, is that right . . .'. Certain displays of hesitation also have phrase boundaries: 'she was like a, sort of, you know, like one of those film stars'. Certain relative clauses also require phrase boundaries: 'You grow your own fruit which is fantastic' (= your fruit is fantastic); 'You grow your own fruit, which is fantastic' (= it's fantastic that you grow your fruit (which may or may not be fantastic)).

Chapter 5

1. and 2. The answers you come up with will depend on your own dialect.

3. Here are the sorts of transcriptions many Anglo-English speakers would produce:

record	'rɛkɔːd (n)	rɪ'kɔːd (v)
alternate	'ɒltəneɪt (v)	ɒl'tɜːnət (adj)
object	'ɒbdʒɪkt (n)	əb'dʒekt (v)
minute	'mɪnɪt (n)	maɪ'njuːt (a)
permit	'pɜmɪt (n)	pə'mɪt (v)
present	'prɛzənt (adj, n)	prə'zɛnt (v)
produce	'prɒdjuːs (n)	prə'djuːs (v)
frequent	'friːkwənt (adj)	frɪ'kwɛnt (v)
invalid	'ɪnvəlɪd (n)	ɪn'valɪd (adj)

4. Your transcriptions are most likely to contain function words, including auxiliary verbs (e.g. 'have', 'is', 'will', 'can'), pronouns (e.g. 'he', 'her', 'you'), prepositions (e.g. 'for', 'to', 'from') and conjunctions (e.g. 'and', 'or'). If you look at the weak forms overall, you will see fewer vowels than in the set of strong forms (and probably many of them will be [ə] or [ɪ]), and they are unlikely to contain [h].

Chapter 6

1. Most speakers will find that they have more heavily velarised laterals when a consonant follows; and that when a vowel follows, the lateral will be more velarised when syllable final than when syllable initial. Many speakers will also find that pronouns behave differently from other words in e.g. 'fill it' vs. 'fill ink . . .', with less velarisation before pronouns. Place of articulation will most probably be dental if there is a following dental; and these will generally be more velarised than in other positions.

2. Check whether your production of words in (d) is like that in (a)–(c). For (b), the plosive probably shares many features with [r]; compare e.g. the [k] sounds of 'creep' and 'keep'. It may be useful to check the lips in a mirror.

Chapter 7

1. Pay particular attention to the duration of the various articulations. When considering plosives in verbs, the plosive is in different positions in each form of the verb. When followed by <-ing>, there is a central release, with the possibility of aspiration. When word final, or when followed by <-ed>, the release may not be evident. [t] between vowels may be produced as a tap. The degree of aspiration will probably be greatest when the plosive is word final.

2. The waveforms and spectrograms match up as follows: 1: (f). The voicing stops at the same time as closure is made. After release, there is a short period of aspiration before voicing starts again. [-pʰ-]. 2: (d). There is voicing throughout the closure, though it dies away in the later portion. Full voicing starts again soon after release. [-b-]. 3: (e). Voicing dies away gradually, and there is a little friction before complete closure is made. There is a lot of aspiration on release, and voicing starts late. We could transcribe [-ʰkʰ-]. 4: (g). This has a short period of closure which looks incomplete. On release there is a lot of noisy friction,

reminiscent of [ʃ]. F3 is low, which indicates [r]. [-n̪t̪r̥-]. 5: (b). This has a long closure compared with the simple plosives at 1 and 2. There is a transient just before 1.1 s which may correspond to velar release. The alveolar release has a lot of aspiration and voicing starts late. [-k(˺)tʰ-].

Chapter 8

1. The transcriptions below capture some of the details of most Anglo-English speakers. The last one represents a common pronunciation in conversational speech.

future	ˈfjuːtjə	fʲj̊ʉ̟ːʔtçə
shop	ʃɒp	ʃʷɒ̰pʷ
this shop	ðɪs ʃɒp	ðɪʃ ʃʷɒpʷ, d̪ᶞɪʃ ʃʷɒpʷ
disgusting	dɪsgʌstɪŋ, dɪzgʌstɪŋ	dɪz̥g̊ʌstɪŋ
sneezing	sniːzɪŋ	sniːz̥ɪŋ, sn̥niːz̥ɪŋ
all the horses	ɔːl ðə hɔsɪz	ɔːl̪ːə ɦɔsɪˈz̥, ɔːl̪ːə ɔ̤sɪˈz̥
from the summer	frəm ðə sʌmə	fˠʷɹˠʷəm n̪ə sʌmə
a thin veil	ə θɪn veɪl	ə θɪɱ b̪eɪl, ə θɪn͡ɱ b̪eɪl
for his father	fər ɪz fɑːðə	f͡ɹ̩ˠʷɪz̥ fɑːð̞ə
to hush up	tə hʌʃ ʌp	tə ɦʌʃʷ ʌp
thank you	θaŋk juː	ɦãŋk̩jʉ̟, ã̤ãŋk̩jʉ

Chapter 9

1. In the following words, the nasal and following consonant share their place of articulation:

> emphasis [ɱf], hangar [ŋg], unreal [n̠r], anthropology [n̪θ], in that (manner) [n̪ð]

In other words and phrases, productions may vary between e.g. alveolar + another place of articulation; one (non-alveolar) place of articulation; possibly a double articulation:

> unbalanced [nb, mb], ungrateful [ng, ŋg], in good (shape) [ng, ŋg, n͡ŋg].

In the phrase 'I'm going to'/'gonna', the nasal is often velar. Usually it is nasals which are basically alveolar which exhibit this change in place of articulation.

3. In these cases, the complete closure needed for the final nasal is produced early, and instead of close approximation (which would result in friction). The result is a cluster of two consonants with a shared place of

articulation. The first part of the cluster has oral airflow, the second has nasal airflow, and the transition from the oral to nasal airflow is achieved through lowering of the velum.

4. English does not use nasalised vowels; but some speakers mimic them in their pronunciation of French words: [gratã, kwasã]. Another strategy is to use a vowel similar to the French one and put a nasal consonant after it, e.g. [bɒn məʊ, kruːtɒn]. Words can also become completely nativised, such as [lieɪzən].

Chapter 11

2. You should find that there are five short vowels, not six, in stressed syllables; and that while the qualities of the vowels are different from a standard variety like RP, the overall vowel system is pretty similar to other non-rhotic British English varieties.

3. Salford is a non-rhotic variety. Evidence includes: the lack of [ɹ] or [r] before consonants; long vowels for vowel + /r/.

5. Glottalisation is a common realisation of /t/, which is alveolar; in place of alveolars finally, we often find a place of articulation that matches the next consonant, which in this case is bilabial; the combination of [dən] has been reduced to a syllabic nasal.

6. There are two possible (and compatible) explanations. One is that 'd'you ...' is often produced as a kind of affricate, with a plosive + fricative release. The other is that the end of the previous utterance is voiceless, and we have seen that across such joins, there is often voicing assimilation. Evidence that Marie hears this as 'd'you' is in the form of her reply, 'I do'.

Further reading

Abbreviations

EWW   *English World-Wide*
JIPA   *Journal of the International Phonetic Association*

Abercrombie, David (1967), *Elements of general phonetics*, Edinburgh: Edinburgh University Press.

Baken, R. J. and Robert F. Orlikoff (2000), *Clinical measurement of speech and voice* (2nd edn), San Diego: Singular Press.

Ball, Martin (1993), *Phonetics for speech pathology*, London: Whurr.

Bauer, Laurie, Paul Warren, Dianne Bardsley, Marianna Kennedy and George Major (2007), New Zealand English, *JIPA* 37: 97–102.

Bell, Masha (2004), *Understanding English spelling*, Cambridge: Pegasus.

Boersma, Paul and David Weenink (2009), Praat: doing phonetics by computer. Version 5.1, <http://www.praat.org>.

Brown, Gillian (1977), *Listening to spoken English*, London: Longman.

Catford, J. C. (1977), *Fundamental problems in phonetics*, Edinburgh: Edinburgh University Press.

Catford, J. C. (2001), *A practical introduction to phonetics*, Oxford: Oxford University Press.

Couper-Kuhlen, Elizabeth (1986), *An introduction to English prosody*, London: Arnold.

Cox, Felicity and Sallyanne Palethorpe (2007), Australian English, *JIPA* 37: 341–50.

Cruttenden, Alan (1997), *Intonation* (2nd edn), Cambridge: Cambridge University Press.

Cruttenden, Alan (2001), *Gimson's pronunciation of English*, London: Arnold.

Crystal, T. and A. House (1988), The duration of American-English stop consonants: an overview, *Journal of Phonetics* 16: 285–94.

Denes, Peter B. and Elliot N. Pinson (1993), *The speech chain: physics and biology of spoken language*, New York: W. H. Freeman.

Dilley L., S. Shattuck-Hufnagel and M. Ostendorf (1996), Glottalization of vowel-initial syllables as a function of prosodic structure, *Journal of Phonetics* 24: 423–44.

Foulkes, Paul and Gerard Docherty (1999), *Urban voices: accent studies in the British Isles*, London: Arnold.

Fromkin, Victoria, Robert Rodman and Nina Hyams (2007), *An introduction to language*, Boston, MA and London: Thomson/Wadsworth.

Gick, Bryan, Ian Wilson and Donald Derrick (2013), *Articulatory phonetics*, Chichester: Wiley-Blackwell.

Giegerich, Heinz (1992), *English phonology*, Cambridge: Cambridge University Press.

Harry, O. G. (2006), Jamaican Creole, *JIPA* 36: 125–31.

Hedevind, Bertil (1967), *The dialect of Dentdale in the West Riding of Yorkshire*, Uppsala: Appelbergs tryckeri, Acta Universitatis Upsaliensis 5, Studia Anglicistica Upsaliensia.

Heselwood, Barry (2013), *Phonetic transcription in theory and practice*, Edinburgh: Edinburgh University Press.

Hillenbrand, James M. (2003), American English: Southern Michigan, *JIPA* 33: 121–6.

IPA (International Phonetic Association) (1999), *Handbook of the International Phonetic Association*, Cambridge: Cambridge University Press.

Jacewicz, Ewa, Joseph Salmons and Robert A. Fox (2007), Vowel duration in three American English dialects, *American Speech* 82: 367–85.

Jacewicz, Ewa, Robert Allen Fox and Samantha Lyle (2009), Variation in stop consonant voicing in two regional varieties of American English, *JIPA* 39(3): 313–34.

Jefferson, Gail (1985), Notes on a systematic deployment of the acknowledgement tokens 'Yeah' and 'Mmhm', *Papers in Linguistics* 17(2): 197–216.

Johnson, Keith (2002), *Acoustic and auditory phonetics* (2nd edn), Oxford: Blackwell.

Jones, Daniel (1975), *An outline of English phonetics* (9th edn), Cambridge and New York: Cambridge University Press.

Kelly, John (1967), On the phonology of an English urban accent, *Le Maître Phonétique* 127: 2–5.

Kelly, John and John Local (1989), *Doing phonology*, Manchester: Manchester University Press.

Labov, William (1972), *Language in the inner city: studies in the Black English Vernacular*, Philadelphia: University of Pennsylvania Press.

Ladd, D. Robert (1996), *Intonational phonology*, Cambridge: Cambridge University Press.

Ladefoged, Peter (1995), *Elements of acoustic phonetics* (2nd edn), Chicago: University of Chicago Press.

Ladefoged, Peter (1999), American English. In International Phonetic Association, *Handbook of the International Phonetic Association*, Cambridge: Cambridge University Press, 41–4.

Ladefoged, Peter (2005), *Vowels and consonants: an introduction to the sounds of languages* (2nd edn), Oxford: Blackwell.

Ladefoged, Peter (2006), *A course in phonetics* (5th edn), Boston, MA: Thomson/Wadsworth.

Ladefoged, Peter and Ian Maddieson (1996), *Sounds of the world's languages*, Oxford: Blackwell.

Ladefoged, Peter and Anthony Traill (1994), Clicks and their accompaniments, *Journal of Phonetics* 22: 33–64.

Laver, John (1994), *Principles of phonetics*, Cambridge: Cambridge University Press.

Lecumberri, Maria Luisa Garcia and J. A. Maidment (2000), *English transcription course*, London: Arnold.

Lindau, Mona (1985), The story of /r/. In V. A. Fromkin (ed.), *Phonetic linguistics*, London: Academic Press, 157–68.

Local, John and John Kelly (1986), Projections and silences: notes on phonetic and conversational structure, *Human Studies* 9: 185–204.

Local, John and Gareth Walker (2012), How phonetic features project more talk, *JIPA* 42(3): 255–80.

Local, John K., John Kelly and William H. G. Wells (1986), Towards a phonology of conversation: turn-taking in Tyneside English, *Journal of Linguistics* 22(2): 411–37.

McCarthy, Owen and Jane Stuart-Smith (2013), Ejectives in Scottish English: a social perspective, *JIPA* 43(3): 273–98.

Nolan, Francis, Tara Hoist and Barbara Kühnert (1996), Modelling [s] to [ʃ] accommodation in English, *Journal of Phonetics* 24: 113–37.

Ogden, Richard (2013), Clicks and percussives in English conversation, *JIPA* 43(3): 299–320.

Pandeli, H., J. Eska, M. J. Ball and J. Rahilly (1997), Problems of phonetic transcription: the case of the Hiberno-English flat alveolar fricative, *JIPA* 27: 65–75.

Pike, Kenneth L. (1943), *Phonetics: a critical analysis of phonetic theory and a technic for the practical description of sounds*, Ann Arbor: University of Michigan Press.

Pullum, Geoffrey K. and William A. Ladusaw (1996), *Phonetic symbol guide* (2nd edn), Chicago: University of Chicago Press.

Rathcke, T. and J. Stuart-Smith (2015), On the tail of the Scottish Vowel Length Rule in Glasgow, *Language and Speech* 59(3): 404–30, <http://dx.doi.org/10.1177/0023830915611428>.

Roach, Peter (2004), British English: Received Pronunciation, *JIPA* 34: 239–45.

Rogers, Henry (2000), *The sounds of language: an introduction to phonetics*, New York: Longman.

Shockey Linda (2002), *Sound patterns of spoken English*, Oxford: Blackwell.

Sivertsen, Eva (1960), *Cockney phonology*, Oslo: University Press and New York: Humanities Press.

Slomanson, Peter and Michael Newman (2004), Peer group identification and variation in New York Latino English laterals, *EWW* 25(2): 199–216.

Stuart-Smith, Jane (2007), A sociophonetic investigation of postvocalic /r/ in Glaswegian adolescents, *Proceedings of the 16th International Congress of Phonetic Sciences, Saarbrücken*, 1307–10.

Thomas, Erik (2003), Secrets revealed by Southern vowel shifting, *American Speech* 78: 150–70.

Trudgill, Peter and Elizabeth Gordon (2006), Predicting the past: dialect archaeology and Australian English rhoticity, *EWW* 27(3): 235–46.

Watson, Kevin (2007), Liverpool English, *JIPA* 37: 351–60.

Watt, Dominic and William Allen (2003), Tyneside English, *JIPA* 33: 267–71.

Wells, J. C. (1982), *Accents of English*, vols 1–3, Cambridge: Cambridge University Press.

Wells, J. C. (2006), *English intonation: an introduction*, Cambridge: Cambridge University Press.

Wolfram, Walt and Ralph W. Fasold (1974), *The study of social dialects in American English*, Englewood Cliffs, NJ: Prentice Hall.

Wright, Melissa (2007), Clicks as markers of new sequences in English conversation, *Proceedings of the 16th International Congress of Phonetic Sciences, Saarbrücken*, 1069–72.

Wright, Melissa (2011), On clicks in English talk-in-interaction, *JIPA* 41(2): 207–29.

Zsiga, Elizabeth C. (1994), Acoustic evidence for gestural overlap in consonant sequences, *Journal of Phonetics* 22: 121–40.

Index

Note: this index covers the main chapters of the book, not the Glossary, where many of the terms listed in the Index can also be found.

dental, 12–13
  click, 159–64
  diacritic, 107
  fricative, 30, 120–2, 129–30
  lateral, 86, 178
  nasal, 145, 178, 192
  plosive, 14, 109, 128
devoicing, 77–8
diacritic, 8, 13, 22, 31, 50, 62, 72
  advanced, 110
  breathy, 53
  closer, 74, 94, 137
  creak, 53
  dental, 13, 109, 129
  inaudible release, 115
  labialisation, 85
  long, 8, 69
  more open, 30, 74, 95
  nasalisation, 29, 53, 148
  palatalisation, 87
  postalveolar, 107
  raised, 92, 135
  retracted, 110
  retroflexion, 66
  rounding, 63, 87
  short, 147
  slit-t, 135
  syllabic consonant, 86
  velarisation, 85
  voicelessness, 27, 77, 82, 84, 86,
    126–7, 133
  vowels, 74
digraph, 21
diphthong, 27, 66, 67, 68, 73–4, 76, 92,
  174–5
dorsum (dorsal), 15, 98, 100, 108,
  109–10, 115, 137, 138
double articulation, 83, 93
duration, 23
  aspiration, 105
  finality, 188
  fricatives, 124, 126, 127, 135, 137,
    138
  laterals, 87
  nasal, 192
  pause, 173

plosives, 100, 102, 112, 118, 133, 168,
  170
taps, 94
transcription, 68, 107
vowels, 66, 68, 74, 79, 116

ejective, 164–9
English
  African American Vernacular, 92
  American (USA), 14, 16, 17, 60, 61,
    64, 66, 68, 69, 70, 71–6, 79, 84, 86,
    87, 116, 129, 152
  Australian, 16, 63, 64, 65, 68, 70,
    71–6, 79, 86, 88, 131, 135, 144,
    151–2
  Canadian, 64, 116
  Cockney see English: London
  Dent (Cumbria), 13
  Glasgow, 56, 97, 171, 196
  Irish, 13, 66, 67, 68, 88, 93, 130,
    135–6, 137, 139
  Liverpool, 94, 117, 135–7, 139, 149,
    196
  London, 108, 137, 150, 155
  Manchester (UK), 87, 138
  New York, 13, 87, 97
  New Zealand, 63, 64, 68, 70, 75, 92,
    107, 124–6,
  Nigeria, 13
  northern England, 61, 68, 87, 114,
    138, 172
  Northumberland, 95
  Received Pronunciation (RP), 3,
    60, 63, 64, 65, 67, 68, 70, 71–7,
    94, 111, 117, 123–4, 142–3,
    145–6
  Scottish, 14, 17, 21, 24, 64, 66,
    67–8, 79, 86, 92, 113, 136; see also
    Glasgow
  Tyneside, 71, 88, 106, 104
epiglottis, 10

falsetto, 54–6
float symbol, 64–5
formant, 34, 35–7, 65–6, 84–5, 90–1,
  95–6, 100, 143